MAKE IT WITH WOOD

MAKE IT WITH WOOD

*Tricks of the Trade
from over Forty Years Experience
in the Cabinet Shop*

EDGAR RANDALL BEARD

VNR VAN NOSTRAND REINHOLD COMPANY
NEW YORK CINCINNATI TORONTO LONDON MELBOURNE

Copyright © 1983 by Van Nostrand Reinhold Company Inc.
Library of Congress Catalog Card Number 82-11085
ISBN 0-442-21176-7 (hardcover)
ISBN 0-442-21175-9 (paper)

Printed in the United States of America
Designed by Ginger Legato

Published by Van Nostrand Reinhold Company Inc.
135 West 50th Street
New York, NY 10020

Fleet Publishers
1410 Birchmount Road
Scarborough, Ontario M1P 2E7, Canada

Van Nostrand Reinhold
480 Latrobe Street
Melbourne, Victoria 3000, Australia

Van Nostrand Reinhold Company Limited
Molly Millars Lane
Wokingham, Berkshire, England RG11 2PY

16 15 14 13 12 11 10 9 8 7 6 5 4 3 2 1

Library of Congress Cataloging in Publication Data

Beard, Edgar Randall.
    Make it with wood.

    Includes index.
    1. Woodwork.   I. Title.
TT180.B4 1983   674′.8   82-11085
ISBN 0-442-21176-7
ISBN 0-442-21175-9 (pbk.)

In memory of my late son, Roger,
who worked with me on many projects.

CONTENTS

ACKNOWLEDGMENTS

To my wife, Arthel, and daughter, Karen, who encouraged me through months of writing and drawing the contents of my first (and last) book.

To Carolyn Rains, Pauline Robinson, and Cheryl Cooper for typing the manuscript.

To L.D. Akridge and Marshall Nelson for their help in copying and organizing the text.

INTRODUCTION

When I was a kid, I enjoyed visiting some cousins who owned and operated a cabinet shop. Instead of playing with the youngsters, I would spend my time in the shop watching Mr. and Mrs. Canfield turn rough pieces of wood into beautiful and useful things.

He had made all his machines and at that time powered them with a gasoline engine by means of belts and a line shaft. I was fascinated as I watched the shavings fly from pieces of wood being turned in the lathe and seeing a table leg or bed post take shape. A special treat was seeing the edge of a board being sawed in graceful curves on the band saw and then shaped with a fancy molded edge as it was held against the rubbing collar of the spindle shaper.

I wondered how anyone could call this work when it seemed to be so much fun to cut, assemble, and finish pieces of furniture, cabinets, store fixtures, boats, and anything else that could be made of wood.

At home, about the only experience I was getting in woodwork was in helping my dad and neighbors build a barn or outhouse. So when I was older, I happily accepted my cousin's offer to let me help him in his shop. Although he paid me fair wages, I think I would have worked for free.

By this time, he had bought larger factory-made machinery, powered by electric motors, and his two sons were now helping in the shop. As I look back, I know that this was when I decided what I really wanted to do whether I could make a living at it or not.

In 1937 I bought my first power tools from Sears and set up a small shop in the rural area where I lived. I also got married about that time and my first job was making our furniture, of which we were very proud.

We managed to live fairly well those first two or three years from the odd jobs I did in my shop and by doing some carpentry work to supplement my income. This experience in shop and construction work proved advantageous later during the war when I closed down my shop and worked on various defense jobs as carpenter, saw filer, and saw operator. During most of the last two years of the war I served in the Navy where I acquired some experience in machine-shop work, which also proved beneficial.

After the war I set up a shop in the town where I now live. I replaced most of my power tools with larger heavy-duty machines and had to hire two or three hands to keep up with the demand caused by the "building boom" that was taking place. We not only built cabinets but all kinds of millwork for home and business construction as these were in short supply the first year or two after the war.

Also hard to find were tools and accessories. I found a few good buys in war surplus machines, but still had to make many of the tools, machines, and cutters that were needed in the wide variety of work we were doing. Some

of these I am still using and have included in this book.

In the last ten years my health has forced me to slow down, so I have limited my work to only a few select jobs that I could do alone and at my leisure. This has given me a chance to do many things that I never had time for before. So, partially as a hobby, I chose projects of interest that offered a challenge.

Over a period of more than forty years and a wide variety of jobs, I have developed many ideas and techniques that have been helpful in my work. I feel that some of these are worth passing on to other craftsmen who like to make things for themselves.

I have included several projects especially for the home craftsman, such as a guitar, wooden wheel clock, some furniture, novelties, and toys along with some woodworking machines that he can make of wood and a few metal parts.

I know from experience that the professional cabinetmaker has to save time and material without sacrificing quality and I would like to share a few ideas to help achieve this purpose.

Accuracy is also a very important part of shop-built cabinetry and millwork. I have found that jigs, templates, and lay-out strips reduce the chance of costly mistakes in measurements, lay-outs, cutting, and assembly. They also save time by freeing the cabinetmaker from a lot of figures, which usually involve a bunch of fractions and headaches.

Included also are some molding heads and cutters that the craftsman can make himself and some tips on the maintenance of power tools.

In the following pages I have tried to present this information mostly through drawings, at which I am better suited than I am at writing. I hope the reader will be able to understand them and find the book beneficial.

A WORD OF CAUTION

I still have ten fingers, but I admit that I have had some close calls with woodworking tools. Carelessness can cause serious accidents even when operating the most expensive machines with the best safety features. A home-built machine can be dangerous if it is not well constructed and/or poorly maintained and operated.

Try out newly constructed tools at slow speeds, making sure that all cutters and fittings are securely fastened. Let the machine idle for a few minutes before feeding in material. Watch for excess vibration, which may indicate that something is out of balance. Fix guards over exposed cutters and saws and be careful at all times. Unfortunately, fingers do not grow back when "pruned" from the hand.

Since building custom kitchen cabinets has been my occupation for the past thirty-five years, I feel I should begin this book with a discussion on their construction. Because it would take a whole book to cover the many styles, types, shapes, and methods in kitchen cabinet construction, I will explain only the two basic methods of construction I have used most over the years. I will devote another chapter to door and drawer construction since they determine the style and appearance of the cabinets more than anything else.

It is assumed the reader is a craftsman who has access to tools such as a drill press, router, band saw, table saw, radial arm saw, jointer, and shaper and some experience in cabinet or furniture construction. I will share some ideas about cutting, framing, and installing that have saved me time and material and have given my customers their money's worth.

BASE CABINET CONSTRUCTION

Figure 1-1 shows details of a base cabinet framed for a preformed top. The front is strips of $3/4''$ birch plywood or board lumber, dadoed at the joints to make a flush half-lap. The framework is $1 1/2''$ strips notched as shown for strength. The floor and shelving is $5/8''$ particle board or fir plywood. The doors are lipped at the top and vertical edges. Double doors that meet in the center have a square edge with a slight bevel on the meeting edge to permit a close fit without rubbing. The drawer fronts are lipped on four edges.

The overall depth of the cabinet (including the Masonite backing) should be about $24''$. This will permit about $1''$ hangover of the preformed top at the front.

This type of cabinet is generally used where raised panel or early American style doors are used. Details for cutout and construction are shown in Figures 1-3 and 1-4.

The cabinet shown in Figure 1-2 is simpler to build than the one shown in Figure 1-1 since it has no joints to fit in the front. The vertical facings are dadoed at the top to receive the $1 3/4''$ strip that goes along the top front. It is not dadoed as half of it extends out over the drawer fronts. The bottom end of the facings are cut out to fit the floor. Posts are cut as shown in Figure 1-5 with notches for shelf supports and the two strips (F) that support the drawer slides. The top support is $1 1/2'' \times 21 3/4''$ and the shelf support $1 1/2'' \times 20 1/4''$ (or $1 1/2''$ shorter than the top one).

Nail the frames together, then nail the frame to the facing from the back side with 6 d coated nails. A little glue along the edge of the front post will give extra strength.

The floor is built as shown in Figures 1-2 and 1-4. Lay out the location of the facings and frames. Notch the back edge of the floor to receive the $3/4''$ tenon on the bottom end of the back post.

Set the assembled frame in place, nail the back post into the floor edge and the front facing into the front edge. Also nail up through the floor into the front post.

In Figure 1-2, the two strips (F) are notched the same as the ones in the floor. Nail them into the notches in the posts. Then the facing strips (E) are glued and nailed in place across the top front.

This base (Figure 1-2) is made for a shop-built top, which is nailed to the frames before the Formica is glued on. Cut the top and nail flush with front facing (E).

This leaves about a $1''$ hangover on the back side, which permits nailing the backsplash from underneath. Clamp it in place and use No. 6 box nails. The backsplash board should be soft pine; a hard grained board may turn the nails into the Formica covering.

Do not forget to fasten the $1 3/4'' \times 22''$ pieces underneath the top, which keep the drawers from tilting when pulled out. Center them over the drawer slides (Figure 1-4). See Figure 1-13 for making the top. Of course, if you wish to use a preformed top just add $1''$ to the width dimensions of the cabinet framework.

Wall cabinet construction and installation are shown in Figures 1-7 to 1-10, including ceiling hung cabinets over a bar.

MEASURING AND LAYOUT

I have learned the hard way that a mistake in measuring or cutting out a set of cabinets can cost time and money. It is easy to make a mistake in reading your rule or writing down the measurements. Once I hauled a large section to the job and it would not fit through the door. Sometimes in building a cabinet for a bathroom you can have problems if the bathroom door is narrow or if it enters from a hallway where the cabinet cannot be turned to enter the door.

If you have been in the cabinet-making business for a while, you already know these problems. I am going to give the beginner a few tricks that have helped me to cut down on mistakes.

In measuring for kitchen cabinets, go to the job and measure the room yourself. Do not depend on the building

KITCHEN CABINETS

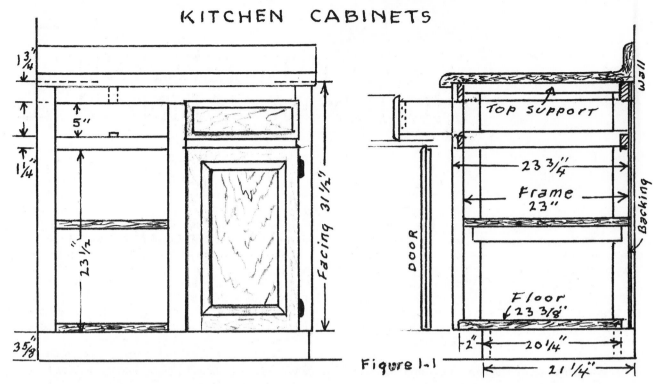

Figure 1-1

Type A. The front is 3/4" material, half-lapped at the joints. The doors and drawer fronts are lipped, except the bottom of door, which is a square cut. The depth of cabinet is 23 3/4" to receive a preformed top.

Type B, below, the doors and drawer fronts are lipped only on vertical edges. The base is framed for shop-built top. See details Fig. 1-5.

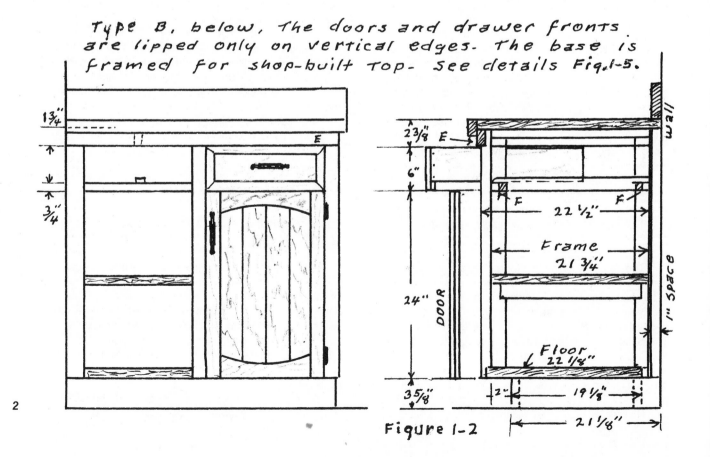

Figure 1-2

2

FACINGS AND POST
For half-lap Cabinet front.
Use gauges to reduce chance of error.

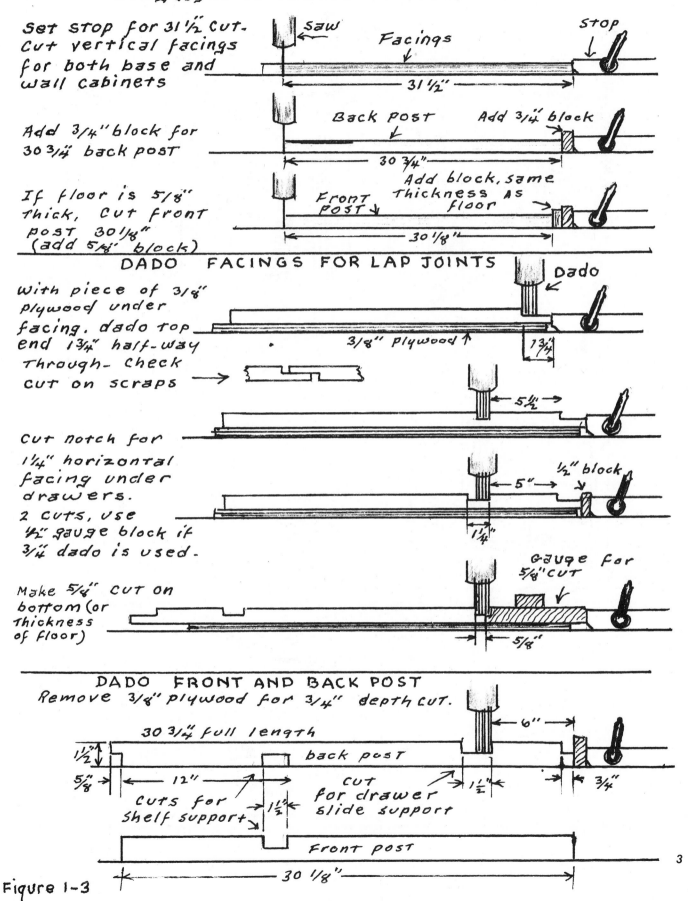

Set stop for 31½" Cut. Cut vertical facings for both base and wall cabinets

Saw — Facings — STOP

31½"

Add ¾" block for 30¾" back post

Back Post — Add ¾" block

30¾"

If floor is 5/8" thick, Cut front post 30⅛" (add 5/8" block)

Front POST — Add block, same Thickness as floor

30⅛"

DADO FACINGS FOR LAP JOINTS

Dado

With piece of 3/8" plywood under facing, dado top end 1¾" half-way Through- Check cut on scraps →

3/8" plywood ↑   1¾"

5½"

Cut notch for 1¼" horizontal facing under drawers. 2 cuts, use ½" gauge block if ¾" dado is used.

5"   ½" block

1¼"

Make 5/8" cut on bottom (or Thickness of floor)

Gauge for 5/8" CUT

5/8"

DADO FRONT AND BACK POST
Remove 3/8" plywood for ¾" depth cut.

30¾" full length

6"

1½"   back post
5/8"   12"   Cut for drawer slide support   1½"   ¾"
Cuts for Shelf support   1½"

Front post

30⅛"

Figure 1-3

3

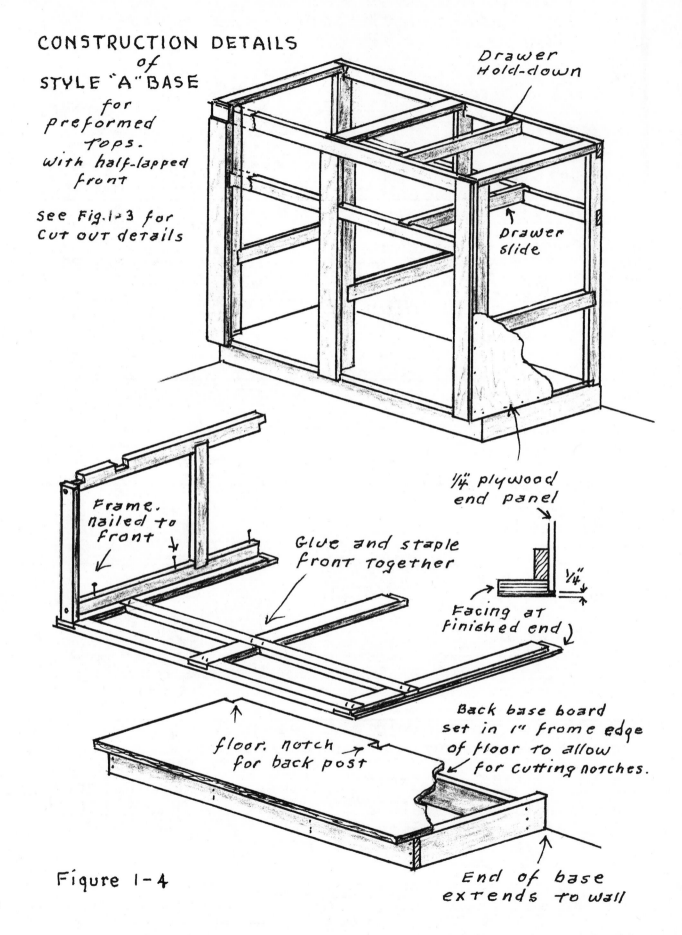

CONSTRUCTION DETAILS
of
STYLE "A" BASE
for
preformed
tops.
with half-lapped
front

see Fig. 1-3 for
cut out details

Drawer
Hold-down

Drawer
slide

1/4" plywood
end panel

1/4"

Frame.
nailed to
front

Glue and staple
front together

Facing at
finished end

Back base board
set in 1" frome edge
of floor to allow
for cutting notches.

floor. notch
for back post

Figure 1-4

End of base
extends to wall

4

DETAILS OF SHOP BUILT-SEMIFLUSH
BASE WITH BUILT ON TOP AND BACKSPLASH

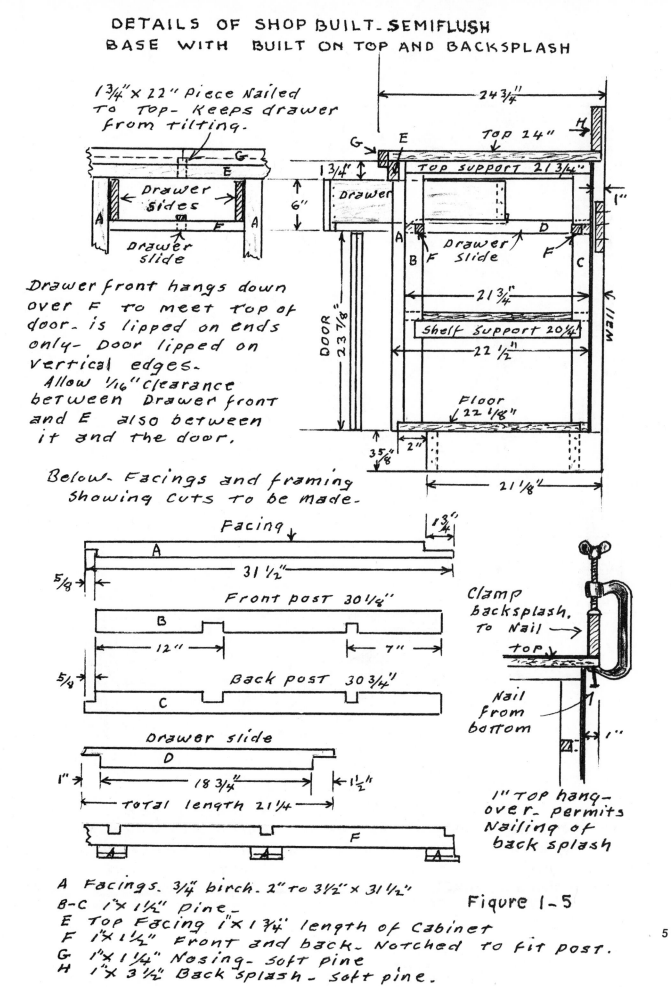

1 3/4" x 22" Piece Nailed
To Top- Keeps drawer
from tilting.

Drawer
Sides

Drawer
slide

Drawer front hangs down
over F to meet top of
door. is lipped on ends
only- Door lipped on
vertical edges.
Allow 1/16" clearance
between Drawer front
and E also between
it and the door.

Below- Facings and framing
Showing Cuts to be made.

Facing

Front post 30 1/8"

Back post 30 3/4"

Drawer slide

total length 21 1/4

24 3/4"

Top 24"

Top support 21 3/4"

Drawer
Drawer Slide

21 3/4"

Shelf Support 20 1/4"

22 1/2"

DOOR 23 7/8"

Floor
22 1/8"

3 5/8"   2"

21 1/8"

31 1/2"

12"   7"

18 3/4"   1 1/2"

Clamp
backsplash,
To Nail
top

Nail
from
bottom

1" Top hang-
over- permits
Nailing of
back splash

Figure 1-5

A Facings. 3/4" birch. 2" to 3 1/2" x 31 1/2"
B-C 1"x 1 1/2" pine.
E Top Facing 1"x 1 3/4" length of Cabinet
F 1"x 1 1/2" Front and back- Notched to fit post.
G 1"x 1 1/4" Nosing- soft pine
H 1"x 3 1/2" Back splash- soft pine.

TYPICAL CONSTRUCTION FOR CORNER
For Type or style B

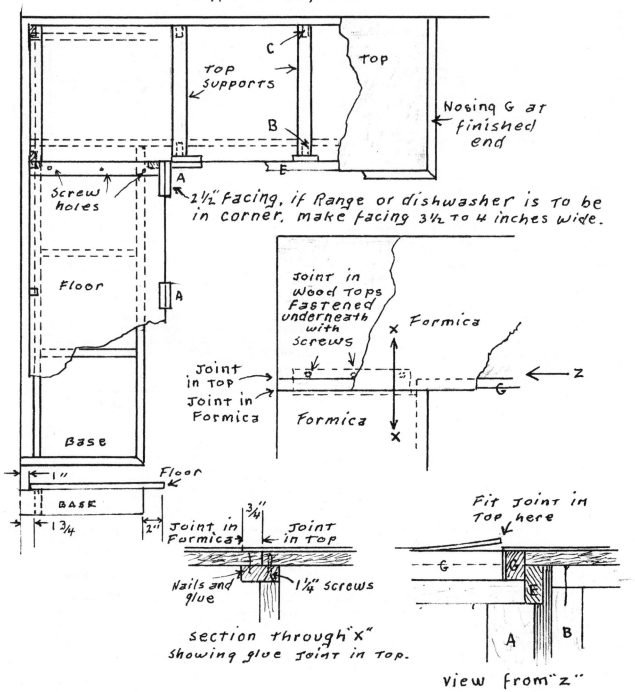

Top supports

C

B

A

TOP

Nosing G at finished end

Screw holes

Floor

Base

2½" facing, if Range or dishwasher is to be in corner, make facing 3½ to 4 inches wide.

Joint in Wood Tops fastened underneath with screws

Formica

Joint in Top

Joint in Formica

Formica

X

X

Z

G

A

Floor

1"

BASE

1 ¾

2"

Joint in Formica

¾"

Joint in Top

Nails and glue

1¼" screws

section through "x" showing glue joint in top.

Fit Joint in Top here

G

G

E

A

B

view from "z"

If shop built, fasten the two sections together with screws so they can be taken apart to move to job. Be sure not to glue the 3/4" lap in the topping until ready to install. Use contact cement, and the three 1¼" screws from underneath to secure the joint.

Figure 1-6

WALL CABINETS

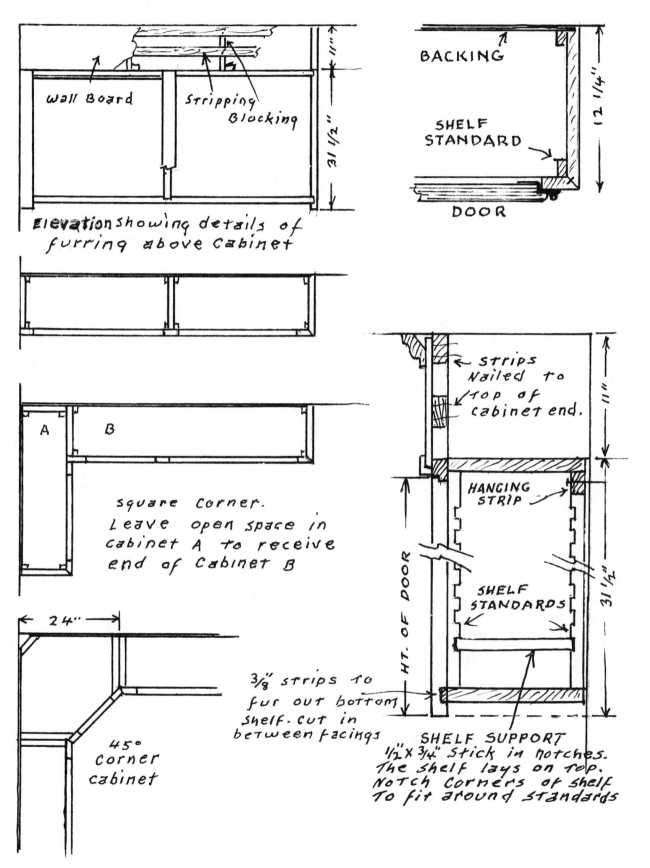

Wall Board

Stripping

Blocking

31 1/2"

Elevation showing details of furring above Cabinet

BACKING

12 1/4"

SHELF STANDARD

DOOR

A B

Square Corner. Leave open space in cabinet A to receive end of Cabinet B

24"

45° corner cabinet

3/8" strips to fur out bottom shelf. cut in between facings

strips Nailed to top of cabinet end.

11"

HANGING STRIP

HT. OF DOOR

SHELF STANDARDS

31 1/2"

SHELF SUPPORT
1/2" X 3/4" stick in notches. The shelf lays on top. Notch corners of shelf to fit around standards

Figure 1-7

WALL CABINETS

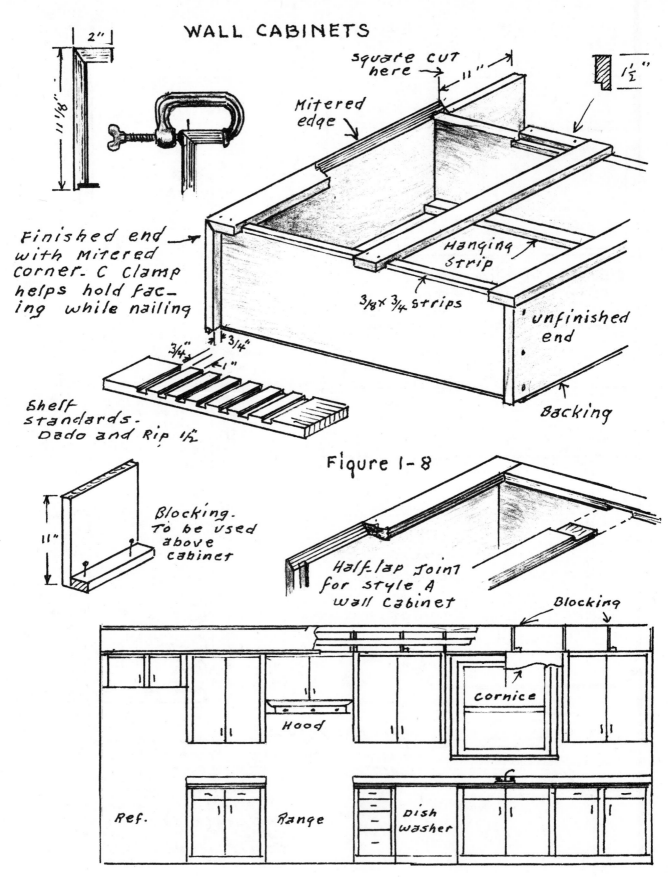

2"

11 1/8"

square cut here

11"

1 1/2"

Mitered edge

Finished end with Mitered Corner. C Clamp helps hold facing while nailing

Hanging Strip

3/8 x 3/4 strips

unfinished end

3/4"   3/4"

1"

Backing

Shelf standards. Dado and Rip 1/2

Figure 1-8

11"

Blocking. To be used above cabinet

Half-lap Joint for style A wall cabinet

Blocking

cornice

Hood

Ref.

Range

Dish washer

Elevation of typical kitchen, check sizes of appliances to be used.

Figure 1-9

CEILING HUNG CABINET OVER BAR

To suspend cabinet to ceiling, drill two holes in a piece of 2"x 4" cut hole in ceiling over cabinet. reach through and lay across two joists

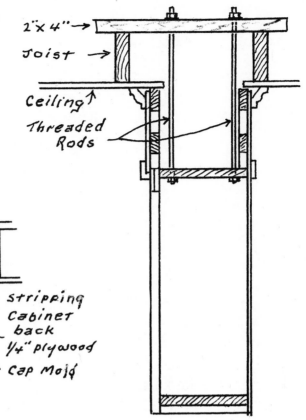

2"x 4"

Joist

Ceiling

Threaded Rods

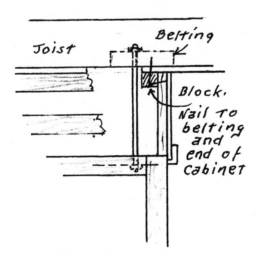

2 nd. Floor →

Belting

Blocking to keep cabinet from slipping sideways. see below

stripping
Cabinet back
1/4" plywood
Cap Mold

Method for two story building

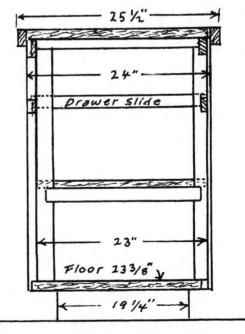

Joist

Belting

Block.
Nail to belting and end of cabinet

25 1/2"

24"

Drawer slide

23"

Floor 23 3/8"

19 1/4"

In case a dishwasher or Range is to be installed in the bar. it will probably need to be made wider. Check dimensions, add the extra inches accordingly.

Detail of Bar Construction.

Figure 1-10

MEASURING AND LAY-OUT

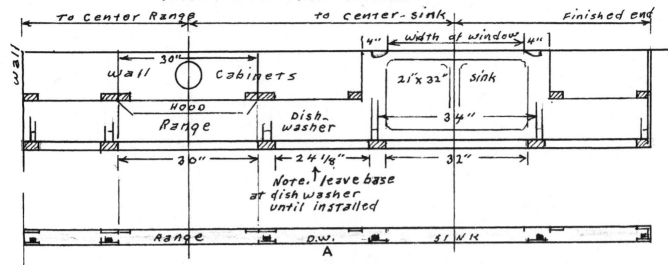

To Center Range   to Center-sink   Finished end

wall

30"   Wall   Cabinets

width of window   4"

4"

21"x 32"   sink

HOOD

Range   Dish-washer

3 4"

30"   24 1/8"   32"

Note: leave base
at dish washer
until installed

Range   D.W.   SINK

A

"Lay-out strip" for Cabinets above. Showing location of frames. Facings. Appliances. Top edge for wall cabinets. bottom edge for base Cabinets.

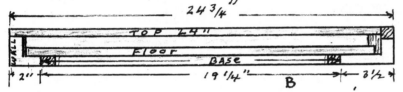

24 3/4"

TOP 24"

Floor

BASE

2"   19 1/4"   3 1/2"

B

Template for Type A Construction with shop built-on top. Make one for each type.

By using This Lay-out strip, The doors and drawer fronts can be cut out before assembly.

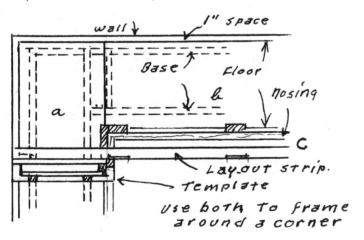

wall↓   1" space

Base   Floor

a   b

Nosing

C

Lay-out strip.

Template

Use both to frame
around a corner

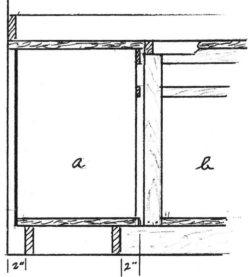

a   b

2"   2"

The drawing at right shows the two sections joined at corner. The base of section b extends under the floor of section a There is a two inch space between the wall and the base, and one inch between wall and edge of floor. If preformed top is used, these dimensions can be reduced by 3/4". However The cabinet will need to be 3 1/4" wider to keep the front 24" from the wall.

10

Figure 1-11

plans. Draw a rough floor plan of the kitchen and put in all dimensions. Locate the center of the sink, usually under a window. Locate the exact center of the window on the drawing, along with the width of finished window casings. Locate the dishwasher, which is usually next to the sink.

As ranges and refrigerators vary in size, it is important to have correct measurements. If the range is a built-in type, get the specifications from the dealer. It is best to allow room for a large refrigerator even though a smaller one is being used. Lots of work and time is involved if you have to cut out for one later. If a vented range hood is to be used, try to locate it (and the range or cook top), so the vent pipe goes between two ceiling joists. If you do not, it will hit one of them dead center every time.

Figure 1-11 shows how to ensure accuracy when cutting parts for cabinets. By using this method you can cut all parts including the doors and drawers before assembly.

On strips of wood the same length as each cabinet section, mark off the locations of the sink and appliances. On the edge next to you, lay out the location of all the facings and frames (A). On the back edge, lay off the wall cabinets and their facings. This will permit getting the measurement for the width of the doors and drawer fronts.

If the doors are to be lipped for 3/8" offset hinges, cut them 5/8" larger than the opening. In case of double doors, make each 1/4" larger than half the width of the opening.

Figure 1-11B shows a template or strip about 2" wide and 25" long, showing the dimensions through a cross section of the "Type A" construction (where you make the top yourself). By marking off the base, floor, and top, as well as the facings, you can use it in cutting them to size as well as helping get around a corner where two sections join at right angles as shown in Figure 1-6.

Just add this template to the lay-out strip as shown in Figure 1-11C or copy off the marks from it onto the end of the lay-out strip. This will give you the length of the base along with the floor and top. Make a work drawing showing the top plan and a separate one of the base. Add in the floor sizes, allowing for cutout of dishwasher but let the two 1" x 31/2" baseboards go on through and cut them out after the cabinet is installed. (Just before setting, saw the backboard nearly through leaving about 1/2".)

Cut the floors 1" shorter than the top at the end where the cabinet is to fit against a wall. This gives room for the backing and for nailing the backsplash from underneath (Figure 1-5).

If the cabinet should fit against a wall at each end, you have some extra problems. First the length must be a little less than the length of the wall it sits against in order to slide it in place. The length should be such that a backsplash on each end and moldings on the front facings will cover the gaps. Any door or window facing will have to be removed if the cabinet has to pass by them. If it's a house under construction, ask the builder to leave them off until the cabinet is installed. In order to get a good fit at the ends where the short backsplashes are against the walls, leave the strip of topping off the top edge of the back-

splash until the cabinet is set, then fit it as shown in Figure 1-14. By doing it this way you can have all the backsplashes already fastened on, leaving about 1/4" clearance at the ends.

Of course if a preformed top is used, just cut it the exact length and leave the backsplashes off. Fasten it down after the cabinet is set.

Figure 1-12 shows how some other problems may be solved. In case a hood vent does hit a joist, it can be bypassed by using one of the swivel-type elbow joints that are used in stove pipes or air conditioning ducts. In a two-story building the hood can be vented to the outside as shown. Of course a self-vented hood will solve this problem but they are not as efficient.

If you have tried to fasten the clamps under a sink, you know how hard it is to get to the ones along the front edge. The way I do it is to attach "buttons," which are blocks fastened to the panel with screws so they will turn and hold the panel in place. They are easy to remove for access to the clamps.

The jacks for holding wall cabinets in place are a "must" if you are in the kitchen cabinet business. For a "one time" job, however, they may not be worth the time it would take to make them.

CABINET TOPS

If you make your own cabinet tops, you will do a neater job if you miter the edges of the topping, especially in the lighter colors. It takes a little more time but is worth it because you do not have the dark line showing around the edges. After a little practice you will be able to do a good-looking top in a short time. I have been mitering them for years. Figure 1-13 illustrates the procedure.

First, after you have cut a 30" piece of laminate to fit the 243/4" top, you should have remaining a strip about 51/2" wide. Run both edges over the jointer until they are straight and free of chipped places. The jointer needs to be sharp to do a good job.

Next, with a fine-toothed blade on the table saw, rip a strip for the nosing a little over 15/16" wide. This should leave about 4" for the backsplash. You will also need enough of the narrow strips for the top edge of the backsplash, so cut them from scrap material left from the ends of the 30" pieces or waste from the sink cut out.

Figure 1-13A shows the strips for the nosings and backsplash being beveled to 45° on the jointer with holding blocks. Make the blocks about 12" or 14" long with a handgrip on top.

Cut to a sharp edge but do not cut into the finish as it might chip.

Glue on the nosing strip with contact cement, using two coats on the wood strip. When the cement has set fifteen or twenty minutes, lightly touch the strip to the wood nosing with the bevel even with the wood top. With a scrap for a gauge, move along the edge pushing the nosing up or down for a perfect miter, press tight with fingers then with small roller.

ODDS AND ENDS

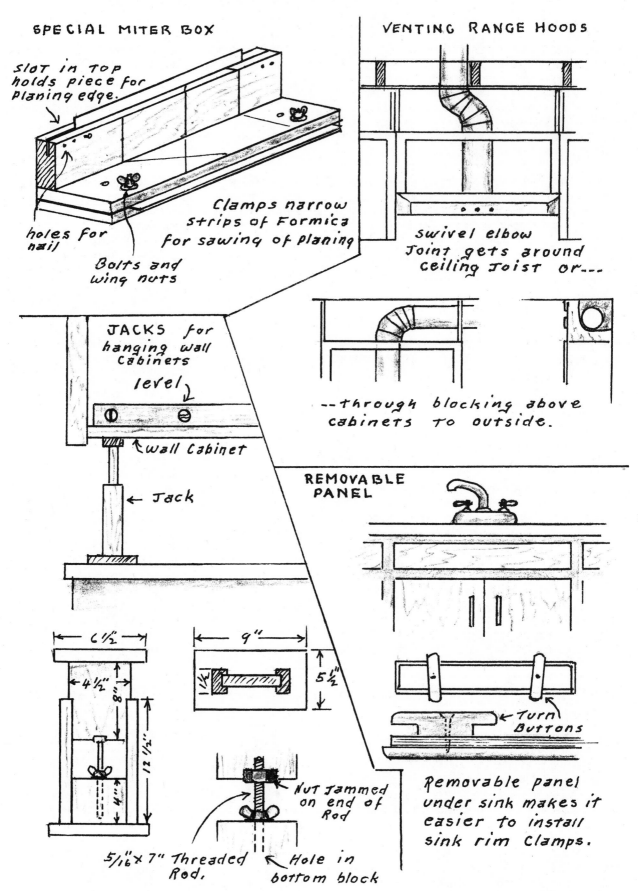

SPECIAL MITER BOX

slot in top holds piece for planing edge.

holes for nail

Bolts and wing nuts

Clamps narrow strips of Formica for sawing of planing

VENTING RANGE HOODS

swivel elbow joint gets around ceiling joist or...

--through blocking above cabinets to outside.

JACKS for hanging wall Cabinets

level

Wall Cabinet

Jack

6½

4½"

8"

12½"

9"

½

5½"

5/16"x 7" Threaded Rod.

Nut jammed on end of Rod

Hole in bottom block

REMOVABLE PANEL

Turn Buttons

Removable panel under sink makes it easier to install sink rim Clamps.

Figure 1-12

SHOP-BUILT CABINET TOPS

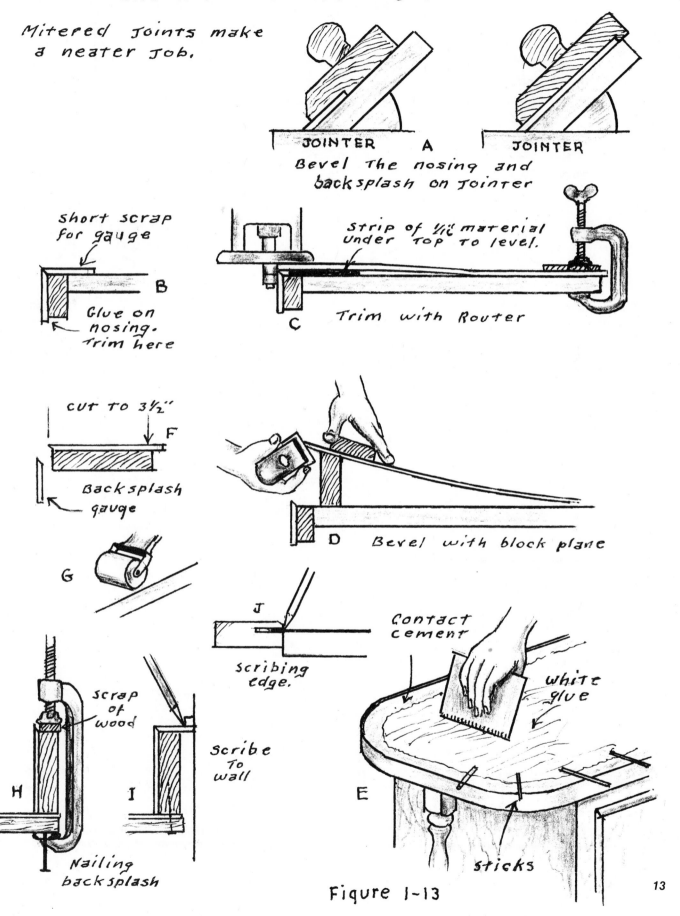

Mitered joints make a neater job.

JOINTER A JOINTER

Bevel the nosing and backsplash on jointer

short scrap for gauge

B

Glue on nosing. Trim here

Strip of 1/16" material under top to level.

C Trim with Router

cut to 3 1/2" F

Backsplash gauge

G

D Bevel with block plane

J

Scribing edge.

Contact cement

white glue

scrap of wood

Scribe to wall

H I

Nailing backsplash

E

sticks

Figure 1-13

13

BATHROOM CABINETS

Bathroom cabinets are built similar to kitchens except the dimensions in height and width. Below are the dimensions I use when I build the top. If a premade top is used, build to fit.

At right is a vanity with a small bar at one end.

The towel rack is made of 1¼" dowels, with ½" dowels for the cross rods.

Below, at the right are two cabinets built to fit spaces that call for a little extra thinking. The first is a tapered cabinet to fit the narrow space between the door and corner of room. The other fits between two walls.

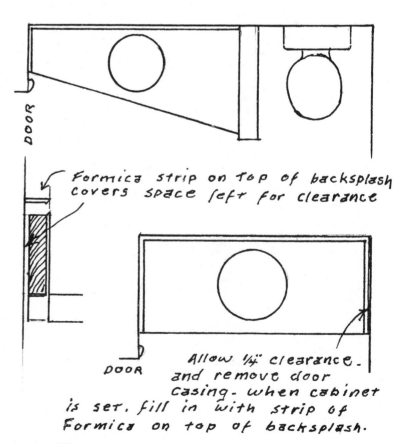

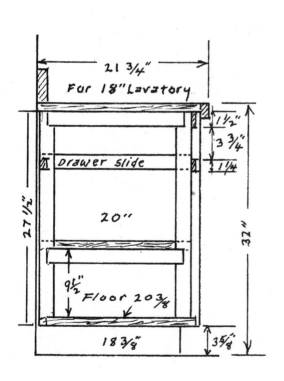

21 3/4"
For 18" Lavatory

1 1/2"
3 3/4"
1 1/4"

Drawer slide

27 1/2"

20"

32"

9 1/2"
Floor 20 3/8"

18 3/8"

3 5/8"

DOOR

Formica strip on top of backsplash covers space left for clearance

DOOR

Allow 1/4" clearance and remove door casing. When cabinet is set, fill in with strip of Formica on top of backsplash.

Figure 1-14

14

Clamp the top at the back edge and lay a piece of topping under the front edge as shown (Figure 1-13C) to keep the top level. (Use the piece for the backsplash for this.)

Trim flush with the face of the nosing with router and laminate trimmer. Bevel the edge underneath with block planes. I use two planes, one set for medium cut and the other fine. They must be sharp. Prop up the edge with a beveled strip, about 2″ wide and 3′ or 4′ long. It should be a light color. I painted mine white, since that makes it easier to see the dark edge of the laminate as it is planed to a sharp edge. Hold the plane as near to 45° to the material as possible. Any places that do not fit may be fitted with a file or sandpaper on a block.

I have found that using contact cement around the edges only is easier than coating the entire wood top and laminate. With a small brush, coat a strip about 1″ wide all around the edges of both the wood and laminate (two coats on the wood). When ready to set, spread white liquid glue over the top with a notched spreader. A spreader is easily made by making small saw cuts along the edge of a piece of Masonite and beveling to a sharp edge. Work up to the contact cement but not on it.

Lay short sticks along the edge and place the laminate on them. Set the ends or corners first by pulling out the sticks one at a time and pressing down lightly. Be sure of a fit along the mitered edge before pressing tight, then pull out the sticks and roll down the whole top. If needed, some weight may be placed on the top until the white glue sets.

Sand the mitered edges lightly with fine sandpaper on a block. Clean off any cement with lacquer thinner.

Run one edge of the backsplash boards over the jointer and glue the laminate to it with contact cement by using the sticks and a scrap of laminate for a gauge at the mitered edge.

Rip to 3⅝″ and square up on the jointer. Seal the edge with a coat of contact cement. Nail the backsplash in place before adding the capping on the top edge. Use C-clamps to hold it in place while it is being nailed from underneath. After the cap has been glued on, set the cabinet in place and scribe against the wall. Trim off excess with a fine-toothed handsaw.

Figure 1-13E shows the end of a bar with rounded corners. If the curves are no less than a 5″ or 6″ radius, the laminate will bend around them. With a smaller radius the strips can be either heated and held in a curve until cooled or sanded thinner on the back side. Lay on a flat board and use a belt sander or cabinet scraper.

Clamp the top on one side while fitting the other, then move the clamps to the other side. The rounded corners can be marked with the gauge (J) called a "preacher." Saw close enough for the router to finish the trimming. Bevel the edge for mitering all around the top.

2 DOOR AND DRAWER CONSTRUCTION

The doors and drawer fronts can either make or ruin the appearance of an otherwise good job, whether it is a piece of furniture or a kitchen cabinet.

In the following drawings, I illustrate a few variations of two basic types of door and drawer fronts. One type is the $3/4''$ plywood door with glued-on moldings or a routed design. The other is the framed panel type. The panel may be $1/4''$ plywood, a raised panel of board lumber with beveled edges, or glass.

Birch is more available than many of the other hardwood plywoods and it can be easily finished to match any other woods.

The doors shown in Figures 2-1 and 2-2 are of $3/4''$ plywood. The trim or molding can be made of bass wood, fir, or white pine. Figures 2-1A and C show two variations of this type; others are shown in Figure 2-2. The top door (Figure 2-1A) has shallow vertical saw cuts about $2''$ to $2\frac{1}{2}''$ apart. The trim is $1/4''$ thick and $1\frac{5}{8}''$ wide with a small bead on the inside edge. The top rail of Figure 2-1C is beaded on the drill press or with a router. The door (Figure 2-1B) can either be made solid or cutout for glass. The simplest way is to saw out the inside and rabbet out the back inside edge to receive the glass or grille wire, which is held in place with small stops. The lower drawing shows the back side and how the top is chiseled or routed out for straight pieces of stops and glass cuts. The small molding on the front is tacked on with a small bead of glue in the center. Do not let the glue work out as it will spot the stain. Tack the moldings in place with small wire brads and pull them out when the glue has dried. The curved molding can be made on the lathe as shown in Figure 2-3.

CURVED MOLDINGS

Curved moldings are complicated to make and are usually used on furniture such as china cabinets or bookcases. Figure 2-3A shows how they can be made on the lathe. Saw a disc a little larger than the outside diameter of the molding. Mount the disc on the faceplate with a threaded rod through the spindle. (See Figure 9-5.) Turn to match the straight molding that is used. The drawing shows a shaped tool ground on an old file being used to shape the curved molding. If only a few pieces are needed, they can be turned the regular way.

Shown in Figure 2-3A are two full circles being made, one on each side of the $3/4''$ disc. This will make four half-circle pieces like the one in Figure 2-1B.

Sand smooth while turning, then use a dividing tool to cut into the center of the edge a little past the inside of the molding and cut off the ring with a sharp skew chisel as shown. The small triple bead molding (Figure 2-3B) is mostly used on French Provincial-type cabinet doors, with one in each corner connecting the straight pieces.

Cut blocks $4''$ square and about $3/8''$ thick. Drill a center hole for attaching to the faceplate and turn with the formed tool as shown. Fix a guide on the tool rest to ensure all the rings are the same size. Make the tool as shown by grinding with a $1/4''$ gumming wheel. Make the spur on the left side of the tool a little longer than the right side so it will cut off the excess material at the corners first. Sand the ring and cut off with the skew.

Figure 2-16A shows a jig to be used in cutting the rings into four segments with the ends mitered to fit the straight sections. With it, five or six rings can be cut at the same time. Just saw out the parts that are outside the crosslike jig.

FRAME AND PANEL DOORS

The frames around the panels can be made in several different ways. They are usually $2''$ to $2\frac{1}{4}''$ wide except when the top rail is to be sawed in a curve as shown in Figure 2-4A. This piece should then be an inch or two wider, but keep the center part about $2''$ wide.

Figure 2-4 shows three or four variations of door framing with $1/4'' \times 1''$ tenons fitting into grooves in the stiles. The simplest is a square butt joint as shown in Figures 2-4A and B. Notice that the groove in the stiles is a little over $1''$ deep at each end, but only about $5/16''$ through the remaining length (dotted line in Figure 2-4A).

If a curved top rail is used, it will have to be grooved on the shaper with a $1/4''$ cutter and rubbing collar (Figure 2-4C). Figures 2-4D and E show a frame that is rabbeted on the back side for glass or removable panels to be installed with stops.

Rabbet all pieces on the jointer $1/4''$ to $5/16''$ deep and $1/2''$ wide, leaving $1/4''$ of the face as shown in Figure 2-4D. The tenon is cut to fit the rabbeted stile (Figure 2-4E). If the curved rail is used at the top it can be installed with just a groove along the edge, as the panel can be slipped up into it, saving the trouble of making a curved stop that would be needed with a rabbeted edge.

Figures 2-4E, F, and G show a beaded edge around the inside of the framing. The door is shown in Figures

CABINET DOORS
3/4" Plywood with Glued-on Molding

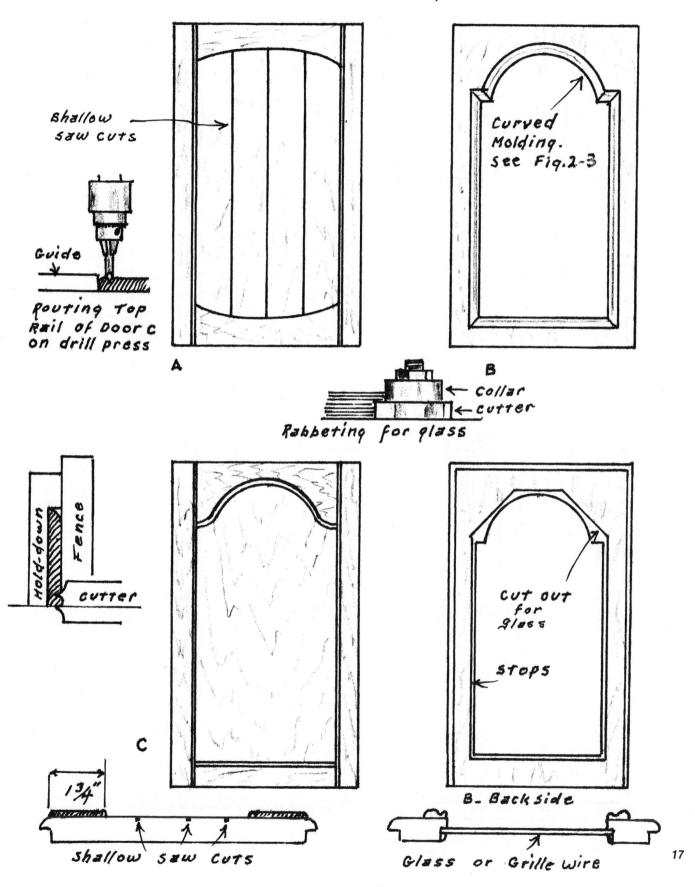

Shallow saw cuts

Guide

Routing Top Rail of Door C on drill press

A

Curved Molding. See Fig. 2-3

B

Collar

cutter

Rabbeting for glass

Hold-down

Fence

cutter

C

Cut out for glass

Stops

B_ Backside

1 3/4"

Shallow saw cuts

Glass or Grille wire

Figure 2-1

17

PLYWOOD DOORS
With Glued-on molding

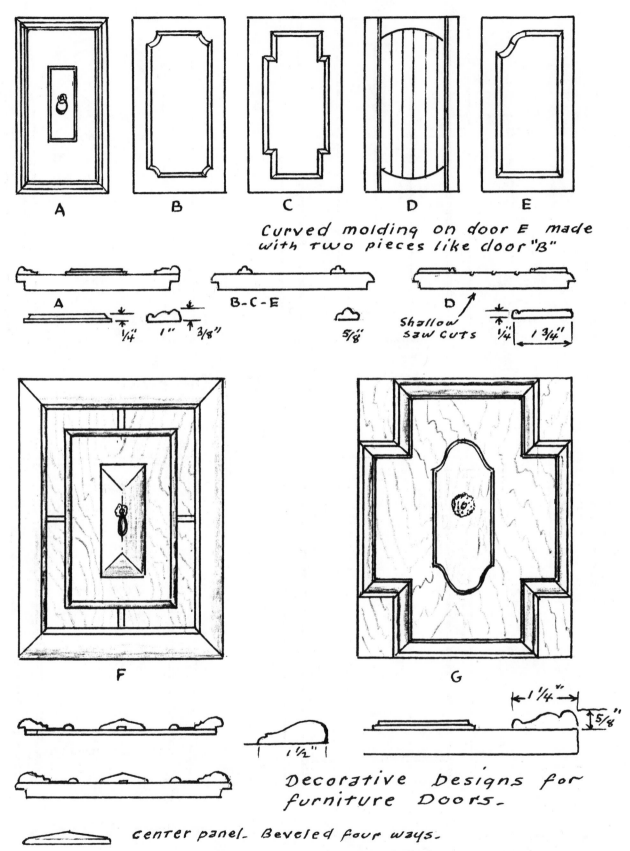

A   B   C   D   E

Curved molding on door E made
with two pieces like door "B"

A

B-C-E

D

1/4"   1"   3/8"   5/8"   Shallow saw cuts   1/4"   1 3/4"

F   G

1 1/2"   1 1/4"   5/8"

Decorative Designs for
furniture Doors.

center panel. Beveled four ways.

Figure 2-2

CURVED MOLDINGS
turned on the Lathe

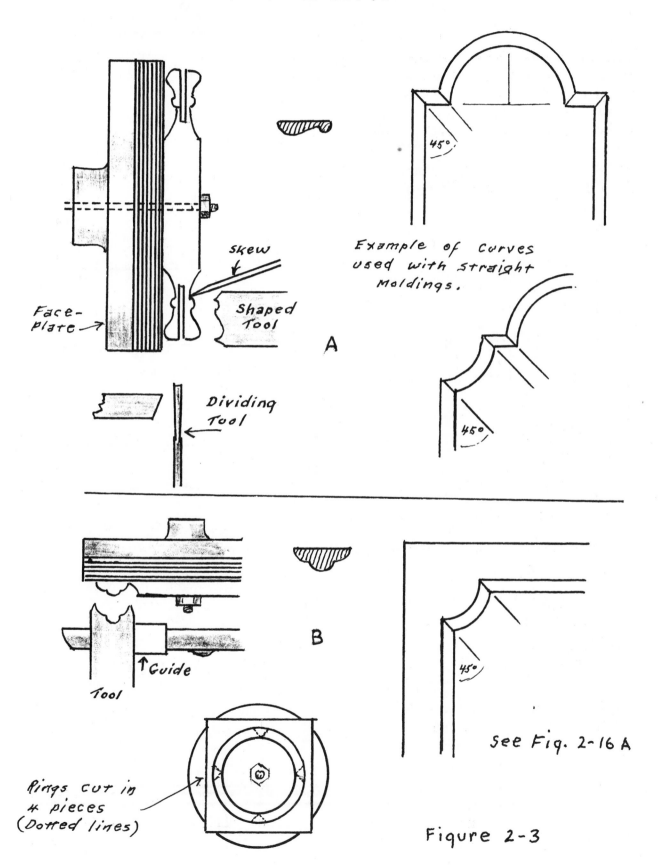

Face-Plate

skew

Shaped Tool

A

Dividing Tool

Example of curves used with straight Moldings.

45°

45°

B

Guide

Tool

Rings cut in 4 pieces (Dotted lines)

45°

See Fig. 2-16 A

Figure 2-3

FRAME-AND-PANEL DOORS

Shown here are two or three
ways to make frame-and-panel
doors. At the right is a simple
butt Mortice Joint,
Below are variations with molded
edges.
the Curved Top Rail is Optional,
it can be omitted or changed
To suit.

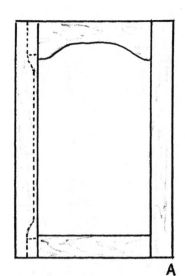

A

D

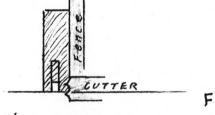

Frame Rabbeted for Glass

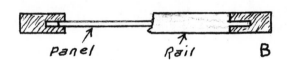

E

Panel   Rail

B

Cutting bead on framing
with shaper.

F

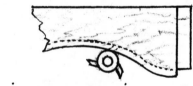

plowing groove in
Top Rail for panel.

C

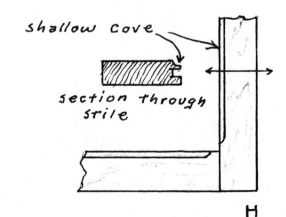

Routing bead on top Rail.
use drill press or router

G

shallow Cove

section through
Strile

H

Figure 2-4

2-1A and G. Another way this frame can be improved in appearance is shown in Figure 2-4H. A shallow cove is made along the edge but the joints are left square. The coped joint is the most professional looking but is the most complicated to make. It is covered in the raised panel doors (Figures 2-5 through 2-8).

RAISED PANEL DOORS

In my opinion the raised panel-type door is far ahead of any other for fine cabinet work, especially in the Colonial styles, and the coped joints in the framing add to the appearance almost as much as the panels. They are complicated to make but are worth the effort when the job is finished. I spent some time making jigs and cutters to speed up cutting the parts and to ensure accuracy.

Figure 2-5 shows a simple gauge that can be used with a yardstick to quickly determine the lengths of the pieces of framing and the size of the panel. This will save time and reduce the chance of mistakes. Detail A shows a section through a door. Note that the panel is let into the frame $1/4''$, but the tenon on the rail (Figure 2-5B) is $1''$ on the back side and $13/16''$ on the front. It fits into the ends of the stiles, which are grooved a little over $1''$ deep. The $3/16''$ added to the shoulder of the tenon is to allow for the cope cut, which is shown in Figure 2-6. Figure 2-5C shows the tenons being cut with a gauge that cuts $13/16''$ on one side and $1''$ on the other.

COPING

Figure 2-6 shows how the cope is made and fitted over the molded edge of the stile. The shaper is fitted with an auxiliary table fastened over the regular one by nailing cleats on the underside to keep it in place and bolts in the holes where the fence is fastened.

The guide (B) is fastened at one end with a screw, the other with a clamp to permit adjusting. Cut the notch just large enough to clear the coping head. The push block shown is a must. The block of $1/4''$ plywood on top holds the stock down on the table and square with the guide as it is fed into the cutter.

Figure 2-6C shows the coping cut being made. The guide is adjusted so the depth of cut is even with the shoulder on the other side, leaving $1/16''$ at the point. The molded bead along the frame is made to fit the cope and so matching cutters are needed for the coping and molding cut. The simplest for this type door is a small cove for the coping and a bead for the molding.

Figure 2-6C shows how they are matched to assure a good fit at the joints. Notice that the radius of the quarter circle is only $3/16''$. You may already have a cutter that can be used for the $3/16''$ bead on the framing but the cope cutter will have to be used in a head that can be mounted at the top of the shaper spindle (Figure 2-6C). (Figure 8-10 shows how you can make the head and cutter.) If a regular cutter is used, it will have to be long enough to

extend out past the spindle at least an inch or the length of the tenon. While the framing is being made, make several tenons and $1''$-deep grooves on scrap material to try out the various set-ups and avoid ruining a piece or two of the framing material. Do the coping cut on the rails before they are molded as they are apt to splinter at the end of the cross-grain cut. The molding cut will remove most of the splintering.

Try the molding set-up on one of the scraps with the groove and check for fit by slipping one of the coped pieces into the groove. Any correction needed for a good fit can be done by adjusting the molding cut.

PANELS

Board lumber is used for the panels. If they have to be glued up, scrape or sand the glue joints flush and cut to exact size by using the gauge (Figure 2-5). The best method to bevel the panels is by using the Sears "three-cutter" molding head on the table saw and shaped cutters (Figure 2-7F). However, the bevel can be made on the jointer (Figure 2-7A) by fastening a board as shown to support the panel at a slight angle or on the table saw as shown in Figure 2-7C. These two methods leave a flat cut with a sharp edge at the end of the bevel, while the shaped cutter makes a smooth, rounded one. Both sides of the panel can be beveled, leaving $1/4''$ in the center, or the back edge can be rabbeted on the jointer as shown in Figure 2-7E. Sand the panels before assembling the doors. Spread glue in the groove where the tenon fits into the stile with a thin paddle or squeeze bottle and pull together with a clamp. Nail each corner with $5/8''$ wire brads if needed. Finish by sanding the joints and trimming to correct size. Figure 2-8 shows curved panels being beveled on the shaper.

Figure 2-9 shows a half-lap version of the frame and panel door. Both the rails and stiles are cut the full width and height of the doors. A $3/8''$ ogee cutter is used for both the coping and molding. The panel is beveled halfway through the thickness and is glued and tacked in from the back side. With thinner panels or glass, small stops are used.

ROUTING TEMPLATE

About the easiest way to decorate a cabinet door is by routing a groove around the edges with a router and a template or frame that clamps around the door to guide the cutter. As these templates are rather expensive, I made my own (Figures 2-10 and 2-11). It will take a door up to 24" x 48" but is not handy to use on drawer fronts, so a smaller version for that purpose is shown in Figure 2-12. The advantage of the large one is that it pulls the corners of the doors up against the frame, taking care of any warp the door might have.

The rails (A) are made of strips of $3/4''$ plywood $31/2''$ wide. Two of them are 25" long and the other two are 50".

RAISED PANELS

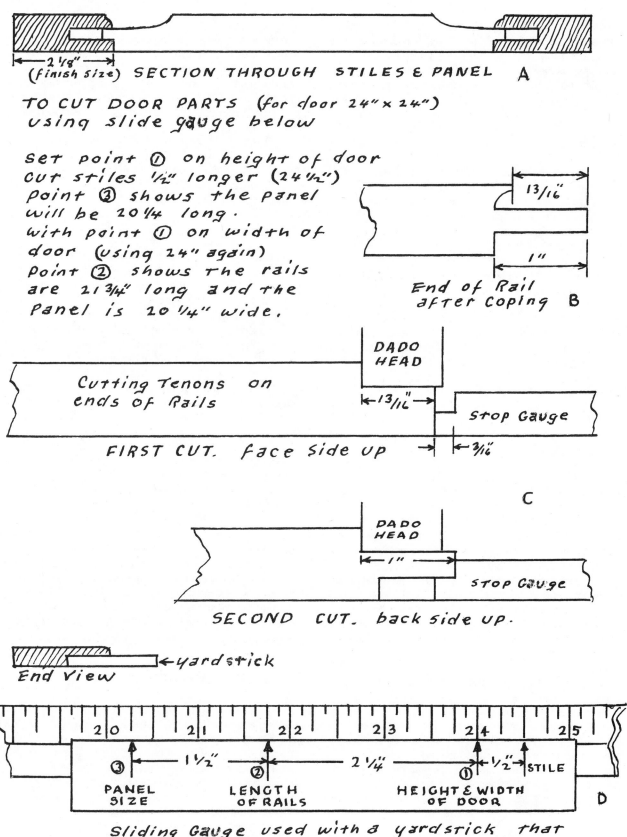

2 1/8"
(finish size) SECTION THROUGH STILES & PANEL   A

TO CUT DOOR PARTS (for door 24" x 24")
using slide gauge below

Set point ① on height of door
Cut stiles 1/2" longer (24 1/2")
Point ② shows the panel
will be 20 1/4 long.
With point ① on width of
door (using 24" again)
Point ② shows the rails
are 21 3/4" long and the
Panel is 20 1/4" wide.

13/16"
1"
End of Rail
after Coping   B

DADO HEAD
Cutting Tenons on
ends of Rails
13/16"
Stop Gauge
FIRST CUT. Face side up   3/16"
C

DADO HEAD
1"
STOP Gauge
SECOND   CUT. back side up.

←yardstick
End View

20   21   22   23   24   25
③   ②   ①
PANEL   1 1/2"   LENGTH   2 1/4"   HEIGHT & WIDTH   1/2"   STILE
SIZE   OF RAILS   OF DOOR
D

Sliding Gauge used with a yardstick that
quickly gives all dimensions in this type
of door construction. see instructions
above.

Figure 2-5

22

COPING
On The Shaper

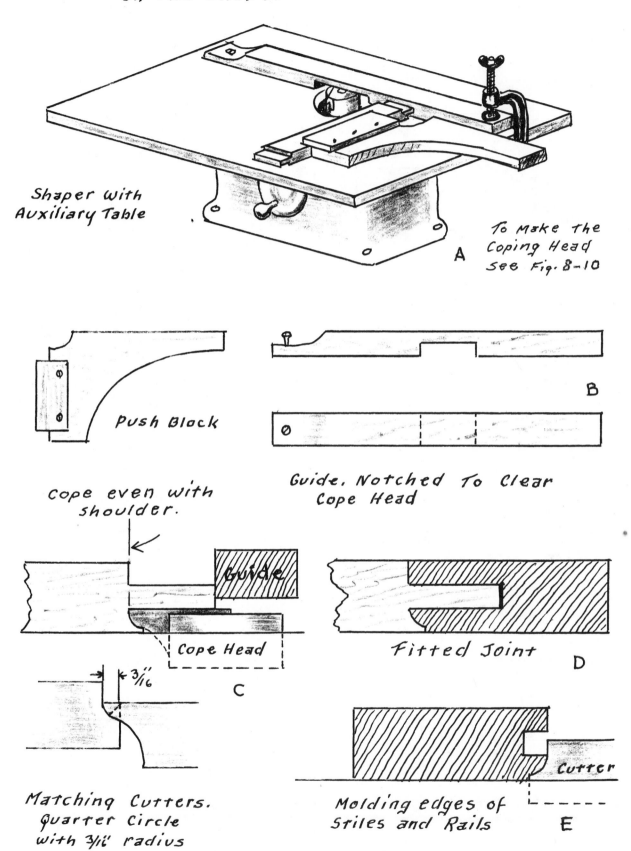

Shaper With
Auxiliary Table

A

To Make the
Coping Head
See Fig. 8-10

Push Block

B

Guide, Notched To Clear
Cope Head

Cope even with
shoulder.

Guide

Cope Head

C

Fitted Joint

D

3/16"

Matching Cutters.
Quarter Circle
with 3/16" radius

Molding edges of
Stiles and Rails

Cutter

E

Figure 2-6

23

RAISING PANELS

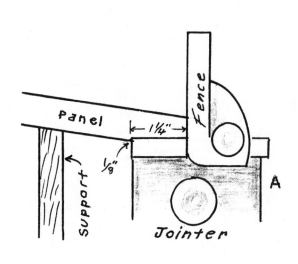

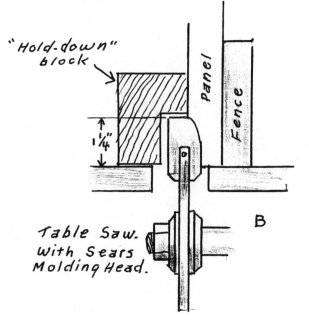

Panel   1¼"   Fence

Support   ⅛"

A

Jointer

panel beveled on
jointer. The support
determines angle
of bevel.

"Hold-down"
block

Panel   Fence

1¼"

B

Table Saw.
With Sears
Molding Head.

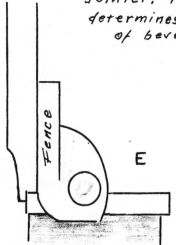

Fence

E

Rabbeting back
side of panel
on jointer

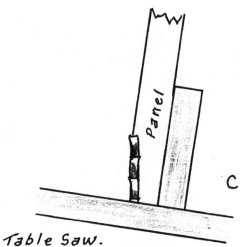

Panel

C

Table Saw.
with table tilted

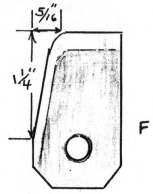

5/16"

1¼"

F

Sears Cutter.
grind as shown.

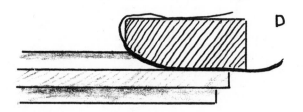

D

Sanding Bevels
(use 100 grit floor sanding
paper)

24

Figure 2-7

CURVED DOOR PANELS

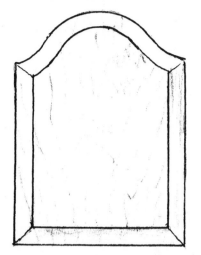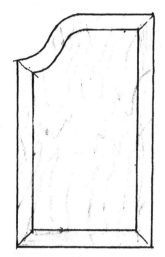

Raised door panels that are curved as shown
here have to be beveled against a rubbing
collar. Below is shown a set-up on the shaper
using a "two knife" head, and an auxiliary table.
Bevel both sides, leaving the center so it
will fit into the groove of the framing.

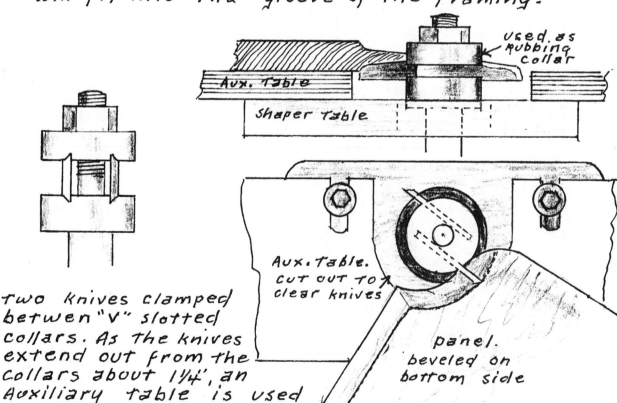

used as
Rubbing
collar

Aux. Table

Shaper Table

Aux. Table.
CUT OUT TO
clear knives

panel.
beveled on
bottom side

two knives clamped
betwen "V" slotted
collars. As the knives
extend out from the
collars about 1¼", an
Auxiliary table is used
in order to keep the
cutters under the work
for safety.

Figure 2-8

CABINET DOOR FRAMES

with half-lap joints for
raised panels or plywood.
Fasten panels in from back
side with glue and small
wire brads.

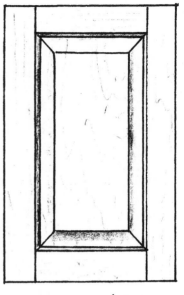

Front side

End view showing coped half-
lap joints

Section through center
showing raised panel.

glue and nail (or staple)
joints

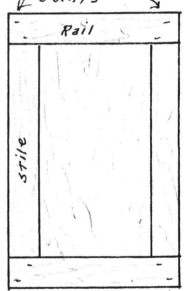

Back side

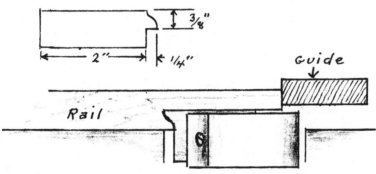

Coping cut on shaper. (cope before
shaping edge)

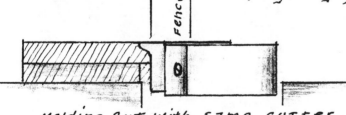

Molding cut with same cutter

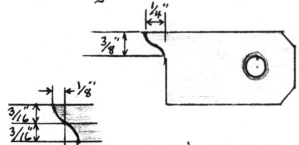

Figure 2-9

Cut framing 2¼" wide,
and height and width
of door. Rabbet back
edge. Cope rails. Shape
front edge.

Grind the cutter in OGEE
pattern at left, with the
upper 3/16" ground in exact
reverse of the lower half.

26

ROUTING TEMPLATE
For Cabinet Doors

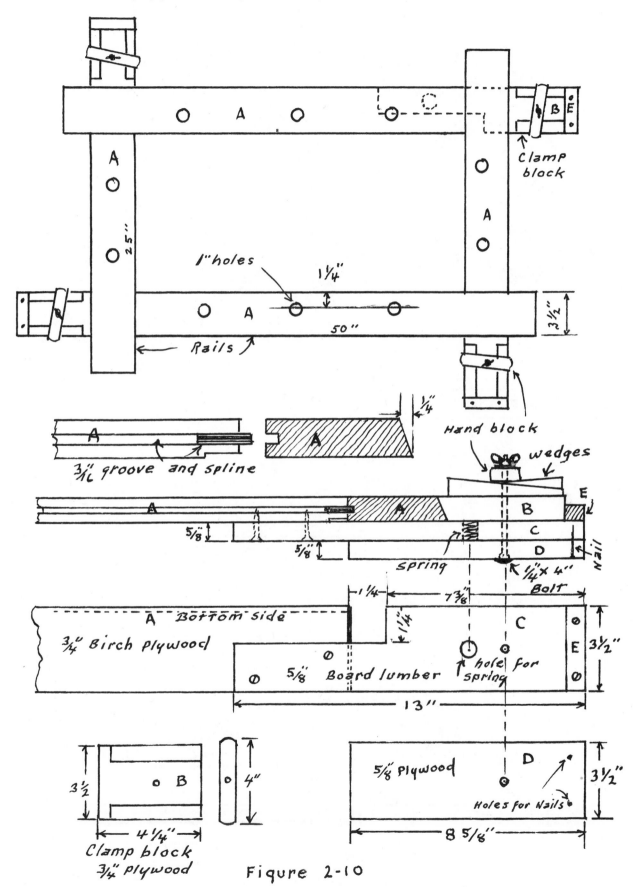

Clamp block

1" holes

1¼"

2.5"

50"

3½"

Rails

Hand block

1"

3/16" groove and spline

wedges

A

B

C

D

E

Nail

5/8"

5/8"

spring

¼" × 4" Bolt

A   Bottom side

¾" Birch plywood

1¼"

1¼"

7⅜"

C

E

3½"

hole for spring

5/8" Board lumber

13"

Clamp block
¾" plywood

3½"

B

4"

4¼"

5/8" Plywood

D

Holes for Nails

3½"

8 5/8"

Figure 2-10

27

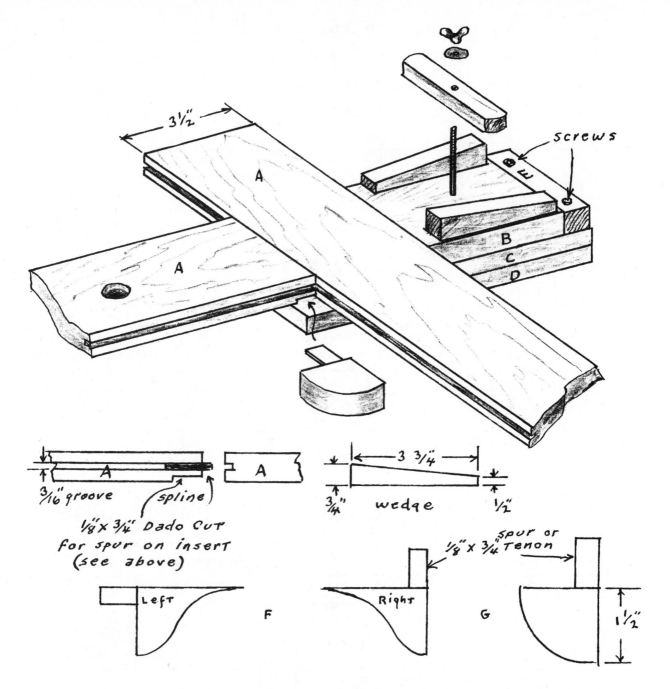

3½"

screws

A

A

B
C
D

E

3/16" groove   spline   A

⅛"x ¾" Dado cut
for spur on insert
(see above)

3 ¾"

¾"   wedge   ½"

⅛"x ¾" spur or
Tenon

Left   F   Right   G

1½"

Inserts for Ornamental Door Patterns.

Hand block tightens clamp
plate B against A and block
D up against door.

Router

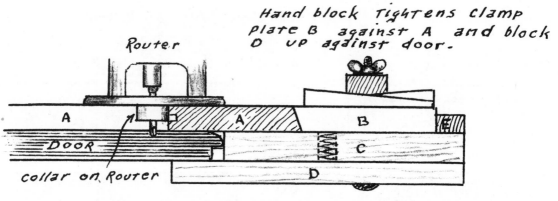

A   A   B

DOOR   C

collar on Router   D

Figure 2-11

TEMPLATE FOR DRAWER FRONTS

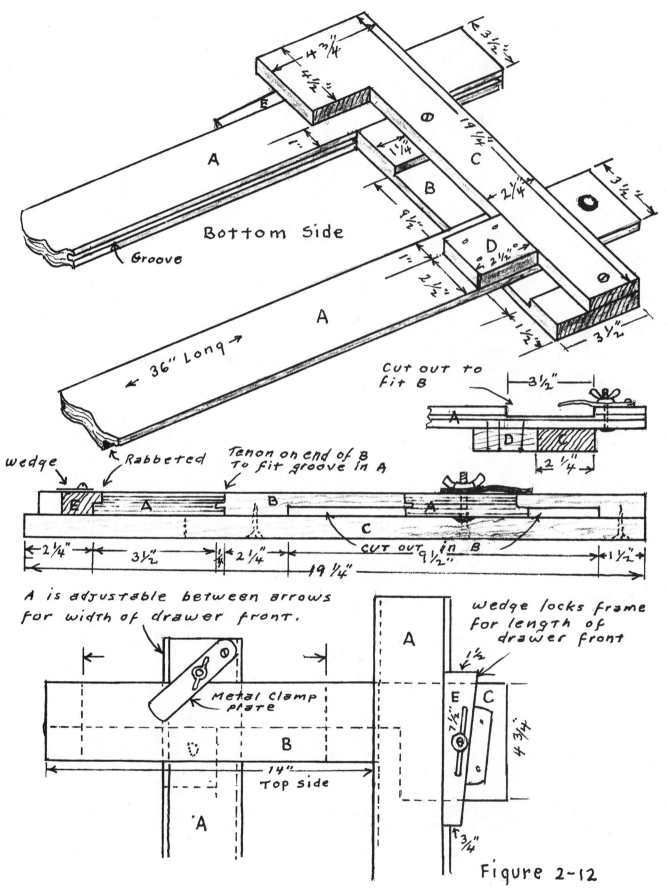

Bottom Side

Groove

4 3/4"

4 1/2"

3 1/2"

19 1/4"

1 1/4"

C

B

9 1/2"

2 1/4"

D 2 1/2"

1"

2 1/2"

1/2"

3 1/2"

3 1/2"

A

36" Long

Cut out to fit B

3 1/2"

A

D C

2 1/4"

wedge

Rabbeted

Tenon on end of B To fit groove in A

E   A   B

C

Cut out in B 9 1/2"

2 1/4"   3 1/2"   1/4" 2 1/4"   19 1/4"   1 1/2"

A is adjustable between arrows for width of drawer front.

Metal Clamp plate

B

14"

Top side

'A

A

wedge locks frame for length of drawer front

1 1/2"

E C

7 1/2"

4 3/4"

3/4"

Figure 2-12

29

SIMPLE DRAWER CONSTRUCTION

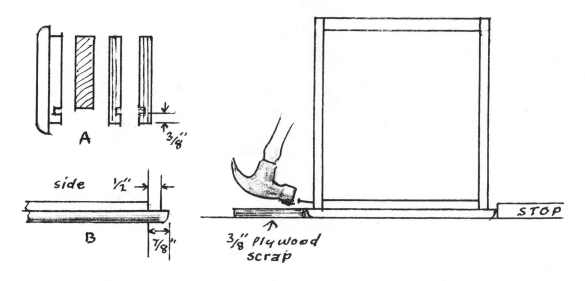

A

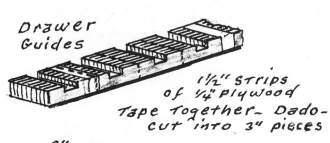

side ½"

B ⅞"

⅜"

3⁄8" plywood
scrap

STOP

Drawer
Guides

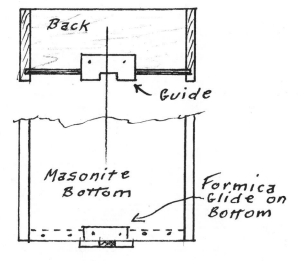

1½" strips
of ¼" plywood
Tape together— Dado—
cut into 3" pieces

Back

Guide

Masonite
Bottom

Formica
Glide on
Bottom

3"

1½"

⅞"

Guide

Formica Slides

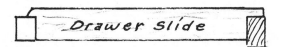

Drawer Slide

Cut Drawer fronts 5⁄8" larger
than opening—
Shape edges with door
cutter—
Dado ends to ⅞" (B)
Sides ½" material— plow
groove for bottom in sides
and front (A).
If sides are of ½" plywood,
sand bottom edge smooth
and rub with paraffin.

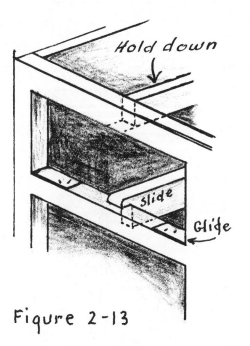

Hold down

Slide

Glide

30

Figure 2-13

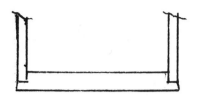  

Front for flush type drawer

Front with lip on each end

Front to match Raised panel doors

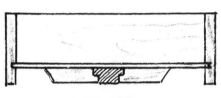 slides each Side to fit groove in drawer side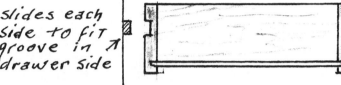

Guide slide

Self-supporting slides - Drawer pulls out level without Tilting -

 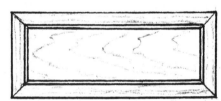

Drawer Fronts with molding to match doors

CURVED FRONTS
for furniture

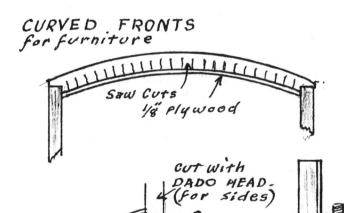

Saw Cuts 1/8" plywood

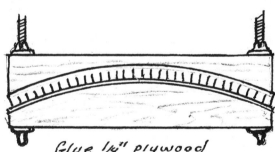

Glue 1/8" plywood To back side - Clamp between blocks. Make oversize. Trim To finish size when dry; fill cuts with Plastic wood, sand.

cut with DADO HEAD (for sides)

Block up end for Rabbeting -

plow groove for bottom on shaper with rubbing Collar

Figure 2-14

PAINT STRIPER

For painting the grooves in routed Cabinet doors. The one shown here can be easily made with parts found in the bathroom wastebasket.

The dark brown stripe greatly improves the appearance of Routed doors

Fasten the glass Tube in the squeeze bottle Cap.

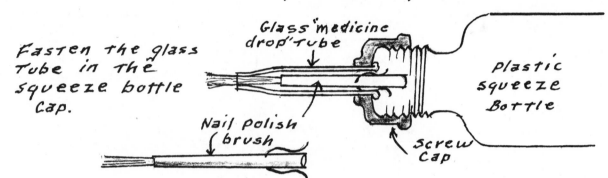

Glass 'medicine drop' tube

Nail polish brush

Plastic squeeze Bottle

Screw Cap

Fine steel wire through stem To keep brush in place

Brush with Thinner

Tear off

THE PAINT

Most paint dealers keep a supply of heavy universal Colors that they mix with paints and stains. Ask for a little black and brown. Mix together for a dark brown. add a little Sandsealer to speed drying.

Wiping pad.
Made by tightly wrapping a strip of Cotton Cloth around a block of wood several times. Keep damp with mineral spirits or paint Thinner. Tear off Outside layer when it becomes saturated with stain.

First, stain the doors. Then seal with one Coat of sealer. Sand with fine paper including The grooves. Fill bottle. keeping the brush down in The groove and lightly squeezing the bottle, paint the entire groove. Immediately wipe off any that gets On the face of door. When dry, apply finishing Coat. Note; Take bottle apart and clean after using.

Figure 2-15

MITERING CURVED MOLDING

At the right, A jig for sawing the segments of curved molding for cabinet doors shown in Fig. 2-3B It is simply two crosses that clamp the turned rings while they are being cut on the band saw. A 1/4" bolt holds them together. recess the head in the bottom cross.

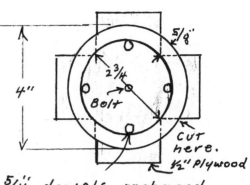

5/16" dowels anchored in bottom cross

A

WOBBLE SAW

Bevel a piece of wood 6"or 7" long. Cut in two pieces. Drill hole size of saw mandrel, clamp saw between, Be sure to match the bevels, the blocks can be marked for this.

Mark for Matching bevels

B

For wide grooves. short bevel   or long bevel for narrow grooving   Drill both pieces together

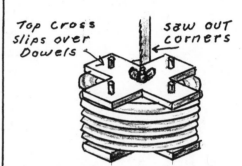

Top cross slips over Dowels   saw out corners

Top cross held down with wing nut.

HINGE GAUGE

Here's a gauge that saves time in hinging cabinet doors. Drill holes from bottom side. use the drill bit that is to be for the hinge screws. and a hinge for template.

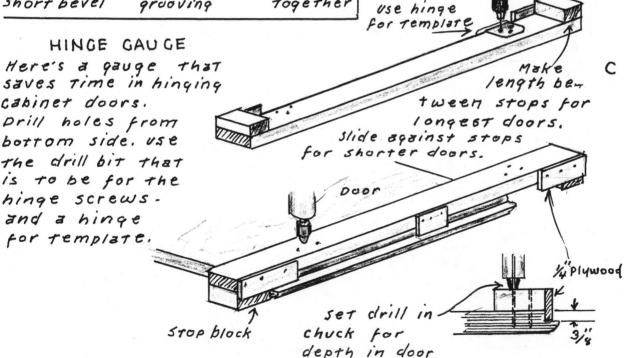

use hinge for template

Make length between stops for longest doors.

C

Slide against stops for shorter doors.

Door

Stop block

set drill in chuck for depth in door

1/4" Plywood

3/8"

Figure 2-16

SHOP HELPERS

Here's some handy gadgets especially the door Rack. The little shelf below serves as a support for drawers while finishing the front and drilling holes for the pulls.
Try using squares of foam rubber for smoothing stain.

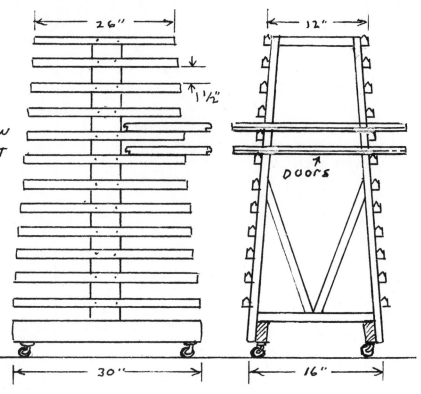

DOOR-DRYING RACK

Do you have trouble finding places for a bunch of wet cabinet doors? this rack permits the doors to lay flat to avoid runs in the varnish. Just load it up and roll out of the way on its casters.

All strips beveled on Top.

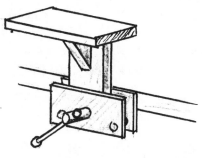

Foam Rubber →

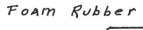

A couple of 2"x 2"s beveled on one edge makes a good support while finishing.

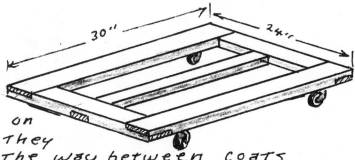

By setting cabinets on dollies for finishing, they can be rolled out of the way between coats

Figure 2-17

34

LOUVERED DOORS

If you have a drill press and a hollow chisel mortising outfit, these louvered doors are fairly easy to make. the frame is two inches wide. Cut the stiles 1/2" over finished height, The Rails 1 1/2" over the distance between the stiles.

Below is the procedure for making the slats.

1. Rip the material for the slats. 3/4 x 1 1/4", in long lengths.
2. Shape both edges as shown below.
3. Split in center. Making two pieces.
4. Plane down to 1/4 thick.
5. Cut slats 3/4 longer than the distance between the stiles.
6. Cut tenons 1/4 x 1/4 and 3/8 long. (Do several at a time)

Shape two slats before ripping

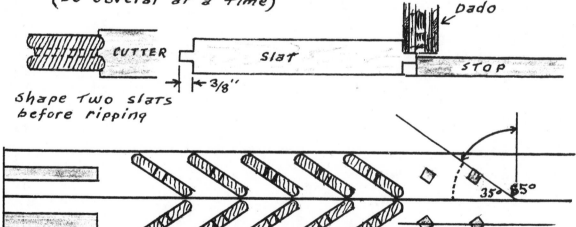

As the angle of the slats is larger than 45° (from the edge of the stile) the hollow chisel will have to reset after one stile has been mortised. Use an adjustable bevel square to set angle approx. 55° with drill press guide) The holes are 1/4" x 1/4" and about 7/16" deep.

Figure 2-18

35

SIMULATED LOUVERS
For Blinds and Shutters

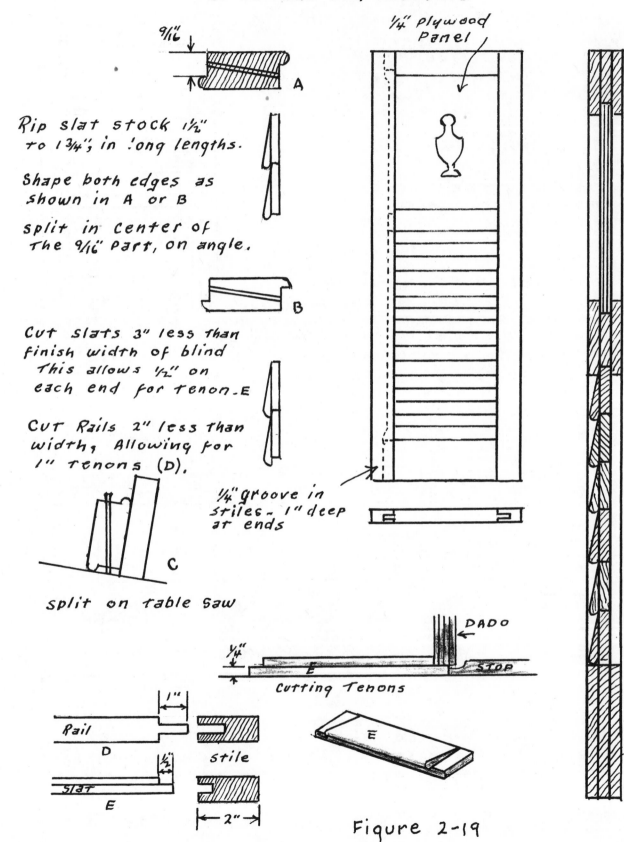

9/16"

A

Rip slat stock 1½"
to 1¾", in long lengths.

Shape both edges as
shown in A or B

split in center of
the 9/16" part, on angle.

B

Cut slats 3" less than
finish width of blind
This allows ½" on
each end for tenon. E

Cut Rails 2" less than
width, Allowing for
1" tenons (D).

C

split on table saw

¼" plywood
Panel

¼" groove in
stiles- 1" deep
at ends

DADO

¼"

E

STOP

Cutting Tenons

1"

Rail

D

stile

½"

slat

E

2"

Ē

Figure 2-19

They can be shorter than this if desired, depending on the size of doors to be routed. They are beveled on one edge and grooved in the other. One end of each is grooved for a spline, which slides along the groove in the edge of the adjacent rail. Be sure it is the end shown in the drawing. The four clamp blocks (B) are 3½" x 4½" are beveled to match the rails. They have two wedge-shaped blocks on top that serve to lock the corners when the hand block is turned to their highest point. It can be adjusted by the wing nut.

Cut parts (C) and (D) as shown and fasten (C) to the splined ends of the four rails with two screws. The hole in (C) is for a coil spring. It pushes the block (B) up and (D) down when the hand block is loosened, allowing the corners of the doors to slip into the corner that is cut in the block (C). Turning the hand block to the right will pull the door up tight against the frame. The bottom block (D) is loosely fastened at the outer end with two nails through slightly larger holes. Place the four small blocks (E), so they will force the clamp blocks (B) tight against the beveled edge of the rails (A), which in turn is against the splined end of the other rail (see Figure 2-10 center). They are all locked in place when the hand block is tightened. The 1" holes along the length of the rails are for checking the position of the door. If it is properly clamped in the frame with all four corners tight in the corners of the (C) block, you should be able to see all four edges through the holes.

Always check this because a groove in the wrong place ruins the door. All four of the rails have a shallow dado cut on the bottom side just under the spline. The spline receives the ⅛" x ¾" tenon on the corner templates that guide the router. Make four of (G) (Figure 2-11)

and one each of (F). These two are alike except the tenon on the right one is on top, the other on the side. They are used at the top of a door to give an arch effect. Other designs can be added as desired. They do not have to be fastened. After the door is clamped in place, just slip them in the slot.

At the bottom of Figure 2-11 is shown a door being routed. A 1" collar guides the router along the rail of the frame. A small frame shown in Figure 2-12 will take drawer fronts up to 12" wide and 30" long. Two wedges with slots for screws lock the frame in the lengthwise positions. The other is changed only when different width fronts are to be routed. It is locked with a metal plate and wing nut.

The long rails (A) are cut out halfway to receive the cross rail and (B) is cut out 9½" long for the cross adjustment.

Figures 2-13 and 2-14 show a few ideas on drawer construction and inexpensive slides and guides.

Figures 2-15–2-17 contain some odds and ends that may be helpful around the workshop.

LOUVERED DOORS

It is usually cheaper to buy louvered doors than make them. In case an odd size is needed, however, they can be made as shown in Figure 2-18, if you have a hollow chisel attachment for your drill press.

The blind is easier as the frame is grooved like a frame-and-panel door and slats are used instead of solid panels. To make simulated louvers, see Figure 2-19.

3 ODDS AND ENDS

In this chapter I have included a few items that can be made in a shorter time than some of the other projects in the book.

In Figures 3-1 to 3-4 are some wooden clamps and templates that are easily made and can be very useful for odd jobs that require special adapted clamps and jigs.

I have most of these hanging over my work bench and have found that the small wooden bar clamps are more convenient for light work than the heavy metal ones. I made the deep-throated C-clamp especially to clamp the bridges on guitar tops (see Chapter 5) but have found many other uses for them.

For quick, one-time jobs, or where a large number of clamps of the same size are needed, the "C-block and wedge" type is the easiest to make and use.

Tape some strips of ³/₄″ plywood together and cut out the notches with a dado saw, then cut into blocks, leaving the notch in the center of each one.

The other items (Figures 3-5 to 3-10) are offered mostly as suggestions of some of the wide variety of gifts, toys, and novelties that can be made in a home workshop from scrap material.

They can be made in lots of a dozen or more by cutting several parts with each set-up. Things like these bring good prices in hobby stores and will give the craftsman extra income and a use for his scrap material.

Toys like the truck (but maybe not as elaborate) can be made in kit form and packaged in plastic bags. The wheels are the main feature in this kind of toy, but are easily made with the proper tools as shown in Figure 3-8.

The "play logs" are lots of fun for kids as well as adults. I've made many sets for gifts. They can be made in any size with any number of pieces desired.

The Tic-Tac-Toe game is very popular and easy to sell.

About the Fun House (Figure 3-9), of course it would be impossible to build as drawn. I included it only as a jest. I used to show a similar drawing to carpenter friends who came to my shop. I would ask if they could build it exactly as drawn for a customer of mine. "Sure," they would say. "No sweat." I would insist that they study the drawing carefully. Most would change their minds later but some still insisted they could build it. Could you?

PICTURE FRAME CLAMP

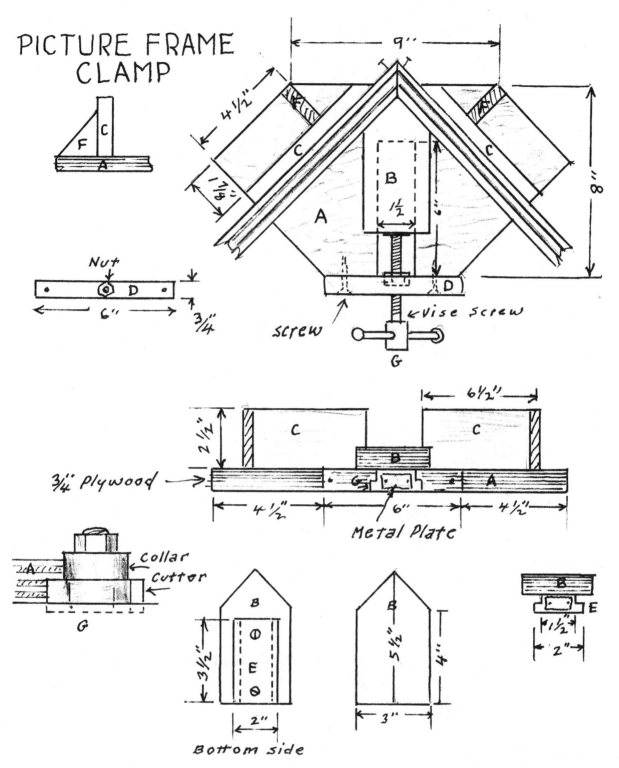

The two pieces of molding are held in place against the two blocks (C) by the pointed block (B) that slides along the slot cut in the base (A). The slot is rabbeted on the bottom (G). To receive block E which is also rabbeted to match And is fastened to B with two screws. The vise screw turns in a nut sunk in block D and against a plate nailed to the end of E.

Figure 3-1

39

FOUR-WAY PICTURE FRAME CLAMP

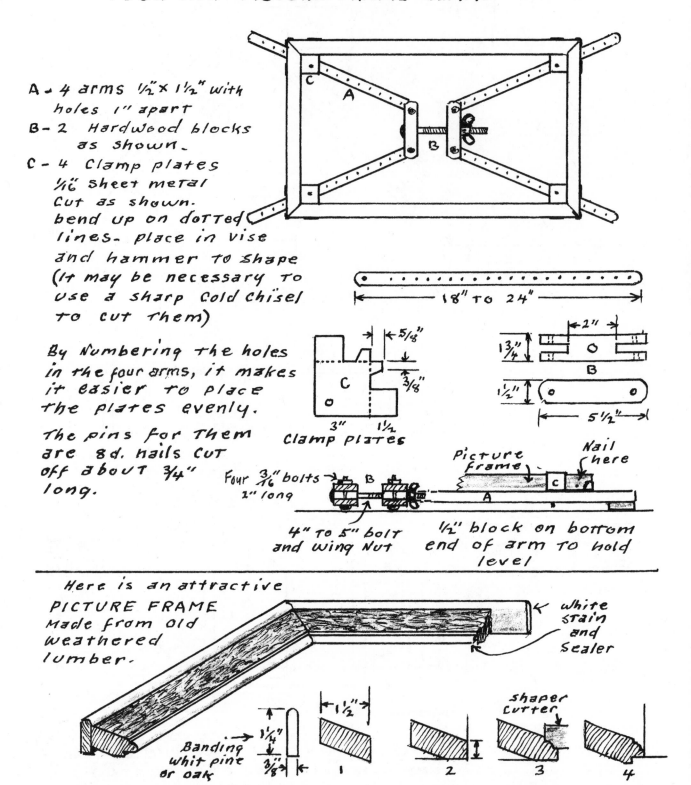

A - 4 arms 1/2" x 1 1/2" with holes 1" apart

B - 2 Hardwood blocks as shown.

C - 4 Clamp plates 1/16" sheet metal cut as shown. bend up on dotted lines. place in vise and hammer to shape (It may be necessary to use a sharp cold chisel to cut them)

By Numbering the holes in the four arms, it makes it easier to place the plates evenly.

The pins for them are 8d. nails cut off about 3/4" long.

18" TO 24"

5/8"
3/8"
C
3"   1 1/2
Clamp Plates

2"
13/4"
B
1 1/2"
5 1/2"

Four 3/16" bolts 2" long   B   Picture Frame   Nail here

4" to 5" bolt and Wing Nut   1/2" block on bottom end of arm to hold level

---

Here is an attractive PICTURE FRAME Made from old weathered lumber.

white stain and Sealer

Banding whit pine or oak
1 1/4"
3/8"
1 1/2"
1
2
shaper cutter
3
4

From old rough sawed oak or pine, saw as shown (1)
Bevel bottom edge square with cut. keep edge marked same
thickness all around inside edge (2) Shape (3) Rabbet (4)
Stain band and shaped edge white - one coat of
sealer over the stain - keep off the rough surface.

Figure 3-2

DRAW PERFECT OVALS

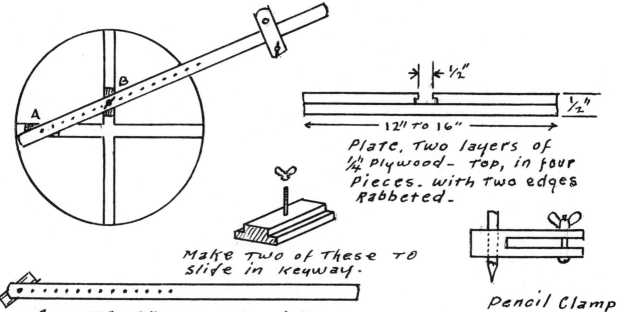

↑ ½"

|← 12" to 16" →| ½"

Plate, Two layers of
¼" plywood- Top, in four
Pieces. with two edges
Rabbeted.

Make Two of These To
slide in keyway.

Pencil Clamp

Arm. 5/16" × ¾" × 30" Holes ½" apart.

The shape of the oval, whether long and narrow or wide
and short is made by adjusting the sliding block (B)
The pencil Clamp is slid along the arm for the size.
The block A can be fastened to arm with a screw.
Only B is used for adjusting.

Dividers

Adjustable Arc Template

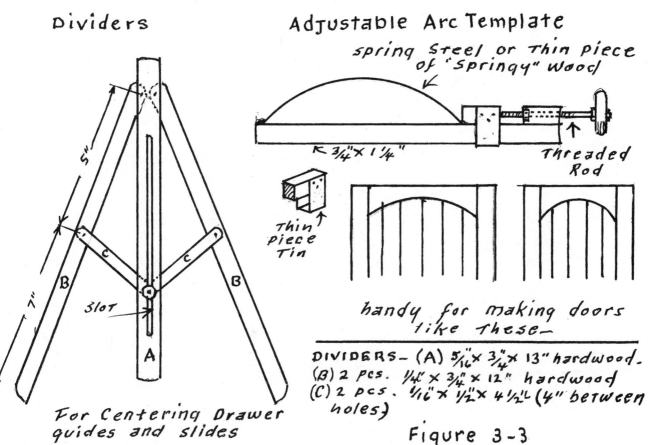

spring steel or thin piece
of "springy" wood

|← ¾" × 1¼"

Threaded
Rod

Thin
piece
Tin

handy for making doors
like these-

For Centering Drawer
guides and slides

Slot

5"

7"

DIVIDERS- (A) 5/16" × ¾" × 13" hardwood.
(B) 2 pcs. ¼" × ¾" × 12" hardwood
(C) 2 pcs. ¼" × ½" × 4½"L (4" between
holes)

Figure 3-3

41

CLAMPS

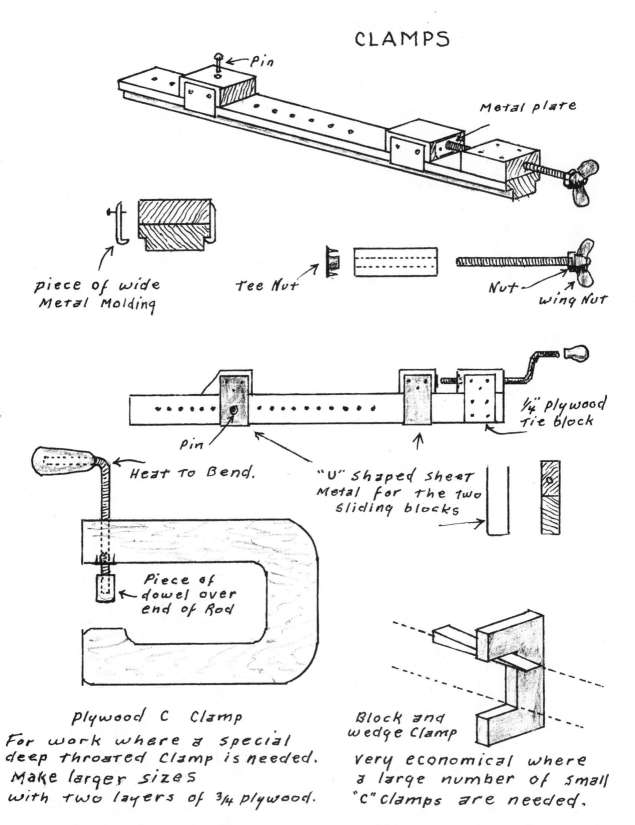

Pin

Metal plate

piece of wide
Metal Molding

Tee Nut

Nut

Wing Nut

Pin

Heat To Bend.

¼" plywood
Tie block

"U" shaped sheet
Metal for the two
sliding blocks

Piece of
dowel over
end of Rod

Plywood C Clamp
For work where a special
deep throated Clamp is needed.
Make larger sizes
with two layers of ¾ plywood.

Block and
wedge Clamp
Very economical where
a large number of small
"C" Clamps are needed.

Useful clamps are Easily made With scrap material, Some
pieces of threaded Rods, "Tee" nuts, & Wing Nuts.

Figure 3-4

SPIRAL BUD VASE

Drill 3/4" hole in 1 3/4" stock of walnut or cherry, Center stock at other end by using jig as shown. Plug with 3/4" x 6" dowel. Turn as shown below, leave tenon on end. Drill 3/8" hole at bottom end of spiral. Starting at hole, wind 3/8" tape around in spiral about three rounds. Do the same with hole on other side. Wind tape exactly in center of other spiral. They should be 3/8" to 1/2" apart. Saw at edge of tape with coping saw, pull out dowel and sand sawed edges.

Glue up blocks for base. Turn and drill for tenon

Insert 3/4" glass test tube.

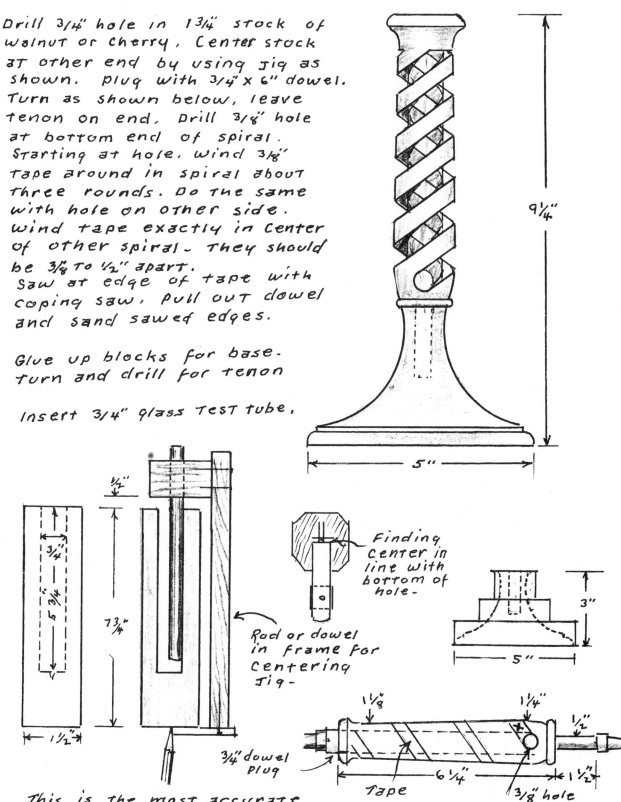

This is the most accurate way to find the center at bottom end. mark from four sides as shown above.

saw out waste (x) with coping saw, sand edges.

Figure 3-5

43

TURN - A - BELL

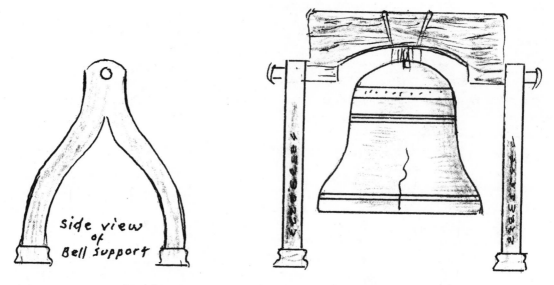

side view
of
Bell support

Suggested Novelty with Wooden Bell
Make size to suit.

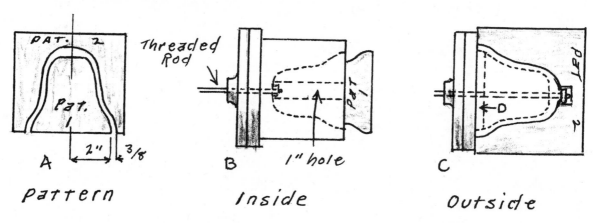

A   PAT. 2   Pat. 1   2"   3/8

Pattern

B   Threaded Rod   1" hole

Inside

C   D   PAT 2

Outside

The pattern — Draw half bell on folded paper — transfer to 1/4" plywood. For 4" dia. cut out about 3/8" for thickness of Bell.

B — Drill 1" hole in center to within 3/4" of end and finish with hole size of threaded rod through lathe spindle. Use pattern for inside

C — Saw and turn a disc to fit inside of bell to keep it on center (D) Turn the outside with pat. 2

Figure 3-6

TOYS AND MODELS
from Scrap materials.

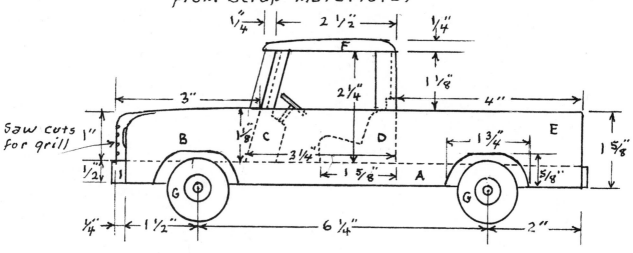

Saw cuts 1"
for grill

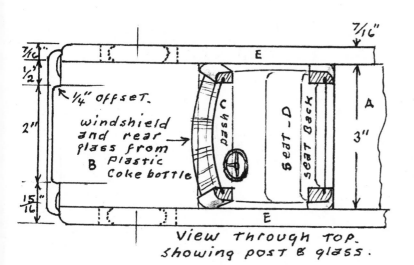

¼" offset.

windshield
and rear
glass from
Plastic
Coke bottle

Dash-C

Seat-D

Seat Back

View through top.
Showing post & glass.

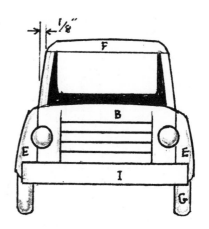

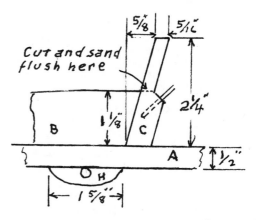

Cut and sand
flush here

A. Base. ½" x 3" x 9 ¾"
B- Hood. 1⅛" x 3" x 3" bevel to fit C
C - Dash & windshield - Cut grooves
     with knife for glass.
D- Seat & Back glass
E - Side panels ⁷⁄₁₆" x 15⁄8" x 9 ¾"
     Bevel as shown
F- Top ¼" 2¾" x 2¾"
G- Wheels. ⅜" x 15⁄16" dia.
     (see wheels for toys)
H. Bearing blocks ½" x ½" x 15⁄8" 5⁄16 hole
     The axle is ¼" dowel. 4"
I - Bumpers. ¼" x ½" x 3⅝"
J - Headlights ½" dowels. 1⅛" long.
K - Steering wheel - ¾" dia.
     Ring type washer.
   After assembly, Sand off sharp corners
     and Joints.

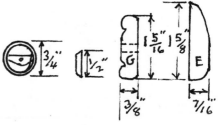

Figure 3-7

45

WHEELS FOR TOYS AND MODELS

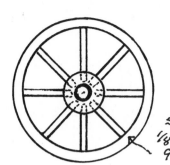

Wagon Wheel

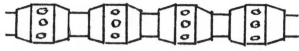

spokes
1/8" dowels-
glue To Rim

Hubs For wagon wheels
Turn Four at same time

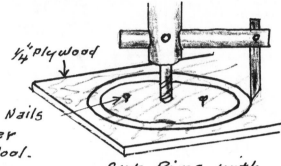

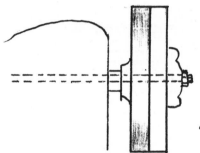

Auto Wheel-
Cut with Circle Cutter
Turn with Formed Tool.

1/4" plywood

Nails

Cut Rims with
Circle Cutter

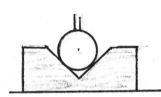

Fasten To
Faceplate
with 1/4" Threaded
rod.

Drilling Hubs
For spokes

KEY RACK

1/4" birch
Plywood

|← 10" →|

Cut out inside as shown.
Rabbet For Plexiglas front.
Glue felt to 1/8" plywood
back- Glue some old keys
To the felt, place some
hooks around edge for
your keys-

3/4" white pine

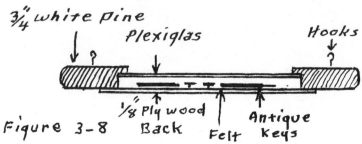

Plexiglas

Hooks

1/8" Plywood
Back

Felt

Antique
keys

Figure 3-8

46

THE FUN HOUSE

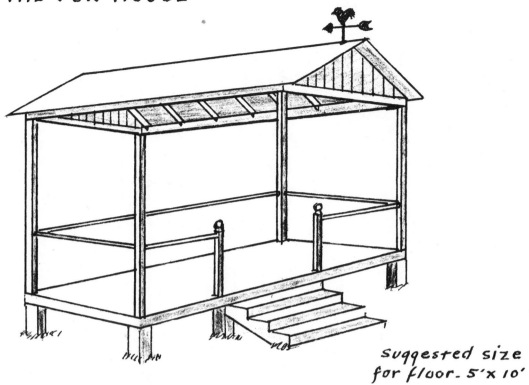

suggested size
for floor - 5' x 10'

Here's something the kids will enjoy in the
back yard And you will have lots of fun
building, Study the drawing Carefully before
you start as it may be a little more
Complicated than it looks at First glance.
Especially the roof and the steps.

PLAY LOGS. Interlocking blocks that keep the
kids busy for hours building all
kinds of Cabins and
other things -

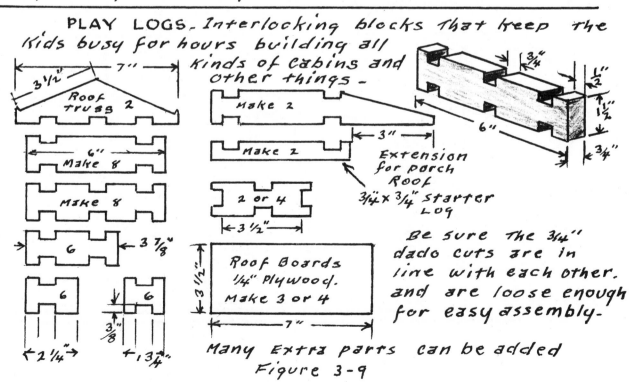

7"

3½"

Roof Truss 2

6"
Make 8

Make 8

6   3 ⅞"

6   6

2¼"   1¾"

3/8"

Make 2

Make 2

3"

Extension
for porch
Roof

3¼" x 3¼" Starter
LOG

2 or 4

3½"

Roof Boards
¼" Plywood.
Make 3 or 4

3½"

7"

¾"

1½"

1½"

6"

¾"

Be sure The 3/4"
dado cuts are in
line with each other.
and are loose enough
for easy assembly.

Many Extra parts can be added

Figure 3-9

TIC-TAC-TOE GAME
With Marbles

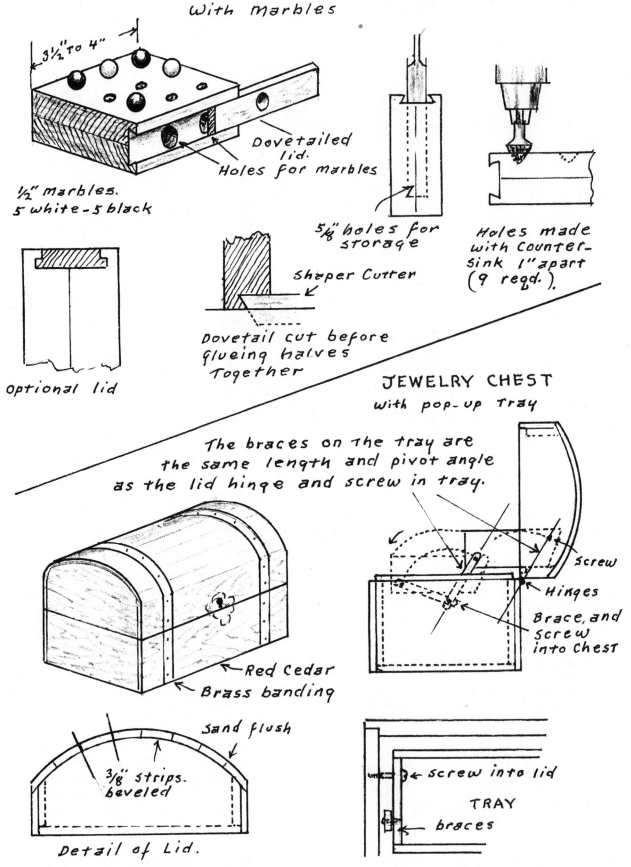

3½" To 4"

Dovetailed lid.

Holes for marbles

½" marbles.
5 white - 5 black

5⅛" holes for storage

Holes made with Counter-sink 1" apart (9 reqd.).

Optional lid

Shaper Cutter

Dovetail cut before glueing halves together

JEWELRY CHEST
with pop-up Tray

The braces on the tray are the same length and pivot angle as the lid hinge and screw in tray.

Screw

Hinges

Brace, and Screw into Chest

Red Cedar

Brass banding

Sand flush

3/8" strips. beveled

Detail of Lid.

screw into lid

TRAY braces

MAKE SIZE TO SUIT
Figure 3-10

FURNITURE 4

Most craftsmen, sooner or later, build some furniture either for themselves or a customer. I have included in this chapter a few odd pieces that seem to be the most popular, especially with the home craftsman. Some of these, such as the drop-leaf desk and typewriter shelf, are included mostly to show construction methods that can be used in any type of cabinet or desk.

I have built variations of all the furniture shown here, including the two small antique tables (pages 56 and 57); however, I have made some changes to simplify construction.

PEDESTAL DINING TABLE

The pedestal shown here (Figure 4-1) is both strong and fairly easy to build. I have made several of them with oak, walnut, and even pine in different sizes as desired by the customer.

The one I have in my kitchen is the size illustrated. It has a 40″ diameter top and a 14″ leaf. If a larger or smaller top is to be made, the pedestal should be sized accordingly. The base is about 12″ less than the diameter of the top (without the leaves).

The base is made of two pieces notched together in the center to form the four feet of the base. They are 1⅝″ × 7½″ x 28″ long and can be single boards or two boards glued up to the proper thickness.

Saw to shape as shown in Figure 4-1. Sand the sawed edges on a drum sander and shape as shown. Hand sand the beaded edges with folded sandpaper until smooth.

The post can be either a solid piece of 5″ x 5″ or glued up. A piece this size would be hard to find and would involve some problems in cutting out the bottom to receive the base.

By gluing up pieces of the same thickness as the base and proceeding as shown in Figure 4-1, Step 5, you will see that they will fit perfectly. Cut two pieces about 26″ long and one piece 5¾″ shorter or about 19½″. They will be cut to exact length later. Notch the two long pieces for a close fit on the base (in this case, 1⅝″ x 5¾″). They can easily be sawed on the band saw but a 5″ or 6″ post would be difficult on a small saw.

A cross-shaped block or jig will be needed to hold the two notches square with each other while the three layers of the post are being glued together. It will also be used to center and hold in the lathe. The block can be made as shown but be sure the small pieces are square with each other. The two pieces can be notched together as was the base to form the jig. When the glue has dried, square the top end, cutting to 25¼″ length (for 30″ table height). Bevel the corners on the jointer to reduce the size and weight for easier turning on the lathe.

Notice that a shallow notch is cut on top of the two pieces of the base in Step 3. This is necessary for a good fit of the beaded pieces into the post. Set the post on the base and mark each side, numbering them in order to reassemble in the same order after the notches are cut.

Turn the post similar to the one shown or use your own design. Keep the diameter as large as the design will permit for strength. Take a shallow cut across the top end with a skew chisel to level it. It is best to "dish" it out slightly about 1/16″, leaving the outer edge a little higher. This will let the plate (Figure 4-2F) that ties the post to the top assembly sit firmly on top when it is fastened with the stud bolt.

TABLE TOP

Cut the top from ¾″ plywood. For the 28″ base, a 40″ diameter top will be about the right size. If a top larger than this is desired, add to the size of the pedestal base accordingly but keep it 10″ or 12″ less than top diameter. With a 14″ leaf this top will be 40″ x 54″. It can be cut from birch or some other hardwood and the edges veneered or a cheaper grade plywood can be used and covered with wood-grain plastic laminate.

With a 20″ "radius stick" mark and saw the 40″ top and split it in the center to form two half circles. Cut the leaf 14″ x 40″. Two 8″ or 9″ leaves can be used by shortening the guide strips that are fastened in the four outside or (D) bars in the expansion assembly (Figure 4-2, Step 5).

The expansion assembly is composed of six pieces of hardwood 1¼″ x 2″ x 24″ with a ¾″ groove plowed 5/16″ deep in the center as shown. The center bar (C) is grooved on both sides. The hardwood guide strips are ⅝″ x ¾″ x 15″ and are fastened in the (D) bars as shown. Do not use glue until the assembly is tried out with the leaf or leaves in place. The center bar has a pin at each end on opposite sides to prevent the outside bar from slipping all the way out.

The center bars are fastened with screws to the plate that is attached to the top of the post. The other bars should slide freely. The grooves and guides should be

49

TABLE PEDESTAL

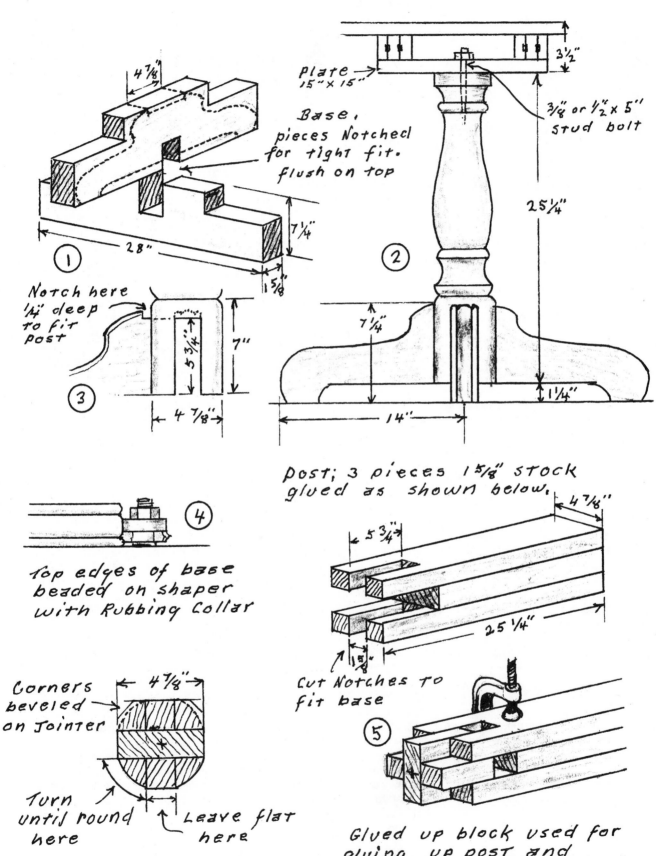

4 7/8"

① 28" 7 1/4" 1 5/8"

Plate 15" x 15"

Base, pieces Notched for tight fit. flush on top

3 1/2"

3/8" or 1/2" x 5" stud bolt

25 1/4"

7 1/4"

14" 1 1/4"

Notch here 1/4" deep to fit post

③ 5 3/4" 7" 4 7/8"

④ Top edges of base beaded on shaper with Rubbing Collar

Post; 3 pieces 1 5/8" stock glued as shown below.

4 7/8"

5 3/4"

25 1/4"

1 5/8"

Cut Notches to fit base

Corners beveled on Jointer 4 7/8"

Turn until round here Leave flat here

⑤ Glued up block used for gluing up post and centering in lathe for turning.

Figure 4-1

EXPANDABLE TABLE TOP
For 28" Pedestal Base

The top expands to 54" with 14" leaf. If a top larger than 40"x 54" is desired, Add to the size of the base accordingly, as it should be about 12" less than the diameter of the top.

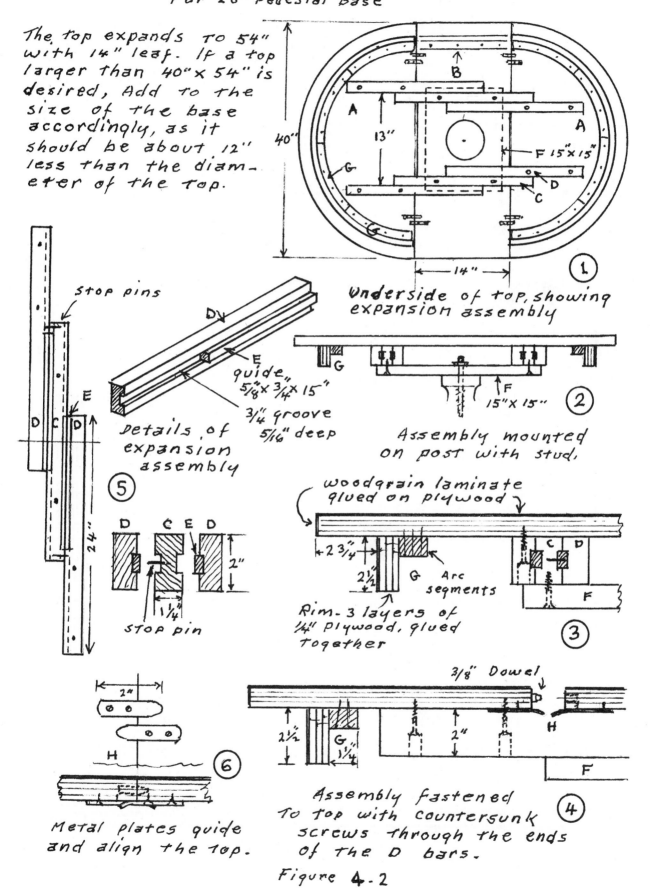

40"

13"

B

A   A

F 15"x 15"

G

D

C

G

14"

① Underside of top, showing expansion assembly

stop pins

D

E

guide
5/8" x 3/4" x 15"

3/4" groove
5/16" deep

Details of expansion assembly

⑤

D   C   E   D

24"

D   C E D

2"

1/4"

stop pin

G

F

② Assembly mounted on post with stud.

woodgrain laminate glued on plywood

2 3/4"

2 1/2"

G   Arc segments

C   D

F

Rim - 3 layers of 1/4" plywood, glued together

③

2"

H

3/8" Dowel

2 1/2"

G
1 1/4"

2"

H

F

⑥

Metal plates guide and align the top.

Assembly fastened to top with countersunk screws through the ends of the D bars.

④

Figure 4-2

51

ROLLTOP DESK

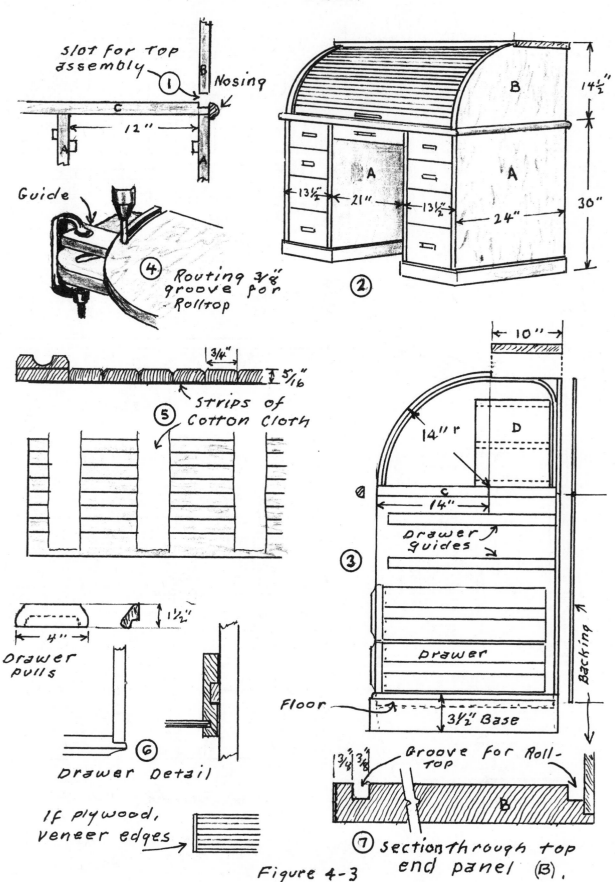

slot for top assembly
① Nosing
C
12"

Guide
④ Routing ⅜" groove for Rolltop

¾"
5/16"
Strips of Cotton Cloth
⑤

② B
A
A
14½"
30"
13½"
21"
13½"
24"

10"
14" r
D
C
14"
Drawer Guides
③
Drawer
Floor
3½" Base
Backing
Groove for Roll-top
⅜" ⅜"
B
⑦ Section through top end panel (B).

1½"
4"
Drawer pulls
⑥ Drawer Detail

If plywood, veneer edges →

Figure 4-3

52

sanded for a slight clearance. Rub paraffin in the grooves and on the guides for smooth operation. The outer bars are fastened to the two halves of the top.

Both dowels and small metal plates should be used for aligning the joints in the top and leaf (Figure 4-2, Step 4). The plates are about 1/2" wide and 2" long. Bend the ends down slightly as shown.

The rim in Figure 4-2, Step 3(G) that hangs down around the edge of the top to conceal the expansion assembly is made by first sawing curved segments from 3/4" pine 1 1/4" wide and with a 16 1/2" radius to outside of the arc. Mark this radius on the top about 3 1/2" from the edge. Glue and nail the segments in place (see Figure 4-2, Step 1).

Build up the rim with three layers of 1/4" x 2 1/2" plywood. Cut across the grain so it will bend more easily. Glue and nail the strips to the curved segments one at a time. Veneer with laminate if the top has been covered. The ends of the leaf can be done in the same way if desired.

ROLLTOP DESK

If you have never made a rolltop desk, here are a few tips that may help. It can be made of whatever materials are available. Oak-board lumber would be ideal but 3/4" birch plywood can be used for the large pieces and oak or birch-board lumber used for the drawer fronts and slats for the rolltop. The overall length and drawer sizes are optional but the dimensions shown in the drawing are minimum for adult use.

Cut the four end panels (Figure 4-3A) 24" x 29 1/4" and the two ends for the top assembly (B) 14" x 24". Round the corners as shown using a 14" radius. Sand the edges smooth and rout a 3/8" groove, 3/8" from the edge. This can be done with either a router or drill press (Figure 4-3, Step 4). The groove runs level across the top and curves down the back edge of the panel making a 2" or 2 1/4" radius at the turn. The 1/4" plywood back serves as the back side of the groove. The 10" board does the same at the top, as it fits in a notch cut down to the groove.

The desk top is rabbeted 1/4" deep at the ends for the end panels of the top assembly to fit in (Figure 4-3, Step 1). The rounded nosing that is glued and nailed around the edges helps to keep it in place.

Floor boards should be evenly placed with the top of the base board at the bottom of each drawer section. The end panels are nailed to them along with the bottom edge of the backing. They are 12" x 23 3/4" for the desk shown.

The drawers can be made and installed as you wish but the beveled-edge type with the wooden drawer pulls are more in keeping with the early American style.

Cut the slats for the rolltop from straight grained material, oak if available. Finish to 5/16" x 3/4" and about 1" longer than the finished length. Make enough so the full width of the slat assembly will be an inch or two wider than the length of the curved part of the groove at the front. Slightly round the corners on the face side of the slats.

The bottom piece is about 5/8" x 1 1/4". Cut it to the correct length and dado the ends on the face so it will slide freely in the grooves. Rout a finger grip in the center or one on each side.

Lay the slats face side down with a thin strip or blocks tacked on each side to hold them together on a flat surface. Cut several strips of heavy cotton cloth about 2" wide. Coat them with white glue and press onto the slats. Glue will not bond to some synthetic materials, which is why I recommend cotton strips. Take care that the glue does not run down between the slats gluing them together. After thirty or forty minutes, carefully flex them and scrape off any glue that may have run between them.

Glue on the bottom piece and cut the ends of the slats square with it. Sand the ends smooth and try the assembly in the grooves. It should work smoothly. If it does not, additional sanding or trimming should take care of any rough spots.

If plywood is used in the end panels, the edges should be covered with strips of matching wood. Thin strips can be bent around the curved pieces by using contact cement.

SMALL TABLES AND GUN AND CHINA CABINETS

In the past when an interesting piece of furniture was brought to me for repairs I made a drawing of it for my files in case I should want to make one like it later on. I am including from that file two small antique tables.

The people who owned the drop-leaf table (Figure 4-6) said it was over 160 years old. I made a few minor changes in the drawings to simplify the construction of the drawer and drawer guides. The outside appearance is the same as the original.

I suggest you make a cardboard pattern of the oval top by the "two nails and string" method or with a jig as shown in Figure 3-3. Notice that the center section is 19 1/2", the leaves 9", and that they lap about 9/16" at the joints. Allow for this when gluing up the board lumber for the top.

The "rule joints" are made as shown in Figure 4-6, Step 3 with two matching cutters and there has to be a true cove cut on the leaves and a matching bead on the top edges. The pin of the hinges has to be at the center or pivot of the 9/16" arc of the joint in order for the cove edge to follow the rounded edge of the top as it drops down.

After the joints are fitted, lay the three pieces together and mark from the pattern.

The general construction is shown in Figure 4-6. The legs are fastened together with the 1 1/2" x 6 1/2" x 17" blocks, which are cut back 1" on the ends for the post. The 1/2" groove and rabbet are for the drawer guides.

The drop-leaf support is a block with a "finger" joint and has a 3/16" wire pin. However, metal hinges could be used here if desired.

The other table (Figure 4-7) has cabriole legs on the front (A) and straight tapered ones on the back (B). The

COMBINATION BOOKCASE AND DESK
With Typewriter Shelf.

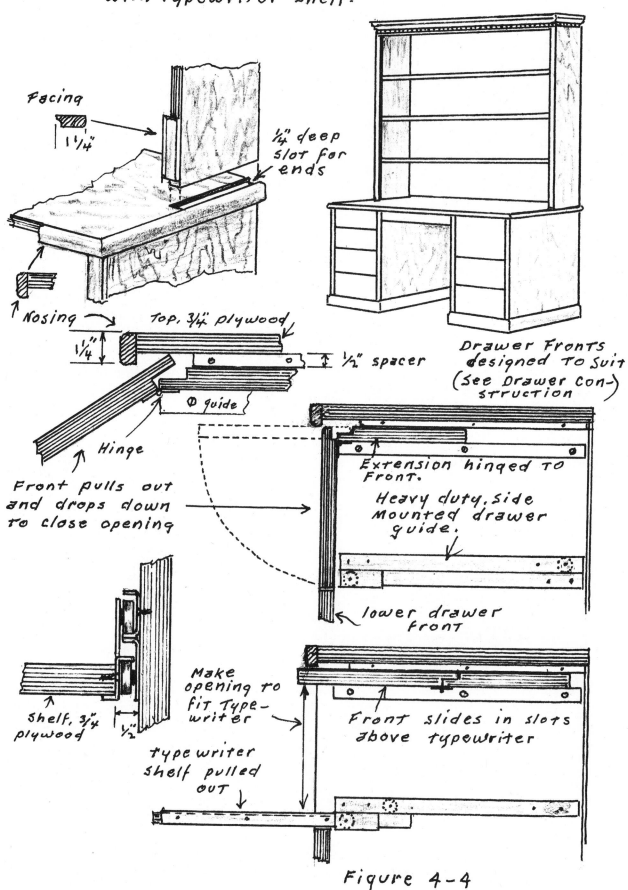

Facing

1 1/4"

1/4" deep slot for ends

Nosing

Top, 3/4" plywood

1 1/4"

1/2" spacer

Ø guide

Hinge

Front pulls out and drops down to close opening

Drawer Fronts designed to suit (See Drawer Con- struction)

Extension hinged to Front.

Heavy duty, side mounted drawer guide.

lower drawer front

Shelf, 3/4" plywood

1/2"

Make opening to fit Type- writer

Front slides in slots above typewriter

Typewriter shelf pulled out

Figure 4-4

54

DROP-LEAF DESK

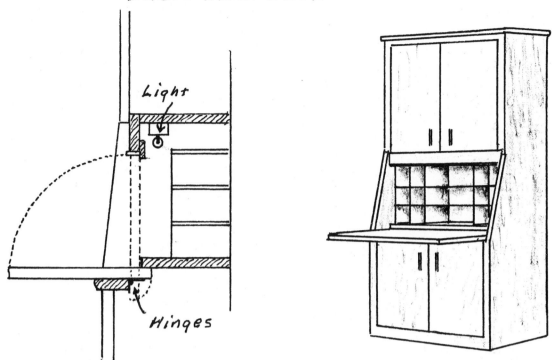

Light

Hinges

Here's a simple way to make a drop-leaf desk in a cabinet similar to the one shown here.

ADJUSTABLE DRAWING TABLE
Make Size to suit

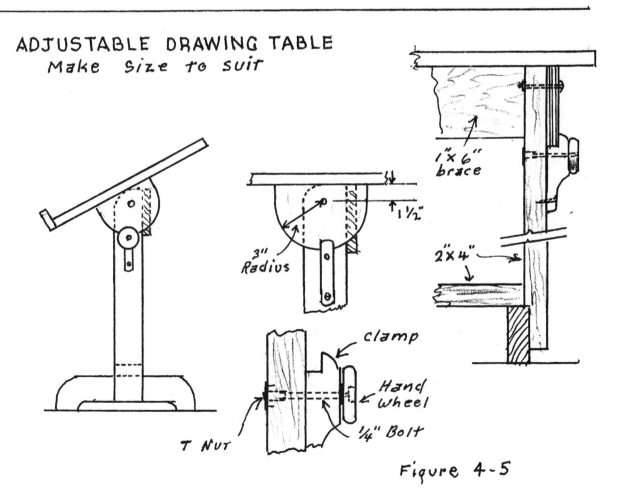

3" Radius

1 ½"

1"x 6" brace

2"x 4"

clamp

Hand Wheel

¼" Bolt

T Nut

Figure 4-5

DROP-LEAF TABLE

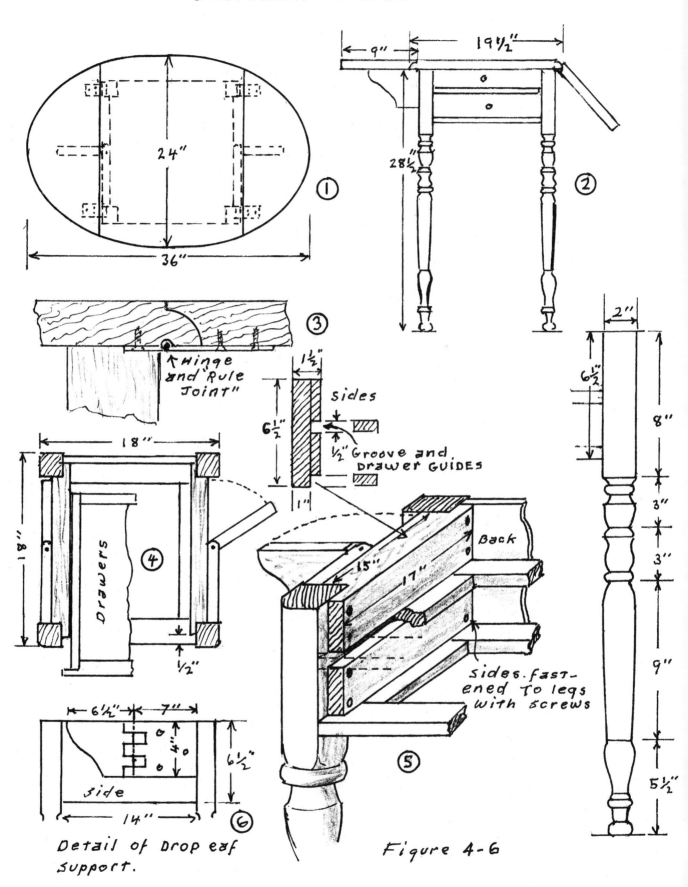

Detail of Drop eaf Support.

Figure 4-6

56

SIDE TABLE

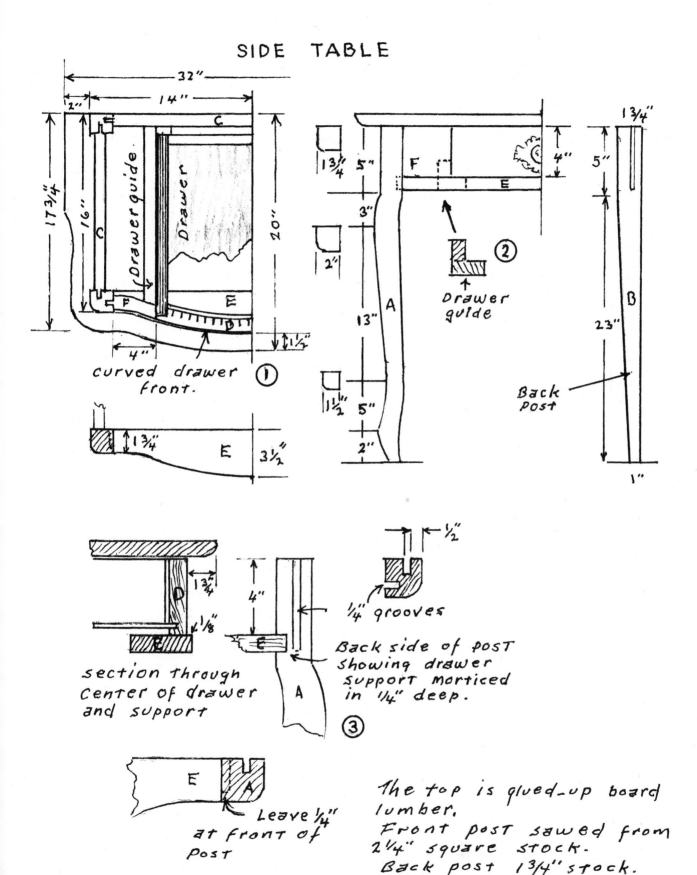

curved drawer front. ①

Drawer guide

Drawer

C

E

F

17¾"

16"

C

20"

1½"

4"

32"

14"

2"

13¾"

5"

3"

2"

13"

1½"

5"

2"

A

F

E

4"

Drawer guide ②

13¾"

5"

23"

1"

B

Back Post

section through Center of drawer and support

D

1¾"

⅛"

E

4"

A

E

½"

¼" grooves

Back side of post showing drawer Support morticed in ¼" deep.

③

E   A

Leave ¼" at front of Post

The top is glued-up board lumber.
Front post sawed from 2¼" square stock.
Back post 1¾" stock.

Figure 4-7

GUN CABINET

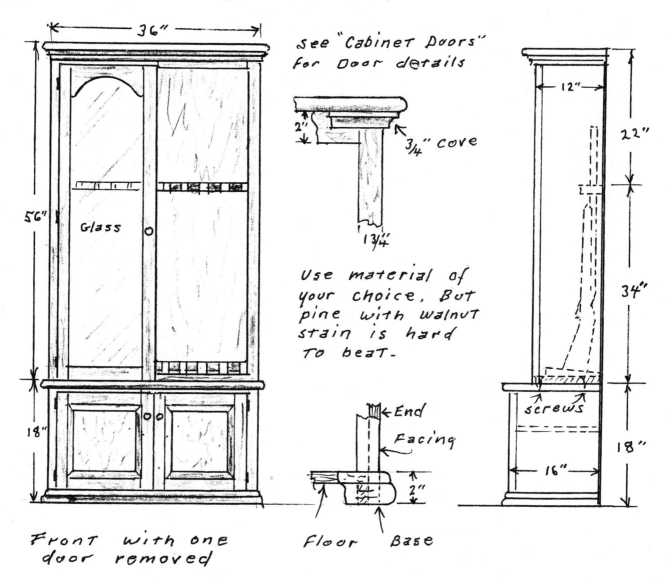

36"

See "Cabinet Doors" for Door details

2"

3/4" Cove

1¾"

Use material of your choice, But pine with walnut stain is hard to beat.

Glass

56"

18"

End Facing

Floor Base

2"

Front with one door removed

12"

22"

34"

screws

18"

16"

Check guns for dimensions as they may differ from those given here.

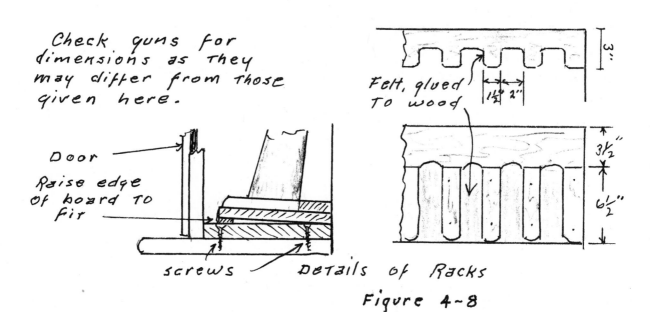

Door

Raise edge of board to fit

screws

3"

Felt, glued to wood

1½" 2"

3½"

6½"

Details of Racks

Figure 4-8

CHINA CABINET

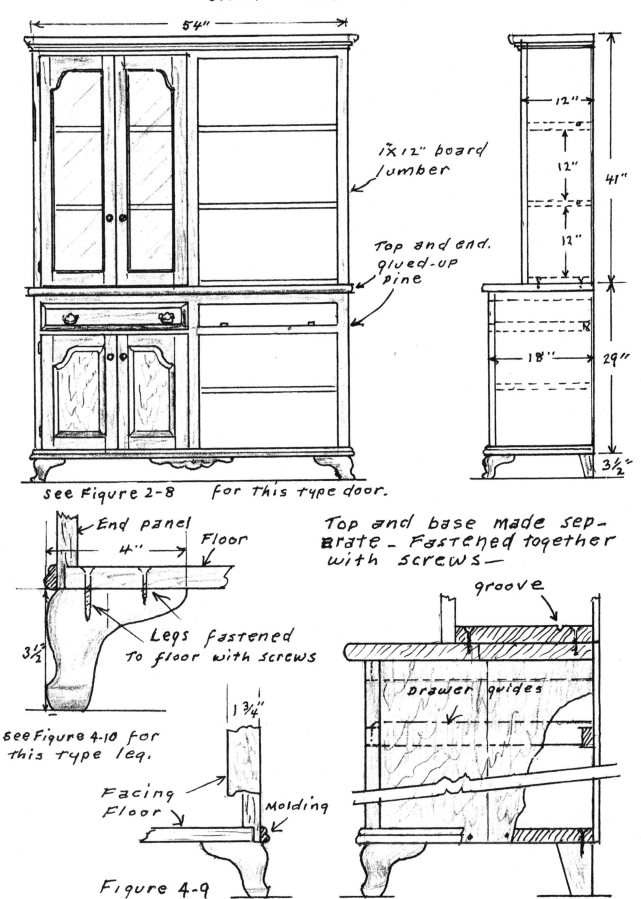

54"

1"×12" board lumber

Top and end glued-up pine

12"
12"
12"
41"

18"
29"

3½"

see Figure 2-8   for this type door.

End panel
Floor
4"

Legs fastened to floor with screws

3½"

see Figure 4-10 for this type leg.

Top and base made separate — Fastened together with screws —

groove

drawer guides

1 3/4"

Facing Floor
Molding

Figure 4-9

FURNITURE LEGS
Made on the Bandsaw

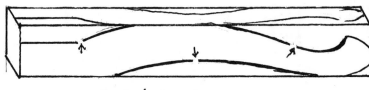

square straight leg

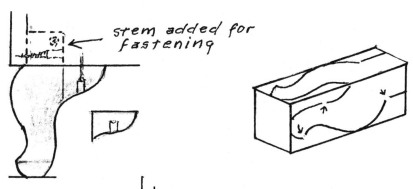

Cabriole leg

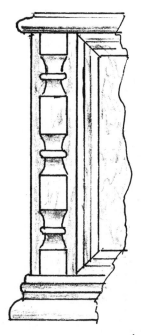

Bandsawed trim added to facing.
make square. split in center, making two pieces

stem added for fastening

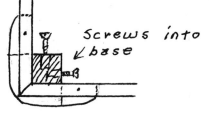

Screws into base

pattern

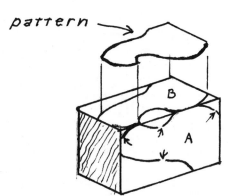

saw side A first. leaving 1/4" at arrows so stock will lay flat and leave outline for sawing side B

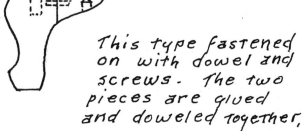

This type fastened on with dowel and screws. The two pieces are glued and doweled together.

Figure 4-10

JENNY LIND BED

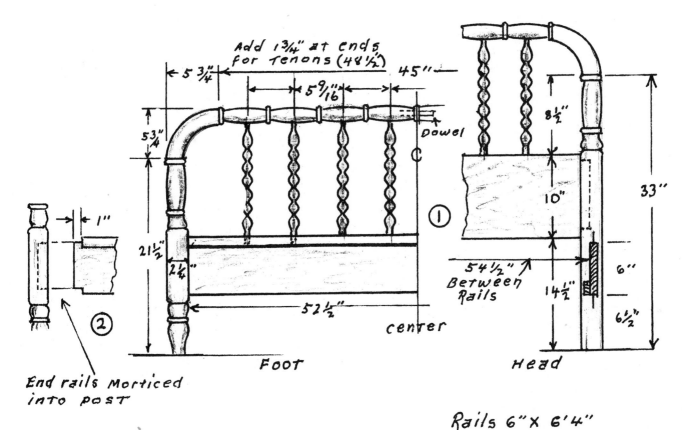

Add 1¾" at ends for Tenons (48½")

5¾"

5 9/16"

45"

Dowel

5¾"

8½"

33"

10"

21½"

2¼"

54½" Between Rails

14½"

6"

6½"

52½"

center

Foot

Head

1"

End rails Morticed into post

②

Rails 6" x 6'4"

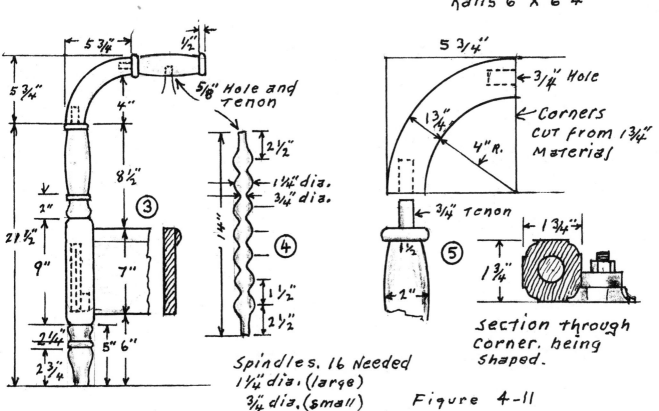

5¾"

½"

5⅝" Hole and Tenon

4"

8½"

2½"

1¼" dia.

¾" dia.

③

④

2"

21½"

9"

7"

1¼"

1½"

2½"

2¼"

5" 6"

2¾"

Spindles. 16 Needed
1¼" dia. (large)
¾" dia. (small)

5¾"

3/4" Hole

1¾"

4" R.

Corners cut from 1¾" Material

¾" Tenon

½"

⑤

2"

1¾"

1¾"

Section through Corner. being Shaped.

Figure 4-11

61

FLUTED TABLE LEGS

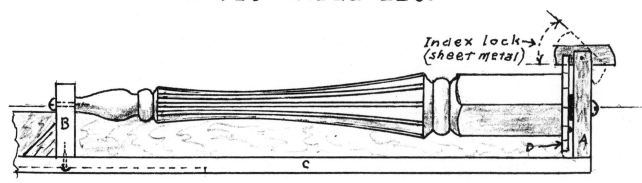

Jig for fluting turned legs on the shaper

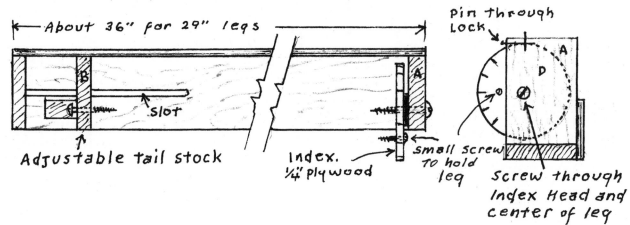

About 36" for 29" legs

Slot

Adjustable tail stock

Index.
¼" plywood

Pin through
Lock

small Screw
to hold
leg

Screw through
Index Head and
center of leg

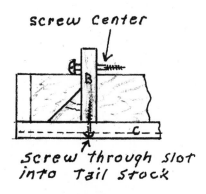

screw center

**Screw through slot
into Tail Stock**

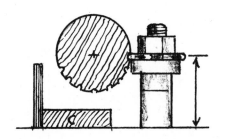

Fluting on Shaper.
with 3/16" round nose
cutter and collar.

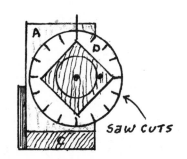

Saw cuts

Inside. showing index
head and leg in
position for fluting.

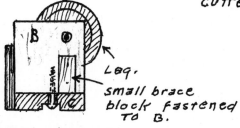

Leg.
small brace
block fastened
to B.

**End view of
Tail Stock**

The dimensions are determined by
the size of the work and the
height that the cutter can be
placed on the shaft (double
arrow) as this is the maximum
height of the screw centers
and Index Head

Figure 4-12

rails (C) are morticed into them with a ¼″ x ½″ tenon. The drawer has a curved front (D) (see drawer construction) and the drawer support piece (E) is sawed to match the curve of the drawer with ⅛″ margin at the bottom of the drawer front. The drawer support is morticed into the front legs 4″ from the top and about ¼″ from the front of the leg (Step 3). A curved block (F) is fastened between it and the top on each side to continue the curved front.

Typical gun and china cabinets are shown in Figures 4-8 and 4-9. Figure 4-10 shows how to saw the cabriole (or Queen Anne) legs on the band saw by sawing two sides of a square piece and finishing on a sander. Figure 4-12 shows how to make fluted table legs.

JENNY LIND BED

I thought that I should include at least one bed in this book and my favorite is the Jenny Lind. I always wanted one for myself so a few years ago I built the one shown here (Figure 4-11) based on pictures I found in magazines.

I had a few pieces of ¾″ walnut, which I used by gluing up three layers for the thicker pieces of the bed. The spindles can be made with solid 1½″ stock or two layers glued up. Other woods such as maple, cherry, gum, or oak would also be suitable.

I had to add an extension to my lathe for the long turnings. I fastened two pieces of angle iron on hardwood blocks at the end of the lathe bed. If you do not wish to go to the trouble you can make the long pieces in two parts and dowel them together. Take care and drill the holes straight into the parts or the joints will not be straight.

The curved corner pieces at the top of the post should be cut from 1¾″ stock into 5¾″ square blocks and drilled before band sawing or clamped to a block so the holes will be square with the ends. Saw to shape, sand the sawed edges, and shape a ½″ bead on the four edges by using a rubbing collar (Figure 4-11, Step 5).

Make a pattern of the spindles (Step 4) by sawing the profile on a thin piece of plywood. A ⅝″ notch can be cut in one end of the pattern to be used to gauge the ends where they fit into the holes. A ¾″ tenon is turned on the top of the post and both ends of the pieces that go across the top. The end rails that tie the post together at the bottom are morticed into the post as shown (2).

Make a template from a strip of wood 52½″ long and mark off the location of the holes for the spindles and the ½″ beads on the top piece. Start with the center bead and mark them 5⁹⁄₁₆ on center. The ⅝″ holes are centered between the beads. Take care and drill them all in a straight line along the round side. A V-block clamped to the drill press with marks made by using a straight edge will help.

The side rails are ¾″ x 6″ x 6′4″ long with ¾″ x ½″ strips glued and nailed to the inside at the bottom edge. The locks can be bought from a specialty hardware place or salvaged from an old bed.

5 CLASSICAL GUITAR

A few years ago when guitars began to be popular I decided to try making one in my spare time. At one time I played the guitar fairly well and I thought this would be an advantage in being able to judge the accuracy and sound of my home-built guitar.

My first attempt was not very good. I had tried to make it the conventional way and ended up wasting time and material. The strings were too high off the fret board for accuracy and the neck was not straight with the center of the soundbox. There was no way to correct the problems since I had glued the neck into the box with the customary dovetail joint which most luthiers use.

I began thinking of a way to make the neck adjustable or devising a method of fastening it so it could be removed and altered without damaging the rest of the instrument. After some experimenting, I found a fairly simple method of making and installing the neck so it could be adjusted or removed if necessary.

Most of the guitars I have made were regular steel-string types with reinforced necks. I had a few requests for classic models, so I changed the method a little, leaving out the neck reinforcing rod. Neck reinforcing is unnecessary in the classic model because the neck is shorter and wider than in the steel-string guitar and with nylon strings, there is not as much strain on the neck.

I will give the step-by-step procedure in making a classic guitar, including instructions for making the necessary jigs and clamps. Some of the dimensions and features of my design are similar to those of different manufactured guitars. I have taken the different features I liked from other designs and during the process of constructing several guitars, have modified those features leading up to my present design. I have developed what I consider a simple design that is easier to make and can sound as good or better than many of the manufactured guitars.

In checking other classic models, I found there were different lengths for fret boards and spacing of the frets. These dimensions and the distance from the nut to the saddle are interdependent and are too complicated to give here. I decided to use an open-string length of 25½" (nut to saddle), which seems to be about average. This "dimension" requires a fret board with the twelfth fret 12¾" from the "nut" or half the length of the span. Whether you buy a fret board from a music store or take measurements from another guitar, remember that the twelfth fret is always located at the midpoint between the nut and saddle.

The spacing of the frets must be very accurate. To obtain measurements from another guitar take a smooth strip of wood about 26" long, lay it along the neck of the guitar with one end against the nut, and with a fine point pencil or knife carefully mark the center of each fret on the strip. Mark the length of the fret board, the location of the bridge, saddle, position dots, and sound hole.

In Figure 5-1, I have given dimensions for the soundbox. Other shapes and sizes can be constructed using similar procedures. If the dimensions are different from those given, you can easily adjust by making patterns and jigs to fit the desired shape.

MATERIALS

I found that expensive imported woods do not improve the tone of a guitar as much as skill and accuracy in the construction. I suggest using what material you can find locally or what you have on hand. I made one or two guitars from pieces of mahogany salvaged from old furniture, such as bedrails and table leaves. If you have some pieces of mahogany, maple, or walnut, I suggest they be used. A piece of white pine or spruce with the proper grain will make a good top. I used bone for the nut, saddle, and position dots. A good hardwood should be used for the fret board. Fret wire and machine heads may be ordered or purchased from musical supply firms.

TOOLS

The power tools needed are a jointer, table saw, shaper, band saw, and drill press. These tools will make the work go faster and easier. However, a good craftsman can usually "make do" with whatever tools are available. A drill press or router can be substituted as a shaper or a shaper can be used as a jointer by using the proper accessories.

Forms, Jigs, and Clamps

The sound box form is made in two halves with brackets at each end for coupling the two halves together. I made the brackets from aluminum angle sections. Use the dimensions shown in Figure 5-1 or your own pattern for the shape of the sound box. Glue up layers of lumber or plywood to the thickness of 2½" and saw both sides exactly alike with the outer edge similar to the sketch. The saw cuts around the inside are to help speed the drying of the sides after they have been boiled and clamped in the

CLASSIC GUITAR
The Form, Clamps, and Boiling Pan.

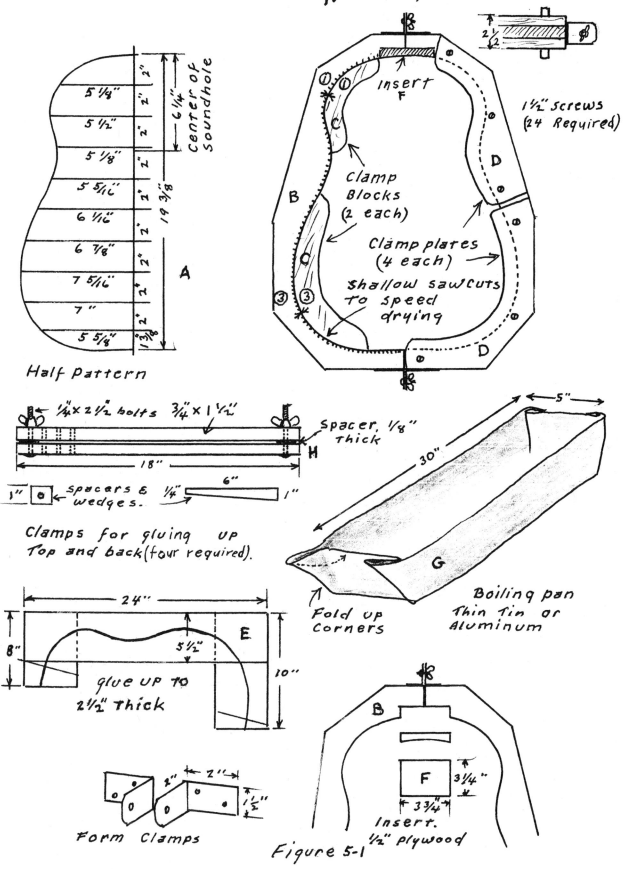

Half Pattern

Clamp Blocks (2 each)

Clamp plates (4 each)

Shallow sawcuts to speed drying

Insert F

1½" screws (24 Required)

Clamps for gluing up Top and back (four required).

Boiling pan Thin Tin or Aluminum

Fold up Corners

glue up To 2½" Thick

Form Clamps

Insert. ½" plywood

Figure 5-1

form. From the waste inside the form, saw the four clamp blocks (C) and mark them so they can quickly be put back in the same place in the form.

The eight clamp plates (D) are to hold the back and top in place while the glue sets. They should extend past the inside of the form about 3/4". Make the plates of 3/8" plywood, drill holes for screws in the plates, and form and mark each one for quick assembly later. The insert (F) is fitted in the notch of the form and is sanded slightly concave to fit the end of the sound box. Its use will be explained later.

The pan (G) for boiling the sides is made by bending up the edges of a thin piece of tin about 12" x 36". Boiling can be done on two burners of a stove.

The clamps (H) are for gluing the pieces together for the top and back. Their use is demonstrated in Figure 5-3. One inch square spacers, 1/8" thick, are placed at each end between the two 3/4" x 1 1/2" x 18" strips. The 1/8" thick wedge is to be driven in between the spacer and the material being glued. These clamps will also be used to clamp the struts or braces to the top and back.

SIDES

The sides should be about 3/32" thick and cut as shown in Figure 5-2A with a 1/4" taper. Mark the corner as shown. The other side will be in reverse. These marks should be made on both sides so they can easily be seen while wet because they have to be placed in the form quickly after being taken out of the boiling water. The wide end of the sides will join on the tail block with the marks together. Note which is the top and bottom edge of the sides. The top, which is flat, will be glued on the straight edge of the sides.

Boiling the Sides

Place the sides in the pan with two or three small scraps about 1/2" square and 4" long between and under them so the water can circulate freely around all surfaces of the sides. Put in a strip of the same material as the sides to check its flexibility before bending the sides. Weight the sides down with something to prevent them from floating. Do not use iron, or other materials that will stain the wood as weights. Boil for about thirty minutes.

Placing Sides in the Form

Separate the form and fasten the clamp plates on one side of each half with 1/2" spacer blocks between the plates and form. Locate the spacers beside each screw (see Figure 5-2B). The sides will be placed in the forms with the top (straight edge) placed down against the clamp plates.

When the sides are ready, take one of them out of the pan and quickly place it in the correct half of the form with the marked corner even with the end (C). Make sure the top or straight edge of the side is down on the clamp plate (D). Clamp the marked end first using the correct clamp block (C) and matching the marks on it and the form. Bend

the side into the other curve and clamp it. Use the same procedure on the other side. Let the sides dry a day or two in the form.

END BLOCKS

The head and tail blocks are made of white pine or spruce and are shown in Figure 5-2. Sand the slight curve to fit the sides at the end joints for a good glue job. Make them a little wider than the sides so they can be sanded flush later. Fasten the form halves together making sure the two ends of the sides that are marked are fitted to each other. This joint will be exposed on the outside and a tight fit is essential. The other ends will be trimmed off later at the edges of the slot in the head block.

Coat the head block and tail block with glue and clamp into place. The correct locations are shown in Figure 5-5D. Be sure the head block is square with the sides and the slot is in the exact center in order for the neck to be properly aligned with the box.

LINERS

Any straight grained wood that bends easily without breaking will do for the liners. To test a piece of wood that you think might be suitable, saw a thin strip about 1/16" thick, and if it bends around the sides without breaking it will probably do.

Shown in Figure 5-2 are four time-saving steps that I use in making the liners. Thin a board down to 5/16" and make the saw cuts for four or five pieces before ripping into strips.

A gauge clamped to the back side of the band saw as shown in Figure 5-2, Step 2 will ensure uniform depth of cuts and the mark will give the 3/8" spacing between cuts.

TOP AND BACK

If your lumber dealer will let you pick through the white pine bin, you should be able to find a board suitable for the top. See Figure 5-3 for details. If your table saw will cut through 2 1/2", you can make the top and back in three pieces. Most tops are made in two pieces but this is hard to do with a small saw. Cut the two sides with the same set-up. Glue the top and back pieces as shown in Figure 5-3.

SOUND HOLE

Whether you make the rosette or buy one, you have to cut a shallow groove around the sound hole for it to fit in. Figure 5-4 shows the best way I know of to do this. It involves the use of a circle cutter in a drill press. I finally made a special cutter to cut the groove at one set up, but it can be done as shown by making three or four separate

SIDES, END BLOCKS, and LINERS

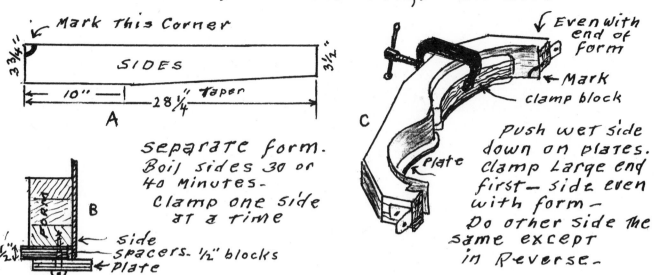

Mark This Corner

3¾"

SIDES

3½"

10" 28¼" Taper

A

separate form.
Boil sides 30 or
40 Minutes-
Clamp one side
at a time

B

½"

Side
Spacers- ½" blocks
Plate

C

✓ Even with
end of
form

Mark
clamp block

Plate

Push wet side
down on plates.
Clamp Large end
first— side even
with form—
Do other side the
same except
in Reverse.

END BLOCKS

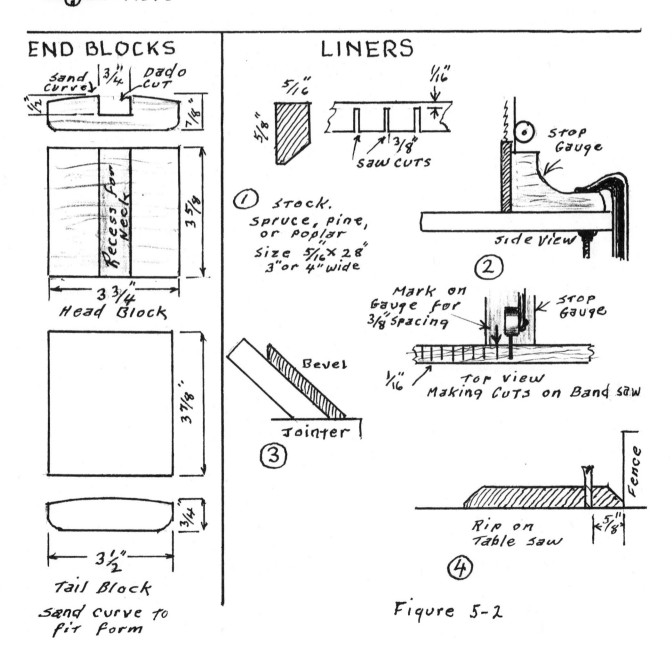

sand
Curve

3¾"

Dado
Cut

½"

7/8"

Recess for Neck

3 5/8"

3 3/4"

Head Block

3 7/8"

3/4"

3½"

Tail Block

sand curve to
fit form

LINERS

5/16"

5/8"

1/16"

saw cuts

3/8"

① stock.
Spruce, pine,
or poplar
Size 5/16"× 28"
3" or 4" wide

stop
Gauge

side view

②

Bevel

Jointer

③

Mark on
Gauge for
3/8" spacing

stop
Gauge

1/16"

Top view
Making Cuts on Band saw

Fence

Rip on
Table saw

5/8"

④

Figure 5-2

67

TOP AND BACK

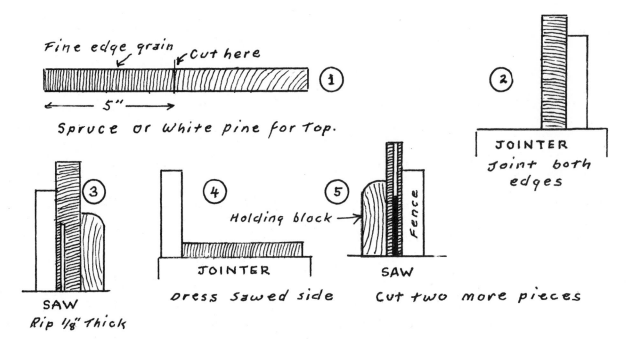

Fine edge grain

Cut here

5"

Spruce or White pine for Top.

1

2

JOINTER
Joint both edges

3

SAW

Rip 1/8" Thick

4

JOINTER

Dress Sawed side

Holding block

5

Fence

SAW

Cut two more pieces

Shown above is a top being cut from a board of regular shelving white pine or spruce, which most lumber dealers stock. Look for a board with a fine straight grain and free of rich streaks. A piece 3/4" x 5" x 20" will make a top or back. However, the back and sides should be made of mahogany or other suitable material

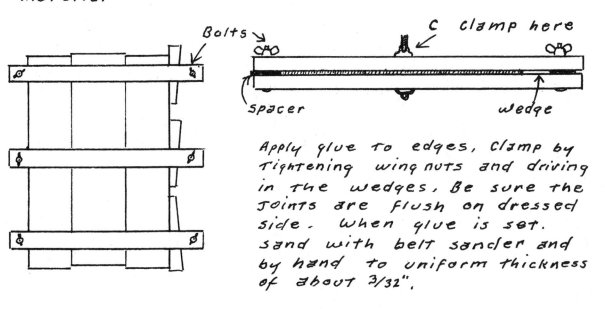

Bolts

C Clamp here

Spacer

Wedge

Apply glue to edges. Clamp by tightening wing nuts and driving in the wedges. Be sure the joints are flush on dressed side. When glue is set. Sand with belt sander and by hand to uniform thickness of about 3/32".

A two piece top and back can be used if a saw is available that will split a 1½" board, or the material can be bought from a music supply company.

Figure 5-3

cuts. Fasten the top to a board so it cannot raise up into the cutter and with a sharp pointed cutter outline the rosette then level the inside with a square cutter (Figure 5-4A, B, and C). Always try new set ups on scrap material first. Cut out the sound hole last.

If you decide to make the rosette inlay, it can either be cut out with the circle cutter or turned on the lathe as shown in Figure 5-4.

Figure 5-5 shows the position of the top and back struts. They are made from straight grained spruce or mahogany. Notice that the three back struts have a 3/16" curvature or crown. Glue them in place by using the same clamps used for gluing the top and back. The small struts for the top can be held in place with a board and weights until the glue sets.

INSTALLING THE LINERS

Clothespins are usually used to hold the liners in place until the glue dries. If you do not have any, you can easily make some that will work just as well by cutting deep grooves in the ends of a short board. Make the width of the grooves a little less than the thickness of the liners plus the side for a tight fit. Make the groove depth about 1 3/4". Cut the board into 1/2" pieces as shown in Figure 5-5.

Coat the liners with glue and clamp flush with the edges of the sides from one end block to the other. If they should break at one of the saw cuts, clamp it at the break with an extra pin or two.

I have shown in Figure 5-6 the procedure for installing the back and top. Be sure the sides, liners, and blocks are even and level. Although the back is glued on first, fit both it and top by "letting" the struts into small notches in the liners as shown in Figures 5-6C and D. Glue on the back and when dry, install the top the same way. The strips and clamp blocks (Figure 5-5D) can be removed through the sound hole after the glue is dry.

THE NECK

If you have looked at the drawings showing the neck construction, they may seem complicated. With a jointer this method is much easier than carving one from a solid piece of wood using a conventional dovetail mortice joint. This method is also stronger and more accurate.

Construct the neck from a straight grained piece of mahogany, cherry, maple, or walnut as shown in Figure 5-7A. The tenon on the end should be square and sized to fit into the slot in the head block. Follow each step as shown and take care in cutting and gluing the end to form the peg head angle (B and C). Make the jig as shown to keep the glue joint from slipping when the clamp is tightened. When dry, taper each side evenly until it is 2" wide at the 12 3/4" mark (D). Shape the back of neck as shown in Figure 5-8M with block planes, rasp, and drum sander. Finish by hand sanding. Add the blocks to each side (Figure 5-7E) to build the peg head width to about 3 1/4".

Smooth the surface with light cuts on the jointer. Be sure and feed with the grain to avoid chipping. Veneer the face with 1/8" walnut or mahogany.

Make a pattern of the peg head from the dimensions given (G), or from another guitar trace onto the neck, and cut the peg head to shape. If you have the machine heads, drill the holes for the rollers, checking the size and distance apart before drilling.

Figure 5-8 shows the details for assembly of the neck to the sound box. The "heel" (H) is glued and bolted onto the underside of the neck with a 1/4" x 3" stove bolt. Mark the outline of the heel on the end of a short piece of 3/4" x 2" wood of the same material as the neck. Do not saw out the heel until the bolt hole has been drilled through it. To drill the hole, make a jig by cutting a 3/4" dado across a piece of 2" x 4" (same as the head block). Place the neck and the heel block in the slot to hold them in line and drill both at the same time. Saw the heel to shape, sand, and round the edges as shown. On the underside of the neck, cut out for the top screw eye. Inlet the bottom screw eye into the bottom of the heel (Figures 5-8I and J).

Drill holes in the head block for the ends of the two screw eyes, taking care that the top of the neck is flush with the top of the sound box. If you wish, a jig can be made as shown in (K).

Countersink the head of the heel bolt and washer in the top side of the neck. The cap that fits on the bottom of the heel is drilled with a shallow hole to cover the nut (K).

With the top screw eye in place, glue the heel to the neck, tightening the heel bolt to serve as a clamp. The cap is added and the joint is sanded flush. The bottom is finished even with the back of the box (L).

BANDING

If the box is of dark wood, make the banding out of light material such as maple, birch, holly, or even white oak, which I have used with a walnut sound box. If the box is light, use walnut or ebony. Whatever you use, it should be straight grained so it will not break while bending around the sides. It should match the rosette, bridge, and peg head veneer.

The edges of the box must be rabbeted to receive the banding. The best way is with a square-edged shaper cutter and a rubbing collar as shown in Figure 5-9. The rubbing collar should have a diameter 1/8" less than the cutter. This will make a cut 1/16" deep. Adjust for 1/4" width (B). A piece of 1/8" Masonite should be fitted around the cutter as shown in (B) to compensate for the arch in the back (it may be removed for the top).

Do not let the cutter go into the neck slot or it will grab and chip the wood. Just ease up to it and stop. Finish with a rasp or file.

Make the banding from a board 2 or 3" wide and about 30" long. Dress it down to a little over 1/4" thick. Run the edges over the jointer and cut as shown in Figure 5-9A. Make a few extra pieces in case some of them break as they are being bent around the box.

SOUND HOLE ROSETTE
Made Of Wood

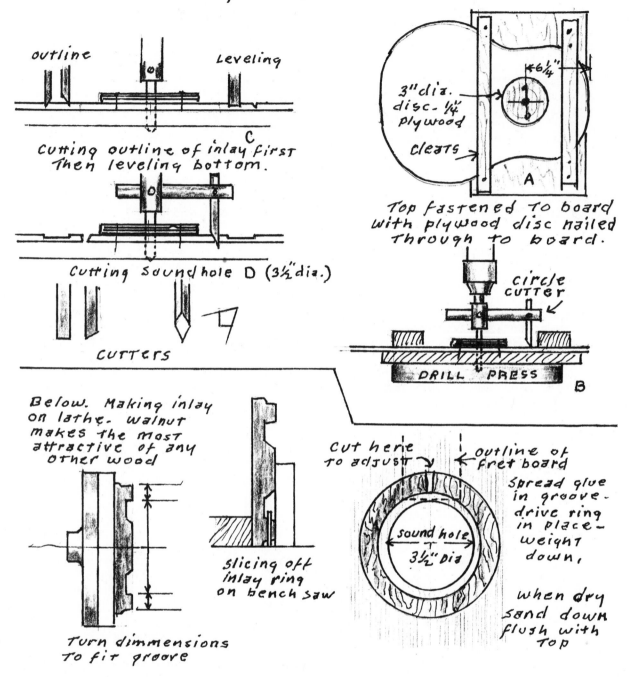

outline   Leveling

Cutting outline of inlay first
Then leveling bottom.

Cutting Soundhole D (3½"dia.)

CUTTERS

3" dia.
disc - ¼"
plywood

CLEATS

←6¼"→

A

Top fastened to board
with plywood disc nailed
Through to board.

circle
cutter

DRILL PRESS   B

Below. Making inlay
on lathe. walnut
makes the most
attractive of any
other wood

slicing off
inlay ring
on bench saw

Turn dimmensions
To fit groove

Cut here
to adjust   outline of
                   fret board

sound hole
3½" dia

Spread glue
in groove-
drive ring
in place-
weight
down.

when dry
sand down
flush with
Top

1   Band saw Top and back. Locate sound hole. Cut them
    ⅛" larger Than pattern.
2   place in frame (A). Saw a 3" disc. drill ¼ hole in center
    nail Over the location of The Soundhole Center the
    hole exactly over Center mark
3   with Circle Cutter, Cut groove for inlay (B and C)
    Cut shallow grooves With sharp pointed Cutter, Then
    level with square one. use slow speed-
4   Cut sound hole last. (D)

Figure 5-4

BACK and TOP BRACES

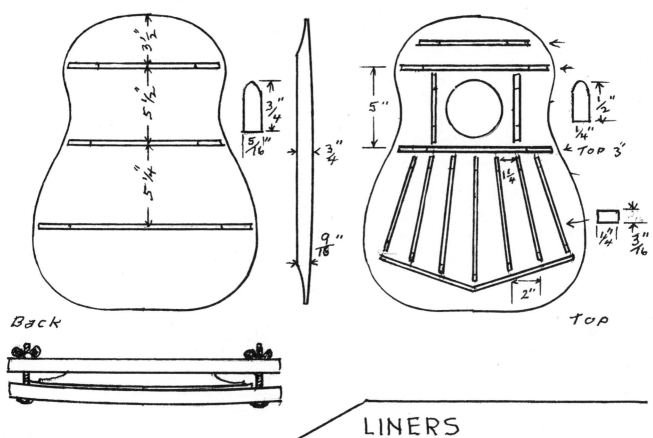

Back

Top

LINERS

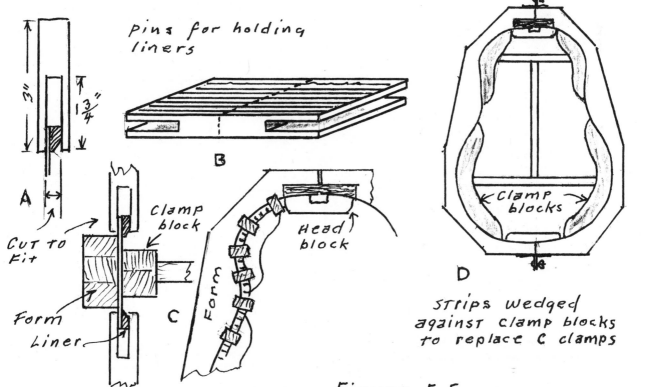

pins for holding liners

Cut to Fit

Form
Liner

Clamp block

Head block

Form

Clamp blocks

strips wedged against clamp blocks to replace C clamps

Figure 5-5

INSTALLING THE BACK

With the sides in the form, use block plane and sanding block to even the sides, liners, head, and tail blocks to assure a fit to top and back. Check with a straight edge

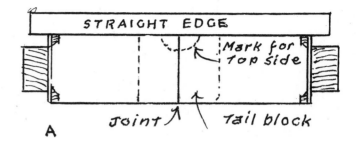

A

Trim sides flush with edges of the neck slot

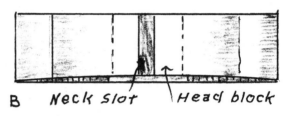

B

Lay sides over top and back. Mark the liners where struts touch them. Be sure the back is on the side that was beveled. The top on the one marked or flat side.

Marking liners for back struts

C

Notch the liners to let the struts rest on them. Be sure the top and back are seated all around the edges.

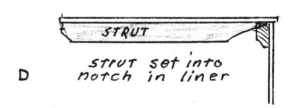

strut set into notch in liner

D

Put the plates on the top side of form with the ½" spacers between the plates and form. Turn over. Coat liners and blocks with glue. Center back over box and clamp down with the other set of plates. Check joint to see if glue is being forced out. When dry turn over and use the same procedure to install top.

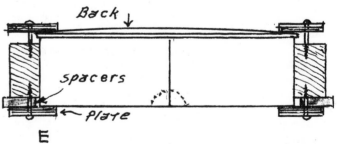

E

Figure 5-6

THE NECK

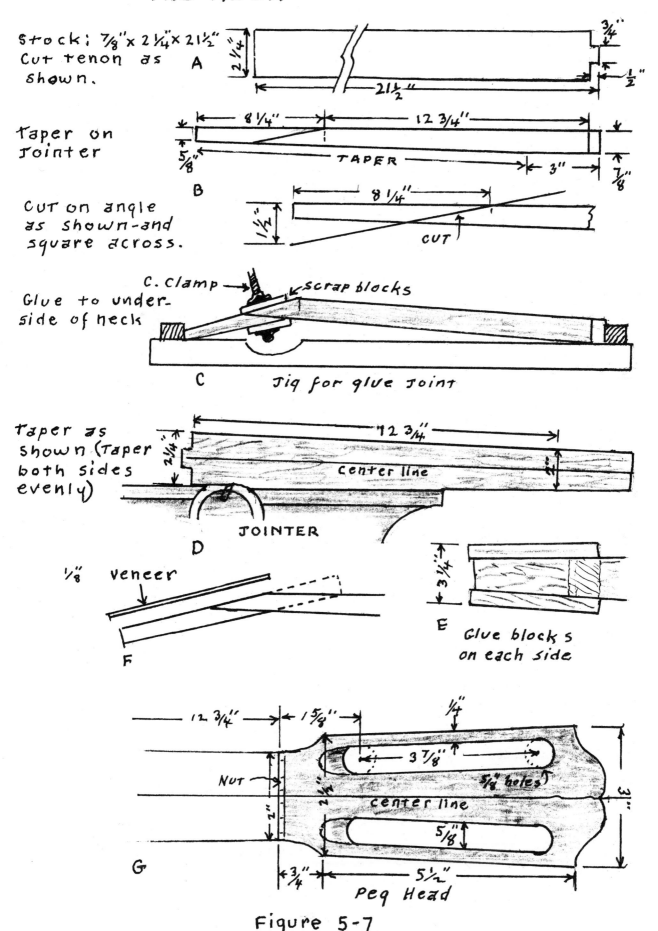

Stock; 7/8" x 2 1/4" x 21 1/2"
Cut tenon as shown.

A

Taper on Jointer

B

Cut on angle as shown-and square across.

Glue to underside of neck

C.clamp → scrap blocks

C   Jig for glue joint

Taper as shown (Taper both sides evenly)

JOINTER

D

1/8" veneer

F

E   Glue blocks on each side

Nut

center line

G   Peg Head

Figure 5-7

THE NECK

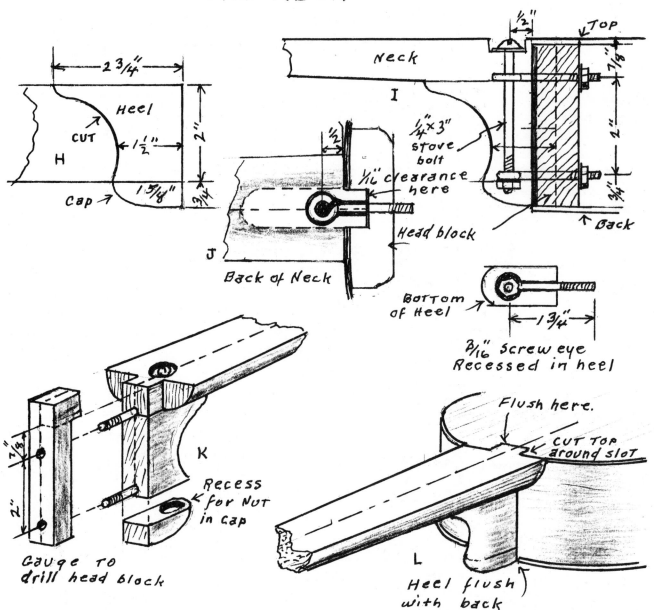

2 3/4"

Heel

CUT

H

Cap →

1 1/2"

1 5/8"

2"

3/4"

Neck

I

1/2"

1/2"

1/4" x 3" stove bolt

1/16" clearance here

Head block

J

Back of Neck

TOP

7/8"

2"

3/4"

← Back

Bottom of Heel →

1 3/4"

3/16" screw eye
Recessed in heel

7/8"

2"

K

Recess for Nut in Cap

Gauge to drill head block

Flush here.

CUT TOP around slot

L

Heel flush with back

The neck is adjusted by tightening, or loosening the Nut on the bottom screweye, As this moves the bottom of the heel in or out slightly, a little clearance is needed inside the headblock dado, see J above.

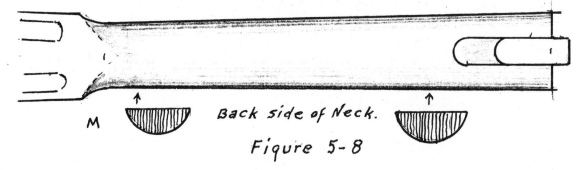

M

Back side of Neck.

Figure 5-8

THE BANDING

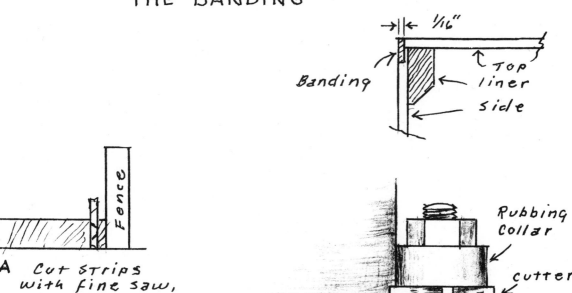

¹⁄₁₆"

Banding

TOP
liner
side

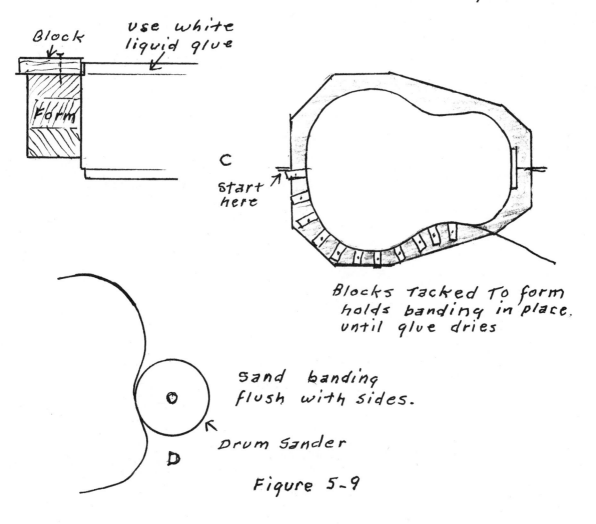

A Cut strips with fine saw, slightly over ¹⁄₁₆" thick

Fence

Rubbing Collar

cutter

B Rabbeting edges on shaper. Cut ¹⁄₁₆" deep, ¹⁄₄" wide.

Block

use white liquid glue

Form

C

start here

Blocks tacked to form holds banding in place. until glue dries

Sand banding flush with sides.

Drum Sander

D

Figure 5-9

INSTALLING THE NECK AND BRIDGE

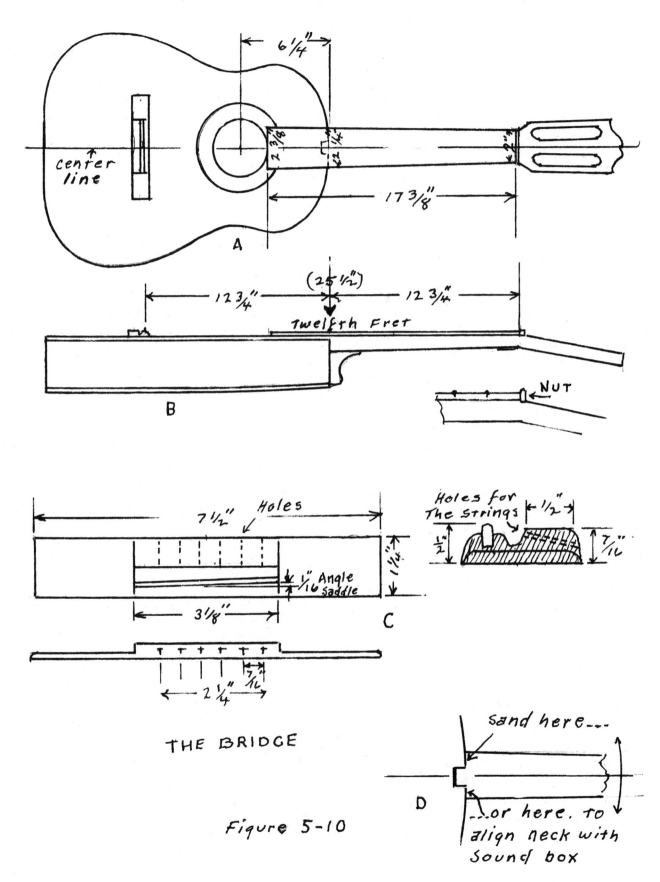

center line

6 1/4"

2 3/8

17 3/8"

A

12 3/4"   (25 1/2")   12 3/4"

Twelfth Fret

B

NUT

7 1/2"   Holes

1 1/4"

1/16" Angle Saddle

3 1/8"

Holes for the strings

1/2"

7/16"

C

7/16"

2 1/4"

THE BRIDGE

sand here...

D

...or here, to align neck with sound box

Figure 5-10

THE FRET BOARD

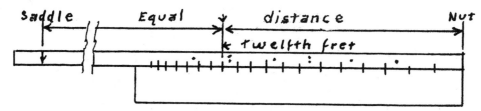

1.
Cut fret board 1/4" x 2 3/8" x 17 3/8" and mark from pattern the location of frets and position dots.

2.
Make a box with a square cut across to saw the grooves for the frets. Cut 3/32" deep and for a tight fit. Drill holes for position dots.

3.
Taper to finish size on jointer (C).

4.
The position dots can made by sawing a piece of bone into 1/4" square strips. Chuck in drill and sand to 3/16" diameter (E).

5.
Drive in hole, use glue (see D and F).

6.
Saw off with coping saw. The piece of thin metal protects the surface from scratches.

7.
Sand flush, seal with a good sanding sealer.

8.
Drive in frets. Rub glue in the grooves and use a hardwood block and hammer or mallet.

9.
Trim frets with file and oil stone.

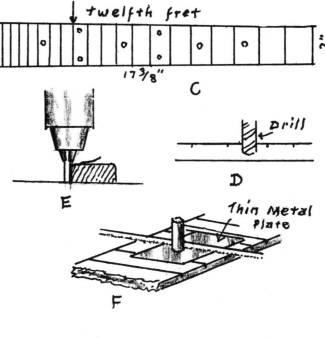

Figure 5-11

Place the box back in the form, leaving the clamp plates off. Cut thirty or forty small blocks from soft wood, about 1/2″ x 3/4″ x 2″ long, to be used to hold the banding in place until the glue dries. Coat the rabbeted edge with glue and start at the back center, place the smooth side of the strips to the inside, push in tight, and tack the blocks to the form (C) to hold the banding. Use as many blocks as needed to hold the banding strips, especially around the curves. Be sure the strips are pushed down to the bottom of the rabbet.

INSTALLING THE NECK

Attach the neck to the sound box and tighten the nuts with a socket wrench through the sound hole. Check with a straightedge to see if the center line of the neck is aligned with the center of the sound box (Figure 5-10A). If it is off center, sand the shoulder of the neck (D) or the box to align the neck. Take care and do not sand too much because a very small amount taken off here will change the angle of the neck with the box.

After aligning the neck, remove it to glue on the fret board.

The details for the bridge are shown in Figure 5-10. It is made of walnut or ebony. Drill the string holes as shown and just large enough for the largest string.

The saddle sits in a groove that is cut with a slight angle. This makes the span of the base string a little longer than the first. File or sand the top of the saddle to a height of about 1/2″ from the bottom of the bridge. It will be trued up later.

Glue the bridge on the top of the sound box at the position shown (B). If your fret board is a different length from the one I have shown, the bridge will have to be adjusted by changing its position on the top.

Be sure the bridge does not slip out of place. Clean off any glue that is forced out around it. Let it dry a day or two before the strings are tightened.

Ask your butcher for a large bone (say it's for your dog). Saw it into smaller pieces and boil the grease out. Split the bone into quarters, put the pieces in the sunlight for several days to bleach them, and you have the best material available for the nut, saddle, and position dots. It saws and sands just like wood.

INSTALLING THE FRET BOARD

If you decide to make the fret board and have the pattern mentioned earlier, follow the steps given in Figure 5-11.

Carefully mark the locations of each fret from the pattern previously made and saw the grooves in a box (B). They should fit tightly enough to require driving in place. Make trial cuts on scrap material first to determine the correct saw thickness. Do not install the frets at this time but saw all the grooves to the correct depth.

Next, taper the fret board on the jointer by taking light cuts on each side until it is the same size as the neck, install the position dots, sand smooth, and, if you wish, finish with two coats of a durable finish. Clean out the grooves by lightly pulling the fret saw back through them before installing the frets. Rub white glue into the grooves and drive in the frets. Start them with a wood or plastic mallet, then drive down with a hardwood block and mallet until the upper part is flat on the fret board. Wipe off the glue with a damp cloth. Trim off the ends of the frets with pliers and finish with a file and stone. The fret board can now be glued onto the neck. Use contact cement in case the fret board has to be removed for any reason. It can be removed by heating it a little and slipping a putty knife between it and the neck. Do not glue the fret board to the top of the soundbox. Scrape and sand the glue joints on each side until they are flush and smooth.

Finish the guitar as you like with varnish or lacquer. Do not use stain because it is hard to keep it off the light wood.

ADJUSTMENTS

As you tune the strings check the height of the first and sixth string from the twelfth fret. When all the strings are tuned, the first should be 1/8″ off the fret and the sixth should be 5/32″.

If they are higher or lower than this, adjust the bottom nut inside the box. Also sand the saddle to a slope of about 1/32″ toward the first string side. Shallow notches can be filed in the saddle and nut for each string. Adjust them at the nut so the strings will just clear the first fret. If they are too low they will rattle; too high and the tone is distorted.

If you have followed the instructions you should have a fine sounding and accurate guitar. If it is not perfect at first tuning, at least you have a chance to correct it without too much trouble or damage to the box.

If you decide to make others later with better materials, you can write for catalogs to "The Guitar Center," P.O. Box 15444, Tulsa, Oklahoma 74115, "International Violin Co.," 4026 West Belvedere Ave., Baltimore, Maryland 21215, or check with your music store.

WOODEN WHEEL 6 CLOCK

On the wall across the room from where I sit hangs a clock ticking loudly as its pendulum swings back and forth. The clock case has a Plexiglas front, which shows that all the wheels and spindles are made of wood along with the dial and hands. It is one of five that I have made in the last three or four years just for fun and the challenge that a project like this can offer.

Over the years, I have been called on to repair a number of Eli Terry "pillar-and-scroll" clocks, which were made in the 1700s and have wooden movements. Most of them had only a tooth or two broken off of a wheel or pinion and were fairly easy to fix by gluing in a small piece of wood and filing or sanding it to match the others. Sometimes a new wheel or spindle was required to restore a valuable antique clock, which in many cases had run for over a hundred years.

Naturally, making a wheel with all the teeth evenly spaced and accurately shaped was an entirely different matter. The operation called for some kind of wood-working milling machine to do the job satisfactorily. Having had some experience in machine shop work in the Navy, I thought I could rig up something to do the milling required. I thought I might even try making a complete clock some day.

The router seemed the best bet for cutting the teeth. I knew it had to be mounted in some kind of jig so it could be accurately moved across the edge of the wheels and pinions. The wheels and pinions had to be fastened to some kind of revolving shaft with an indexing plate in order to cut the teeth on the various sizes needed in a complete clock. The set-up and procedure that I finally found workable follows.

As for the clock, I decided to make a simplified version, using only the gear train for the time side. The original clock had both time and striking trains. I planned to use a case to be hung on a wall instead of placed on a shelf in order to use longer weight cords that permit more time between windings.

I got the idea for the Plexiglas front plate while trying to fit the spindle pins in all the holes while viewing the trouble spots in the gear train. This led to the cutout in the dial, which makes it easy to show your friends that the clock is all wood.

PLATES

The front plate is 6¼" x 9½" and is made of ³/₁₆" or ¼" Plexiglas. The back is 7¼" x 9½" and is of ¼" hardwood

plywood. I suggest using ⅛" Plexiglas for the first front plate. If everything works, it can be used as a pattern to make the permanent one later. Lay out all the holes on the back plate. The ones in the front plate will be drilled from it.

It is very important that the holes be accurately spaced. Start by drawing the center line, and from the dimensions given in Figure 6-1, locate the holes from it. The hole for the two center wheels, Nos. 4 and 6, is 4¹⁵/₁₆" from the bottom of the plate and on the center line. This will place them in the center of the dial. From the center hole, carefully measure and mark the location of the others with a sharp pointed punch. Also mark the holes from 1 to 8 (as shown) for easy reference.

Check the distances between holes by referring to Figure 6-7, which shows the train as it will be in the clock with the correct spacing for proper meshing of the wheel and pinion teeth. Drill ³/₃₂" holes at all locations, including the two center holes located at the top and bottom. The two center holes will be used later to pin the two plates together for drilling the holes in the front plate. Also drill the holes at each corner for the posts that hold the plates together and two on each side of the back plate for screws that will fasten the movement in the case. Some of these will be enlarged later and the dimensions are given in Figure 6-1.

Drill the center holes in the top and bottom of the front plate to match the ones in the back. Pin the two together so they cannot slip, then from the back side of the back plate drill through it into the front. The temporary plate that is ⅛" thick can be drilled through. The ³/₁₆" permanent plate is drilled ⅛" deep for all the pin holes, leaving ¹/₁₆" on the face side. This is easily done by setting the depth gauge of the drill press. When all holes are drilled, separate and enlarge the No. 4–6 hole (in the front only) to ³/₈" and the four post holes to ¼". In the back plate, enlarge No. 8 to ⅝" and the post and mounting holes to ⁵/₃₂" for wood screws that hold the post to the back and the movement in the case.

ROUTER-MILLING MACHINE

The most important thing in making the movement is the accuracy with which the teeth are cut. In order to assure the required accuracy you will need to make a jig for holding the wheels and pinions in the correct position while the teeth are being machined with the router.

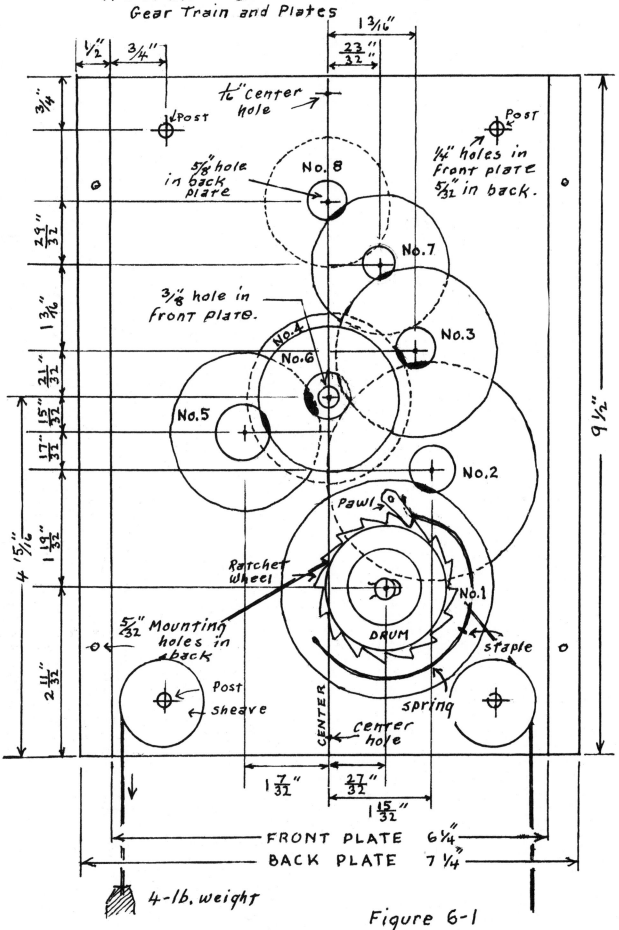

WOODEN WHEEL CLOCK PLAN
Gear Train and Plates

Figure 6-1

80

Figure 6-2 shows a jig similar to the one I used. Of course you will make it to fit your router. It must slide back and forth freely without any "side-play" on the two rabbeted pieces that form a track on top of the jig. They are arranged in a frame that can be shifted to either side since some of the wheels have teeth cut at an angle requiring the router to be set off center.

The tail stock works like the one in your lathe. It can be made of junk parts but it needs to be sturdy, without any loose motion. Use a lock nut on one end of the threaded rod and a crank or handwheel for adjusting. The other end has a 1/4" hole drilled in the center for the inserts that will be used to center the shaft and spindles in the jig for cutting the teeth (see Figures 6-2 and 6-3). Both the lathe and the routing jig will have to be fitted with interchangeable centers or inserts in the tail stock. One should have a 60° point to be used with the metal shaft that the wheels are turned and machined on. The other should have a sharp, slender point, about 3/16" long to center the spindles.

The inserts can easily be made from short pieces of 1/4" rod by using the arbor and chuck in the lathe (Figure 6-4). With a cutting tool ground on the end of an old file, shape the ends as if they were wood. They can also be shaped with a file as the lathe turns.

The inserts for the lathe will probably have to be tapered. This can be determined by removing one from the cup center and using it for a pattern (see Figure 6-4D). The 1/4" diameter of the inserts should extend outside the center about 3/8". The purpose of this extension is to provide an accurate way of centering the two hollow predrilled spindles. This will be explained later and is shown in Figures 6-5B and C.

INDEXING PLATE

It is very important that the indexing plate be as accurate as possible. I made two or three before I finally got one that was satisfactory so I recommend the following procedure.

Drill a 1/16" (or less) hole in a piece of 1/16" aluminum and with a compass or dividers, mark and cut a disk 6" in diameter with the hole in the center.

As it is difficult to lay out and mark all the holes in the small plate, I suggest making a pattern on a piece of stiff cardboard or plywood about a foot square. From a small center hole, draw four circles with radii of 4", 4 1/2", 5", and 5 1/2". Divide these into four equal parts (Figure 6-2G). The drawing here shows only one circle with each quarter divided into the different divisions but you will need a full circle for each set of holes. The first circle is divided into 32 equal parts, the second 36 parts, the third 40 parts, and the fourth 48 parts.

With a sharp pair of dividers, scribe four circles on the plate as shown. Tack it over the pattern with a small nail through the center holes, and another near the edge to keep it from turning. With a metal straightedge against the center pin and on the points of the pattern, transfer them to the plate by marking across the circle with a sharp pointed scribe. Center punch and drill a 1/16" pilot hole at each mark then enlarge to 1/8".

This may seem complicated but I found out (the hard way) that it's the most accurate because the 1/8" drill will sometimes crawl off center. In case a hole should be slightly off center, it can be moved by expanding the metal into one side of the hole and redrilling. To do this, lay the plate on a piece of smooth, flat metal and with a nail set, tap the edge of the hole on the side opposite the direction you wish to move the hole. This will close that side of the hole in slightly. Redrill by forcing the bit against the side in which you wish to move the hole. Sand off the burrs on the back side caused by drilling.

Fasten the plate to one end of a 3/8" shaft about 4" long. It can be fastened by threading and placing a nut on each side of the plate or by drilling a hole in the end of the shaft and threading for a screw. Either way, it must be tight enough so the plate cannot turn on the shaft.

The locking device is a piece of spring steel with a tapered pin in one end that engages the holes in the plate. The other end is fastened to the jig as shown in Figure 6-2B, C, and D. The arbor shown (E) is a 3/8" threaded shaft about 4 3/4" long with a sleeve that is used to fasten it to the index. This arbor will be used to mount the wheel blanks in the lathe for turning as well as cutting the teeth in the router jig.

WHEELS

The wheels are made of well-seasoned black (wild) cherry, preferably quarter sawed. They range in size from 2" to 3" in diameter. Dress the wheel material to 1/4" thick, except for the No. 1 drive wheel, which is 5/16" thick.

The escapement wheel, No. 8 (Figure 6-3D), is made by gluing two layers of wood-grained Formica together, back to back. I found that wood is too soft for this wheel and the sharp points of the teeth soon wear off causing the verge to skip. Clamp the two pieces between blocks of wood until the glue dries (use white liquid). The Formica can be worked like wood and the teeth are hard and smooth. The verge can also be made this way.

Cut the wheel blanks with a circle cutter in the drill press (Figure 6-3), making them about 1/16" oversize. Make several of each size, also a couple from scrap plywood. Enlarge the center holes to 3/8" and mount the wheel blanks on the shaft. Place a plywood blank on each end to prevent the cherry ones from splintering while the teeth are being cut with the router (B).

To make the wheels the exact size with the holes in dead center, mount the shaft in the lathe and turn the blanks to size. If your lathe will take a tapered arbor with a drill chuck, clamp a short piece of 3/8" rod in the chuck for the sleeve of the shaft to fit over. If this is not possible, any other arrangement will do as long as the shaft turns perfectly true between the lathe centers. The threaded end of the shaft should be center-drilled to fit the 60° tail center of the lathe and the indexing jig as shown in Figure 6-2E.

INDEXING JIG FOR ROUTER

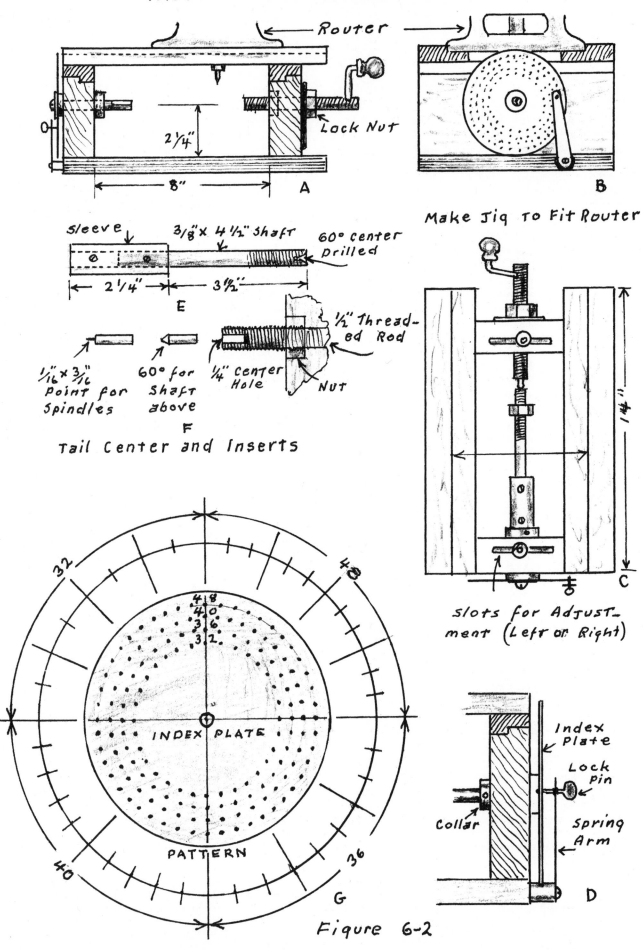

Router

2¼"

8"

A

B

Lock Nut

Make Jig To Fit Router

Sleeve   3/8" x 4½" Shaft   60° Center Drilled

2¼"   3½"

E

1/16" x 3/16" Point for Spindles

60° for Shaft above

¼" Center Hole

½" Threaded Rod

Nut

F

Tail Center and Inserts

14"

C

Slots for Adjustment (Left or Right)

32   40
48
40
36
32

INDEX PLATE

PATTERN

40   36

G

Index Plate

Lock Pin

Collar

Spring Arm

D

Figure 6-2

82

WHEELS

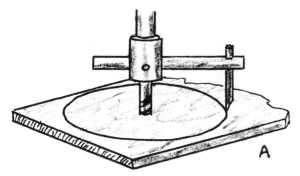

Wheel blanks being cut
with circle cutter
(cut 1/16" over size)

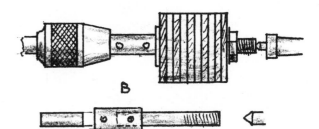

Turn to exact size on
shaft by chucking in lathe.

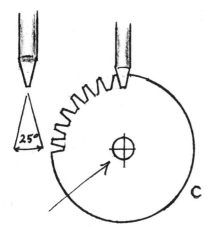

25°

Redrill holes to 3/8 dia.

side
view

42°

Router
bits

Edge of bit
in line with
Center of
wheel

Escapement Wheel

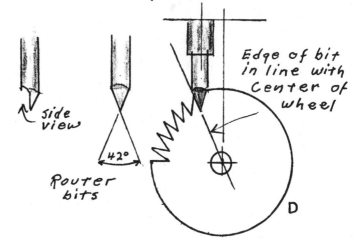

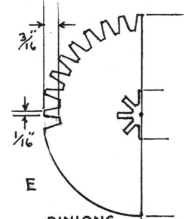

3/16"

1/16"

E

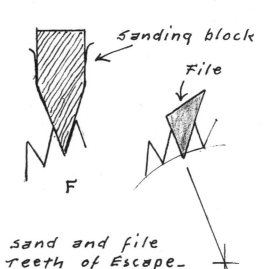

sanding block

File

F

sand and file
teeth of Escape-
ment wheel to
sharp point.

Figure 6-3

	WHEELS		PINIONS	
No	Dia.	No.Teeth	Dia.	No.Teeth
1	3"	40		
2	3"	48	11/16"	8
3	2 3/16"	36	9/16"	8
4	2 5/16"	40	5/8"	9
5	2 3/16"	36	3/4"	12
6	2 1/16"	36		
7	1 15/16"	32	1/2"	8
8	2	32	1/2"	8

TOOLS and ACCESSORIES

Tail Stock

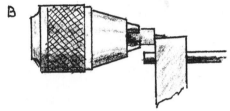

A

Work Arbor with Chuck
with which the small metal parts
shown here can be turned in
the wood lathe, by cutting with
a tool or by filing
(Turn at high speed)

D

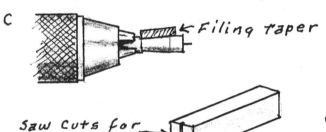

B

Turning inserts on lathe
with tool made from file

Tapered Inserts for
Lathe Cup Center.
(make to fit)

C

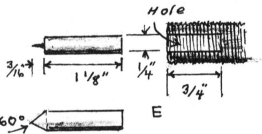

←Filing Taper

Saw Cuts for
Spur Center

Spindle Stock

Hole

3/16" ← 1 1/8" → 1/4" ← 3/4" →

60° ← E

Inserts for Indexing
Jig Tail Stock.

TOOLS FOR TURNING SPINDLES
made from used files.

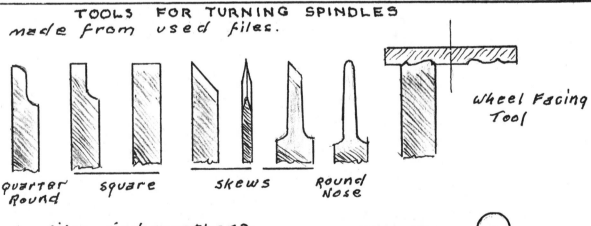

Quarter Round   Square   Skews   Round Nose

Wheel Facing Tool

Two files tied together ↗

Wood filler   3/8"

Sizing gauge for Spindle
at wheel location

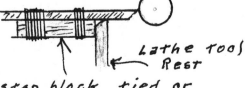

Lathe Tool Rest

Stop block tied or
clamped To tool

Figure 6-4

THE SPINDLES

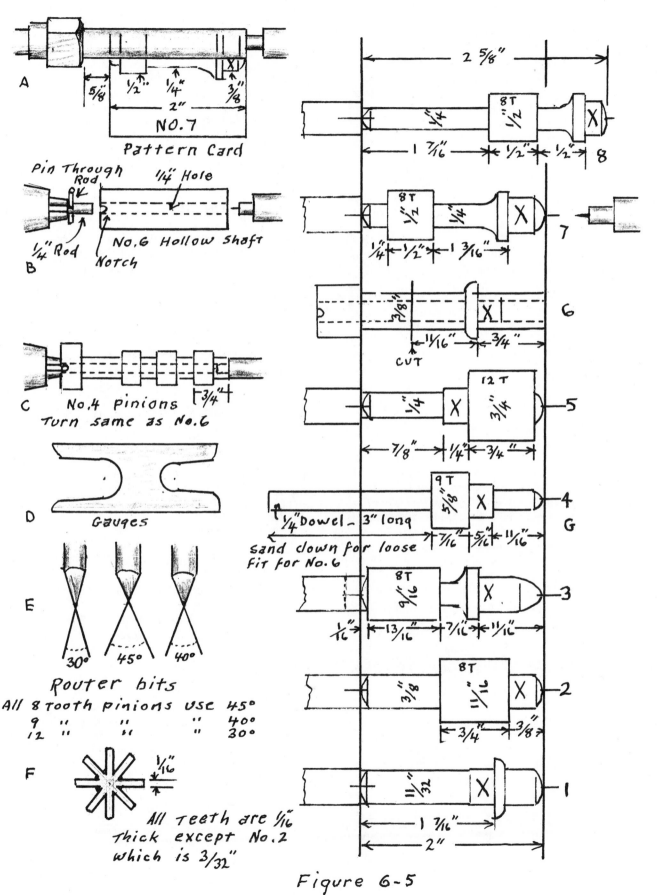

Pattern Card

NO.7

A

B
Pin Through Rod
1/4" Rod
Notch
1/4" Hole
No.6 Hollow Shaft

C No.4 pinions
Turn same as No.6

D Gauges

E Router bits
30°   45°   40°

All 8 tooth pinions use 45°
9 "   "   "   40°
12 "   "   "   30°

F All teeth are 1/16
thick except No.2
which is 3/32"

8
7
6 CUT
5
4
G 1/4"Dowel - 3" long
sand down for loose
fit for No.6
3
2
1

Figure 6-5

85

The router bits can be made from old ¼" drills as shown in Figure 8-1. Two different sizes (or angles) will be needed for the wheels and they should be ground to the 25° and 42° angles as shown in Figure 6-3C and D.

For the first try at cutting the teeth, some experimenting or practicing is advisable so use some extra wheel blanks for the first set-up. Mount them in the jig and set the router in the track on top. Adjust the cutter to route a shallow groove across the top of the blanks. Set the index lock pin in a hole on the circle having the number of holes corresponding to the number of teeth to be cut.

Make three or four passes turning the plate one hole each time. Check the points of the teeth, adjusting the depth of cut until they are ¹⁄₁₆" thick at the tip. There should also be about the same distance between the teeth at the base (however this is not critical). After adjusting the router for the correct cut, lock it into position and proceed to cut the teeth on all the wheels having this size and number of teeth.

If the cut is rough, teeth break off, or wood is burned, the bit is not sharp or does not have clearance behind the cutting edge. Mount the wheel blanks on the shaft with the grain of each turned at right angles to the one next to it and use the plywood blanks on each side. This should reduce the chance of breaking teeth.

If the teeth are not uniform, check for looseness in all parts of the assembly, especially if the shaft is tight in the jig. The set screws could be loose. The index plate may be loose or not accurate. The lock pin should be tight in the holes of the index plate.

If you decide to make the escapement wheel yourself as I did, the glued-up Formica seems to work fine for both the wheel and the verge. I can see no appreciable sign of wear after about four years of use.

Notice in Figure 6-3D that one side of the teeth is in line with the center of the wheel. By using a router bit ground as shown and moving the router off center so that one side of the bit is in line with the center of the shaft, the teeth should be correctly formed. The teeth must be sharply pointed and all the same length from the center. I used the same method that is used to accurately sharpen a circle saw, "jointing and filing until sharp."

Set the bit so a slight flat tip is left on all the teeth to ensure that they are the same length. Finish to a sharp point with a sharp-edged file. File the same side of the teeth to keep them evenly spaced. Figure 6-3 shows the blanks being cut, sized, and machined. In the original clock some of the wheels had teeth cut at a slight angle. I tried them both ways and could see no difference in performance. In order to simplify the procedure, I suggest making the teeth straight as shown (Figure 6-3C and E).

The escapement wheel (No. 8) will have to be made as shown (Figure 6-3D). Special care is needed to make it perfectly round with evenly spaced, sharp-pointed teeth. The original has a brass escapement and steel verge. If you choose, they can be bought or salvaged from an old clock. It will have to be a 32-tooth assembly to work with this gear train.

Make several wheels of each size as it is just as easy as making one or two. Notice that the No. 3 and 5 wheels are alike so make twice as many of them. Number all wheels and spindles as they are made (from 1 to 8) according to their position in the gear train.

A sharp-edged sanding block can be used to advantage if several wheels are being made on the shaft. It should be shaped to fit between the teeth with a piece of fine sandpaper tightly wrapped around it. Move it back and forth in each V groove. This should be done on all the wheels while they are still on the shaft.

SPINDLES OR SHAFTS

Cut the stock for all the spindles a full ¾" square. Five of them should be cut to the working length of 3½". Cut No. 6 to 2¼" and No. 8 to 4". They should be of straight grain maple or cherry. All except Nos. 4 and 6 can be turned in the lathe with the regular spur center. The No. 4 and 6 shafts, which are hollow, need special adapters to assure accuracy. The set-up for turning them is shown in Figure 6-5B and C.

The No. 6 shaft has a ¼" hole through the exact center. The most accurate way is to first drill the hole and center from it, in the lathe as shown (Figure 6-5B). A piece of ¼" rod with a small pin through it is fastened in the work arbor chuck. The drilled stock has a notch sawed across one end in the center of the hole to engage the pin. This keeps it from turning on the rod.

The other end turns on the ¼" extension of the tail center (Figure 6-5B). The pinion for the No. 4 shaft, which is a ¼" dowel, is made in the same way and is shown (Figure 6-5C). For the other spindles the sharp-pointed tail center is used. It starts the holes in one end for the pins that will be redrilled later. Centering the other end will be explained later.

The best way to turn the spindles is to make pattern cards as shown in Figure 6-5A. The pattern should have marks showing where each section is located and the diameter of each. A pattern card for No. 7 spindle is shown.

The cards are 2" long or (except No. 8) the same length as the finished spindles. In order to fasten the spindles to the index head, a ⅜" diameter shank or extension is turned on the left end. This fits into the sleeve that connects it to the index shaft.

The No. 8 spindle pattern is 2⅝" long (this is the longest turned spindle). The No. 4 is made up with a ¼" x 3" dowel and a short pinion and shoulder that is glued to the dowel. Figure 6-5C shows three of these being turned with the adapters that were used on No. 6.

Number the pattern cards according to their order in the gear train. All the spindles and wheels should also be numbered as they are made to avoid confusion and mistakes.

Make two or three extras of each so if some are ruined later you won't have to repeat the whole process. If they all turn out right, you have parts for another clock or two.

Diameter gauges for turning the spindles are easily made and save time in sizing the many different diameters that have to be turned. They can be made by drilling holes in pieces of Formica and cutting to the outside so they can be slipped over the stock while it is being turned (Figure 6-5D). The x mark on each spindle (as shown) is where the wheel is located. It should be carefully gauged and turned for a tight fit in the wheel.

I made a gauge with two flat files tied together with a 3/8″ wood strip between. It has a slight taper so the outer ends of the files are a little farther apart and can be slipped over the spindle while they are turning. It is eased in until the end of the wood strip touches the spindle. If it is accurately made the two files should cut it to the exact size. It is shown in Figure 6-4. Old files can also be used to make small turning tools needed for the spindle work. Some suggestions are illustrated in Figure 6-4.

The shoulders that the wheels fit against can be undercut slightly to assure a good fit and prevent wheel wobble.

PINIONS

Cut off the square ends of the turned spindles but leave the 3/8″ turned extension, as it is used to fasten the spindle in the indexing jig. The sleeve is removed from the shaft part of the arbor and is used to tie the spindle to the routing jig.

Set the router over the center. For all eight tooth pinions use the 45° router bit and the 48-hole index. Using every sixth hole, gradually lower the bit until the tooth is 1/16″ uniform thickness. (Mark every sixth hole on the plate to avoid mistakes.) If the teeth turn out tapered or wedge-shaped the bit is not properly ground (see Figure 6-5F).

Both No. 7 and 8 pinions are routed with this set-up. No. 3 has eight teeth but is 9/16″ in diameter, so raise the router slightly. No. 2 is 11/16″ in diameter and the teeth on this pinion are 3/32″ thick so adjust accordingly. No. 5 has twelve teeth. The 30° bit is needed along with the 36-hole index, using every third hole. The three No. 4 pinions that are still together and have nine teeth are routed with a 40° bit and every fourth hole of the 36-hole index.

Cut all the spindles except No. 3 to the finished lengths shown in Figure 6-5. Leave about 1/4″ of the 3/8″ extension on it until the holes for the pins have been centered and drilled in the ends that were cut off. (The other end has been centered by the lathe center.)

It is important that the pins be correctly centered. This is hard to do by measuring and marking the conventional way. I recommend the following procedure: drill holes to fit the ends about 3/8″ deep in a block. In the center of each hole drill a 1/16″ (or less) hole on through the block. Drive small nails from the back side, letting them protrude into the inside about 3/16″. Cut them off flush on the back side so the block will lay flat on the drill press table (Figure 6-6A). Make some extra holes slightly oversize, and some undersize in case some of the spindles are a little off. They need to fit snugly into the holes to accurately center the turning spindles.

Sand a slight taper on the sawed ends to help them enter the centering holes. Chuck lightly in the drill press and ease the end of the turning spindle into the hole until the nail has entered about 1/8″ deep (Figure 6-6A).

Of course the holes will have to be drilled to the depth of 1/2″ to 5/8″ deep, and straight into the spindle (Figure 6-6B). The point of a nail is centered directly under the drill chuck to hold the spindle in line with the 1/16″ drill.

I used three-penny finishing nails for the pins. Drive them in and cut off with pliers. The ones that go in the back plate can be about 1/4″ long. The front pins go into the Plexiglas front plate only 1/8″ so they should be gauged to 5/32″ (Figure 6-6F and G).

Drive the spindles into the wheels (Figure 6-6D) but do not glue until the complete gear train has been assembled and tried by spinning them by hand. The decorative pattern that is turned on the face of the wheels will have to be done before the spindles are glued. If the gear train works, touch a drop or two of glue inside the holes and set the spindles. Double check for the correct wheel and to see if the decorated or turned side is facing the front.

Lay them in the jig shown (Figure 6-6E) and spin it with your finger to check for wobble before the glue sets. The jig is a block with grooves for the pins to lay in (Figure 6-6E). If there is a slight wobble it could be a bent pin, which can be straightened with pliers. The wheel can also be trued up as shown (H) by sanding lightly while turning in the drill press. The chuck holds one pin and the other one turns in a hole in a block clamped to the table.

Figure 6-7 shows the gear train as it will be in the clock. It is drawn here in a line in order to clearly show the meshing of the gears and pinions. It also shows the distances between the holes in the plates for the pins. Notice that the No. 3 pinion engages both the No. 2 and No. 4 wheel. The No. 6, which has the hollow shaft, turns on the No. 4 shaft. Their ratio of revolutions is regulated by the No. 5 gear and pinion. It turns the No. 6 or hour shaft one revolution for every twelve revolutions of the No. 4 or minute shaft.

The No. 7, which is turned by the No. 3 wheel, is shown at the left with the No. 8 or escapement. Notice that this wheel is outside the back plate (Figure 6-7E) and is mounted with a strip of 1/8″ Plexiglas or 1/16″ metal between two blocks (Figure 6-7E and 6-8I). Be sure the hole for the spindle pin is on center. The ends of the plate should have slots for slight vertical adjustment if needed.

The top and bottom posts that hold the two plates together are shown in Figure 6-7A and B. They are about 5/8″ square and the overall length is 2 9/16″. The shoulder at the outer end holds the plates 2 1/16″ apart, allowing 1/16″ clearance for the 2″ spindles. The ends are turned with a slight taper and so they will easily fit in the 1/4″ holes at the corners of the front plate. A small hole is drilled through

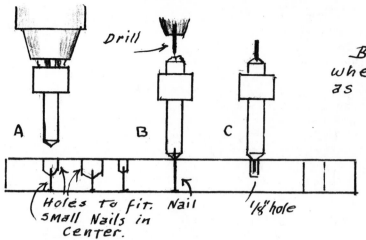

Drill

Centering and Drilling Jig

Holes To fit. Nail
small Nails in
Center.

Nail

⅛" hole

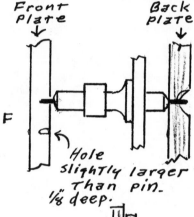

Before installing in
wheels, sand pinions
as shown-

Round
edges

Round
out between
Teeth

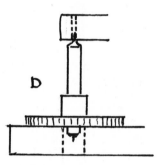

**Driving Spindles
into wheels**

D

E

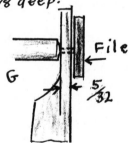

Front
Plate

Back
plate

F

Hole
slightly larger
Than pin-
⅛" deep.

Gauge 5/32" Thick
file flush-Then
file off burr.

G

File

5/32

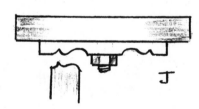

J

A- Centering for pins
B- Drilling ⅛" holes
C- Driving pins
D- Driving in wheel
E- Checking for wobble-
  spin, and adjust-
F, G length of pins-
H- sanding to correct
  slight Wobble or
  oversize
I- sanding No. 4 shaft
  for loose fit of No. 6
  hollow spindle
J- Turning Decorative
  Pattern on face
  of wheels

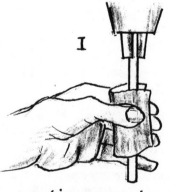

I

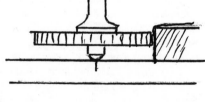

H

**sanding oversize
spindle**

Note: Do Not glue wheels To spindle
until later (if They are tight
enough To stay in place).

88

Figure 6-6

GEAR TRAIN

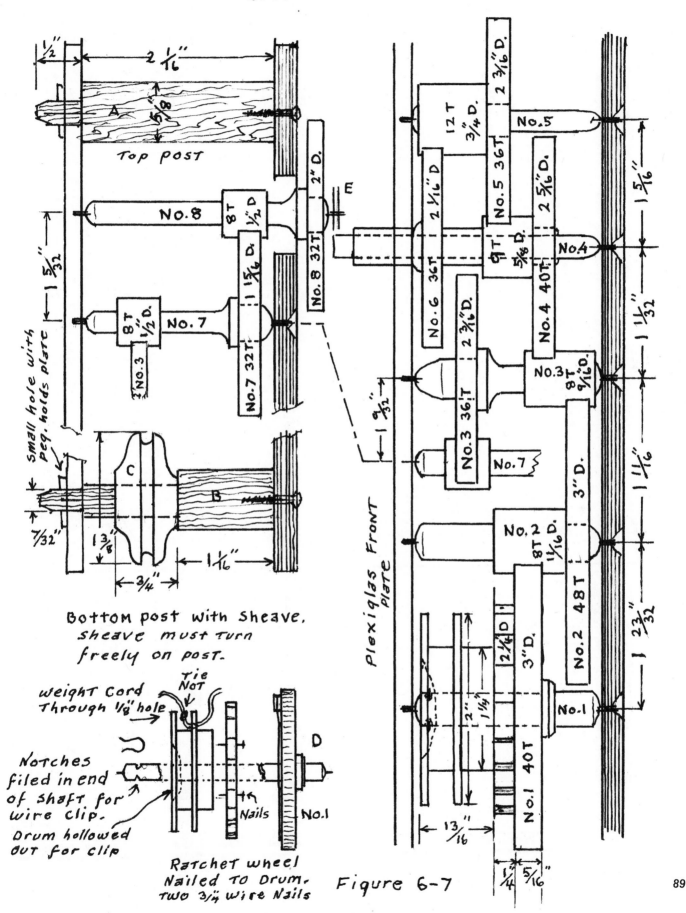

Top Post

½" 2 1/16" 5/8" A

E 2" D.

No. 8 8 T ½" D.

No. 8 32 T 1 15/16 D.

1 5/32"

No. 7 8 T ½" D.

No. 3

No. 7 32 T

Small hole with peg. holds plate

Bottom post with Sheave, sheave must turn freely on post.

C B

7/32" 1 3/8" 3/4" 1 1/16"

Weight Cord through 1/8" hole

Tie Not

Notches filed in end of shaft for wire clip.

Drum hollowed out for clip

D Nails No. 1

Ratchet wheel Nailed To Drum. Two 3 1/4 Wire Nails

Figure 6-7

Plexiglas Front Plate

12 T 3/4" D. 2 3/16" D.

No. 5

No. 5 36 T 2 5/16" D.

No. 6 36 T 2 1/16" D

9 T 5/16" D. No. 4

No. 4 40 T

1 5/16"

No. 3 36 T 2 3/16" D.

No. 3 8 T 9/16 D.

No. 7

1 9/32"

3" D.

1 1/32"

No. 2 8 T 11/16 D.

No. 2 48 T

1 1/16"

2 1/4 D. 3" D.

2" 1 1/4"

No. 1

No. 1 40 T

1 23/32"

13/16" ¼" 5/16"

ESCAPEMENT-PENDULUM & WEIGHTS

A- Escapement Wheel. Turns 1½ Rev. per minute.

B- Verge. Swings 48 Times each minute.

C- Plexiglas plate. Slots in ends for adjusting.

D- Verge support. 1/16" Brass with 1/16" x 1/4" pin.

E- Verge Retainer. Thin spring brass.

F- Hardwood blocks. 7/16" x 3/4". Thick

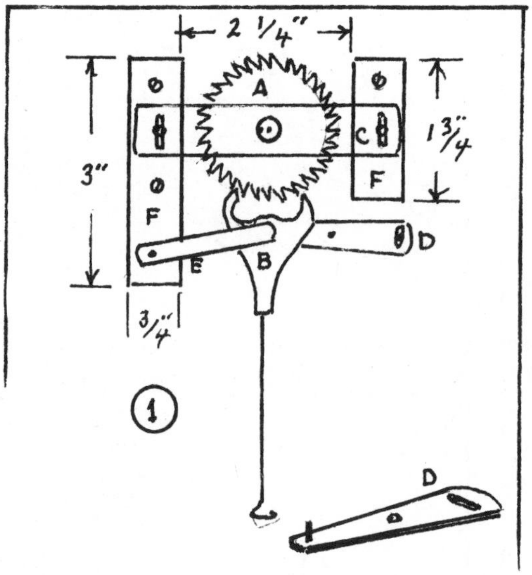

2 1/4"
A
C
1 3/4"
3"
F
F
D
E
B
3/4"
1
D

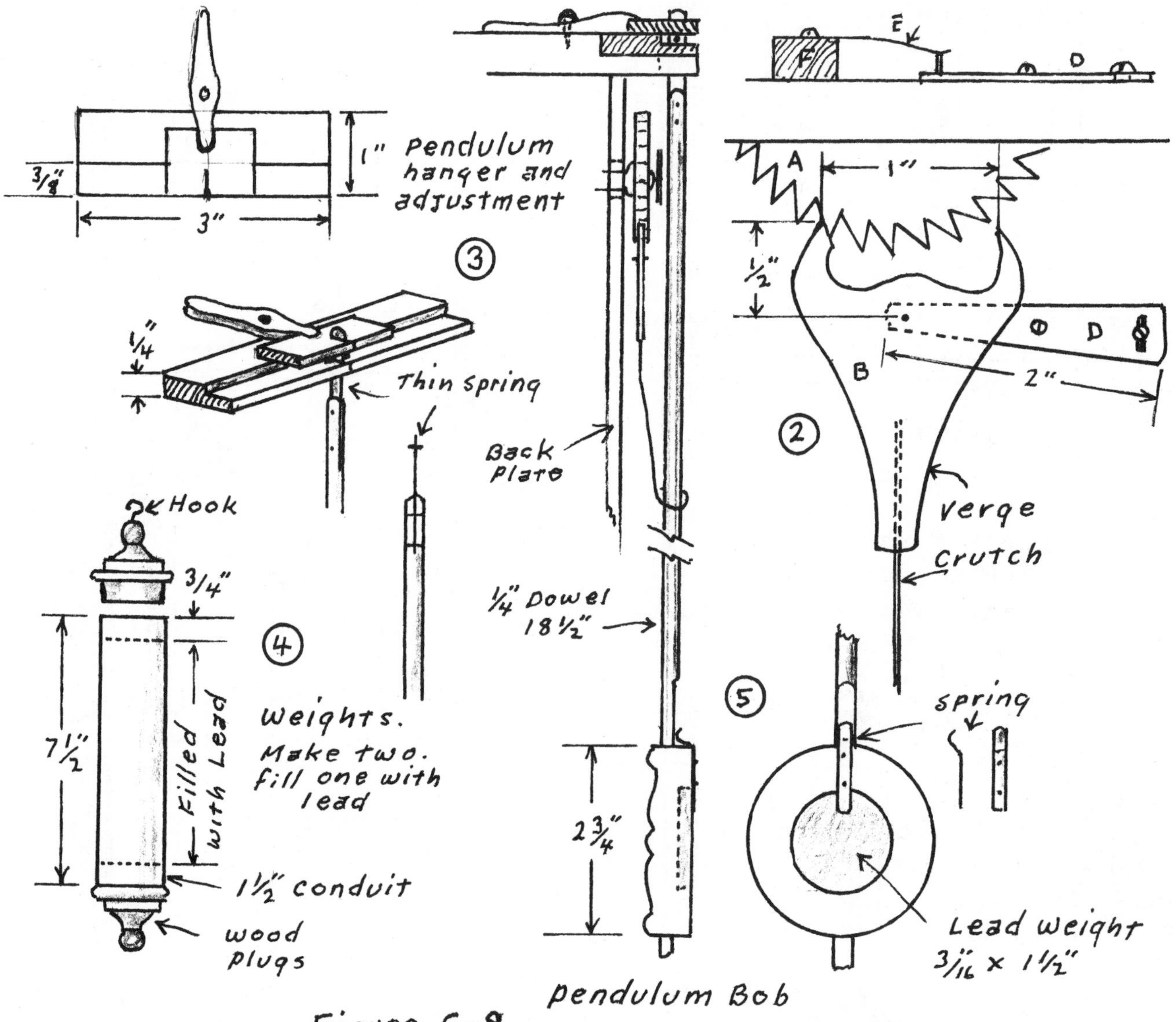

E
F
D
3/8"
1" Pendulum hanger and adjustment
3"
3
1/4"
Thin spring
Back Plate
A
1"
1/2"
D
B
2"
2
Verge
Crutch
Hook
3/4"
4
7 1/2"
Filled with Lead
Weights. Make two. fill one with lead
1 1/2" conduit
wood plugs
1/4" Dowel 18 1/2"
2 3/4"
5
spring
Lead weight 3/16" x 1 1/2"
pendulum Bob

Figure 6-8

each for a small peg (the ends of toothpicks) to hold the plate. They are fastened to the back plate with screws.

The two bottom posts are turned for the sheaves (Figure 6-7C) that guide the weight cords down through the cutouts in the bottom (see Figure 6-1).

The ratchet wheel, cord drum, and No. 1 drive wheel are shown as a unit at the bottom of Figure 6-7. Although the drive wheel is glued to the shaft, the drum and ratchet wheel, which are fastened together with two brads, must turn freely on the shaft. This is why the shaft is reduced in diameter as shown in Figure 6-5.

The drum is turned as shown in Figure 6-7. When fastened to the ratchet wheel it forms two separate sections for the cord. The cord is about 8' long and is threaded through a hole in the center flange and knotted about the middle (Figure 6-7D). Use mason's line or something similar.

The ratchet is 2¼" in diameter. Cut it with the circle cutter the same as the other wheels. The teeth can be sawed on a band saw (see Figure 6-1). The spring and pawl are also shown in Figure 6-1. One end of the spring is bent sharply and driven in a small hole in the wheel. A small staple formed from a piece of paper clip is used to anchor it in place. The other end of the spring is bent up slightly to fit in a groove filed in the top edge of the pawl (Figure 6-1).

The two weights are shown in Figure 6-8, Step 4. They are made with pieces of 1½" conduit with plugs turned to drive in each end. To pour the lead in the heavy weight, set the piece of conduit on a piece of metal and pour the lead to about 1¾" of the top. When cool, jar the lead down into the conduit by pounding on a wood block. Leave spaces at each end for the plugs. The weight should be about four pounds.

The metal can be finished to match the clock case by first painting with a natural wood color latex paint and then staining. Give a wood grain effect by wiping with a piece of foam rubber or brush.

The "verge" (Figure 6-8B) can be made of metal, hard maple, or two layers of Formica. Rough out on the band saw, then sand and file to shape as shown in Step 2. A small hole is drilled in the top center for the support and another at the bottom for the "crutch." The crutch is a piece of spring steel wire flattened on one end to keep it from turning in the hole. A little glue is also added to keep it from working loose. The other end has a hook that wraps around the pendulum rod. A slight clearance is needed in the hook so the rod can swing freely.

The verge support is 1/16" brass or other metal. It has a short pin fastened at one end for the verge to swing on and two screw holes. The outer one is cut out to form a slot to permit vertical adjustment of the verge against the teeth of the escapement wheel.

To fasten the pin to the plate, file a small shoulder on the end as it turns in the drill chuck. Then drive in the hole and peen the back side.

With the wheels in place, adjust the verge so it will let one tooth by with each swing. The left point should slide off the tooth while the right one skips over the point of the sixth tooth and catches the next one. By adjusting and filing the points of the verge (they should be 1" apart) it should click back and forth freely while holding in a vertical position, and pulling down on the cord or the edge of the No. 2 wheel.

If it should hang at the same tooth several times, mark it and file one side as it may be a little unevenly spaced. The teeth and verge must be very smooth for the assembly to work properly.

The movement can be hung in a frame similar to the one shown in Figure 6-11, so all the parts can be seen and trouble spots marked for adjustment. A temporary support for the pendulum can be made to hang over the top of the plates (Figure 6-11). Hang about four pounds of weight on the cord and let it run for a few days while the case is being made.

The details of the pendulum are shown in Figure 6-8. It is turned on the lathe with a hole for the ¼" rod. A piece of lead about 3/16" thick and 1½" in diameter is inset in the back side. The rod has a thin piece of spring (use an old clock spring) ¼" wide fastened at the top with a pin through the end. The bottom end is sanded flat on the back side. Another spring, which is fastened to the pendulum bob fits against the flat (Step 5). The pendulum bob can be slid up or down to adjust the strokes to 48 per minute.

CASE

The case is made of material of your choice in any style, as long as the inside dimensions will allow the movement to fit inside the case. The required dimensions are shown in Figure 6-9. A list of material and the dimensions for cutting are included. The top board (F) and the two fillers (E) can be made of soft pine. The bottom (G) is ¼" plywood and is cut out on each end as shown. The movement fits in between the two fillers and is fastened to their back edge with screws through the outer edge of the back plate.

The most complicated parts of the case shown here are the two small scrolls at the top. They are molded on the bottom edge but are only about 4" long. I have included a step-by-step procedure in Figure 6-10D, showing the safest way to make the short, curved pieces. Since they are mitered around each end, four short, straight pieces will be needed. A piece of straight molding about a foot long should be made with the same set-up for this purpose.

DIAL

The dial is turned on a square block of white pine. Before fastening to the face plate, rabbet the four edges about 3/8" wide and 1/8" deep on the jointer or saw. Turn the face of the dial down flush with it, leaving the ring around the

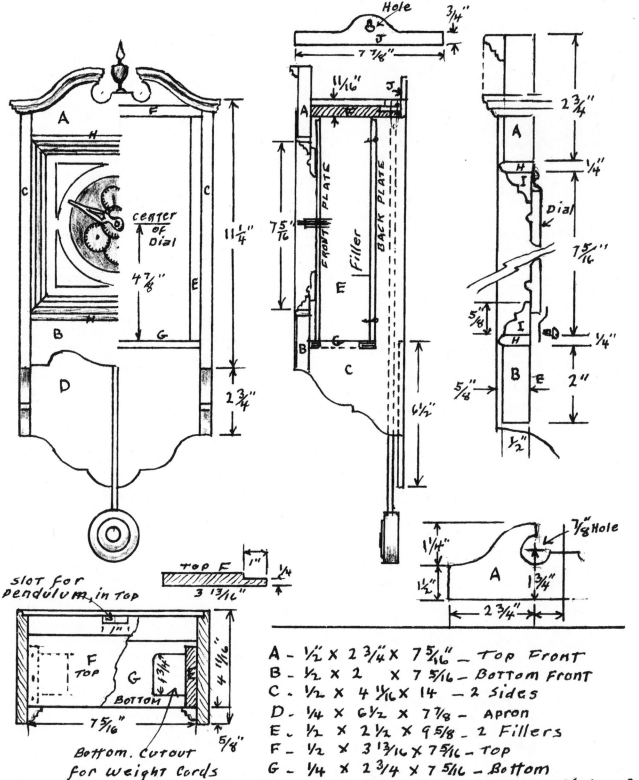

Hole

3/4"

7 7/8"

2 3/4"

1/4"

7 5/16"

5/8"

2"

1/2"

11/16"

7 5/16"

6 1/2"

Center of Dial

4 7/8"

11 1/4"

2 3/4"

1 1/4"

1 1/2"

1 3/4"

2 3/4"

7/8 Hole

Top F

1"

1/4"

3 13/16"

slot for pendulum in top

1 1/4"

F TOP

G BOTTOM

1 3/4"

7 5/16"

4 11/16"

5/8"

Bottom Cutout for Weight Cords

A - 1/2" x 2 3/4" x 7 5/16" — Top Front
B - 1/2 x 2 x 7 5/16 — Bottom Front
C - 1/2 x 4 11/16 x 14 — 2 Sides
D - 1/4 x 6 1/2 x 7 7/8 — Apron
E - 1/2 x 2 1/2 x 9 5/8 — 2 Fillers
F - 1/2 x 3 13/16 x 7 5/16 — Top
G - 1/4 x 2 3/4 x 7 5/16 — Bottom
H - 1/4 x 5/8 x 7 5/16 — Bead Mold (2 pcs.)
I - 9/16 x 5/8 x 7 5/16 — Dial Frame (4 pcs.)
J - 1/4 x 1 3/4 x 7 7/8 — Hanger

Take care in gluing and
Nailing fillers to sides-
5/8" from front and
11/16" from top. (E)

92

Figure 6-9

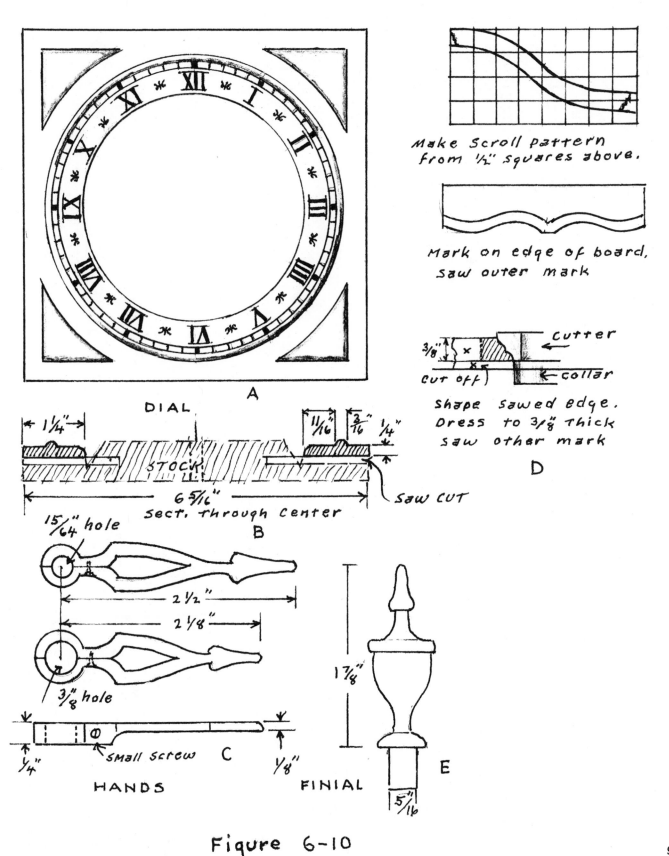

Make Scroll pattern from ½" squares above.

Mark on edge of board, saw outer mark

Shape sawed edge. Dress to 3/8 thick saw other mark

D

DIAL

A

1¼"

STOCK

6 5/16"

Sect. through Center

B

Saw Cut

15/64" hole

2½"

2⅛"

3/8" hole

¼"

small screw   C

⅛"

HANDS

1⅞"

FINIAL

5/16"

E

Figure 6-10

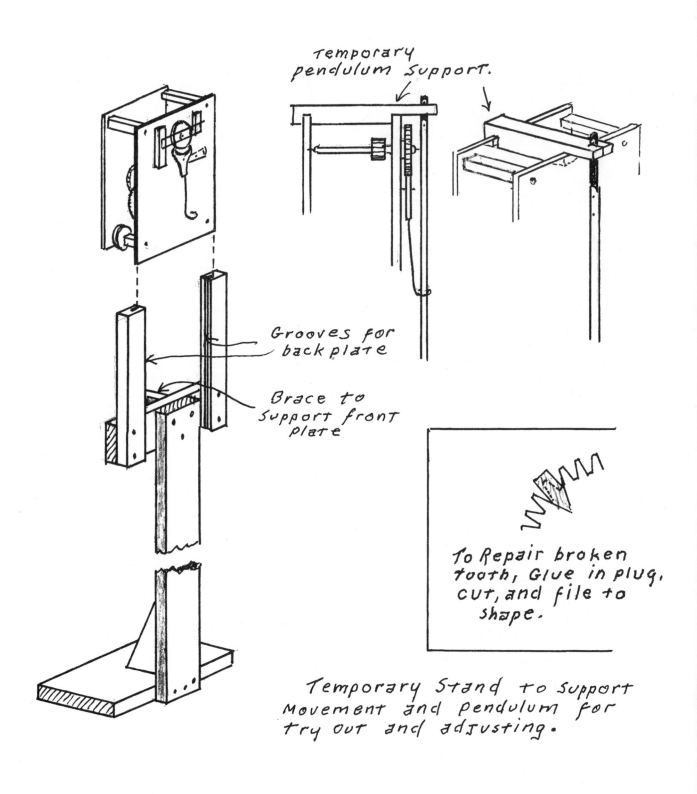

temporary
pendulum support.

Grooves for
back plate

Brace to
support front
plate

To Repair broken
tooth, Glue in plug,
cut, and file to
shape.

Temporary Stand to support
Movement and pendulum for
try out and adjusting.

Figure 6-11

minute marks and the four triangles in relief. A section through the center of the dial is shown in Figure 6-10B. It shows the ring and rounded edges. The dotted lines show how the inside is cut down below the dial. After it has been sanded it is cut from the edges on the table saw. Two can be made by turning both sides of the block.

Stain with a thin coat of white latex paint, wipe off, and finish with clear sealer or varnish. The numerals are laid off similar to the teeth on the wheels and drawn with black ink.

The hands (Figure 6-10C) are made by drilling, sawing, whittling, and sanding. A small screw may be needed to tighten them on the shaft. The finial (E) is turned on the lathe. It sits in a hole in the top center.

The pendulum is hung on an adjustable hanger on the top of the case (Figure 6-8). The hanger lays in the 1/4" x 1" track or groove in the top board. It has a thin saw cut or slot for the spring at the top of the pendulum to fit in. The hanger engages a small lever fastened to the top with a screw. This permits moving the pendulum slightly off center to either side.

This arrangement makes it easy to adjust the clock to the even "tick-tock," which is essential for smooth running. The clock should be hung level and secured so it will not be pulled sideways by the weight. Adjust the pendulum bob for 48 strokes per minute for correct time. This will have to be done through trial and error. Although the length of the rod usually determines the strokes of the pendulum, the weight on the cord and the bob also affect it. The clock can be adjusted by moving the pendulum bob

up or down slightly as needed and timing with a watch or another clock.

The clock will run 36 to 48 hours between windings, depending on the length of the cord. The cord unwinds a little less than one inch per hour.

Weather conditions may affect the movement. Some adjusting of the verge or the pendulum support on top of the case usually corrects it. If it stops often, one of the wheels may be a little oversize or the pin holes too close together, causing the teeth to bind in the pinion. The distances between the holes are shown in Figure 6-7. A slight variation in either the distances or the wheels will cause some trouble. The gear teeth should mesh at about 3/4" of the depth of the flute between the pinion teeth (Figure 6-11).

An oversize wheel can be remedied slightly by sanding off the ends of the teeth as shown in Figure 6-6H. In case a tooth is broken off and you do not wish to change the wheel, it can be repaired as shown in Figure 6-11. Glue in a small wedge-shaped piece, and file to match the other teeth.

Some of the original clocks had brass bushings in the No. 1, 2, and 4 pin holes of the back plates. If you wish, they can be made by drilling in the center of a 1/4" brass rod and sawing 1/4" lengths to inset in the plate by enlarging the holes to fit. The hole in the verge can be bushed the same way if needed. If you have been successful with this clock and wish to make others, you can easily make five or six at one time (and of your own design) since you now have the accessories needed.

7 MILLWORK

I do not claim to be an interior decorator but at times I have been asked to "do something" with a room.

Figures 7-1 and 7-2 show a couple of ideas I have used to dress up a plain room with some moldings and a small amount of other material. It takes 200' to 400' of the small molding for an average room. If you make it yourself, the job is not expensive. A 1″ x 6″ x 10′ board will make about 100′. Cut the strips a little over ³/₈″ thick and dress one side. Shape the other side something like the detail in the drawings. I used a single cutter in the molding head shown in Figure 8-10 and a fitted "hold-down" block, which can be either clamped to the shaper table or held by hand.

The room in Figure 7-1 has wainscoting of ¹/₄″ paneling. The decorative molding is stained to match or painted with the walls. If it is to be stained, do so before installing. Paint or paper the wall space and fasten the finish molding in place by spotting a little glue along the back side and using 1″ wire brads or dark paneling nails.

The other room is a little more elaborate. It is first stripped with pieces of ¹/₄″ x 2″ plywood. If the crown and dental molding (shown in Figure 7-2) is to be used at the top, a 4″ strip of plywood will be needed under it. The small molding is cut to fit around each side of the 2″ strips.

MANTELS

Figure 7-3 shows the construction and installation of a shelf-and-bracket-type mantel that is used when the brick goes all the way to the ceiling or a wood wall. It is fastened to the brick with lag screws and lead shields behind the crown molding. If used on a wood wall, nails or wood screws can be used.

Another style (Figure 7-4) lays on top of the brick, which is usually about 54″ to 60″ high. It can be fastened to wood blocks laid with the brick. A few small nails should be driven into the blocks to help the mortar hold them in place.

DOORWAYS

I feel that at least one doorway should be included in this book so Figure 7-5 illustrates a basic Colonial entrance. Only the front is shown here. It can be added to an existing door frame or the complete entrance can be made by building a conventional frame with the front added.

Its basic construction is the two vertical boards, usually 9″ wide, which rise about 12″ to 14″ above the top of the door frame. They are connected at the top with a 12″ board or lintel. A 1″ x 4″ piece is cut in between the two verticals and fastened to the lintel; it hangs down about 2″, to the bottom edge of the head jam (Figure 7-5B). The fluted pilasters are about 3″ narrower than the 9″ boards. They rest on the base block and cap at the bottom. Another block is at the top with a short beaded piece or "filler" in between. A larger beaded piece with a cove mold under the edge makes the cap for the pilaster.

The main cap is the board and 2″ crown molding that separates the 1″ x 12″ lintel from the head. In case the entrance is to be installed under a cornice or in a porch, this cap should finish against the soffit or ceiling.

The head assembly is made separately and rests on top of the main cap. It is a wide board with the two half circles cut as shown with a pedestal in the center for the finial. It is capped with two 4″ boards and crown mold mitered around each end as shown. The finial is turned from a block of 4″ x 4″ and split in half.

Figure 7-5G shows the pilasters being fluted or beaded on the table saw. Note: this method can also be used in the construction of Colonial mantels by adding the leaf over the cap instead of the head (D).

DENTAL BLOCKING—BUILT-UP MOLDINGS

Sooner or later the woodworker is going to have need, or be called on by others, to make odd sizes or types of moldings. Figure 7-6 shows some ideas on how standard moldings can be used, with some shop work, to produce various sizes and styles. Parts A and B are for cornice work in Colonial-type buildings or as a crown molding in large rooms. The dental block strips used with other molding add a distinctive appearance to a built-up molding but they are hard to find and expensive.

Here are some ideas that I have used in making dental block strips. A good sharp dado set on a radial arm saw is used, with a few minor jigs to speed up the work. Figure 7-6A shows a type mostly for exterior use in Colonial-style homes. The dado cuts are made across the width of wide boards. With the help of the gauge shown (D and E) the spacing between the cuts can be made quickly and accurately. It is a small block fastened to the fence that slips into the groove of the last saw cut. This particular dental

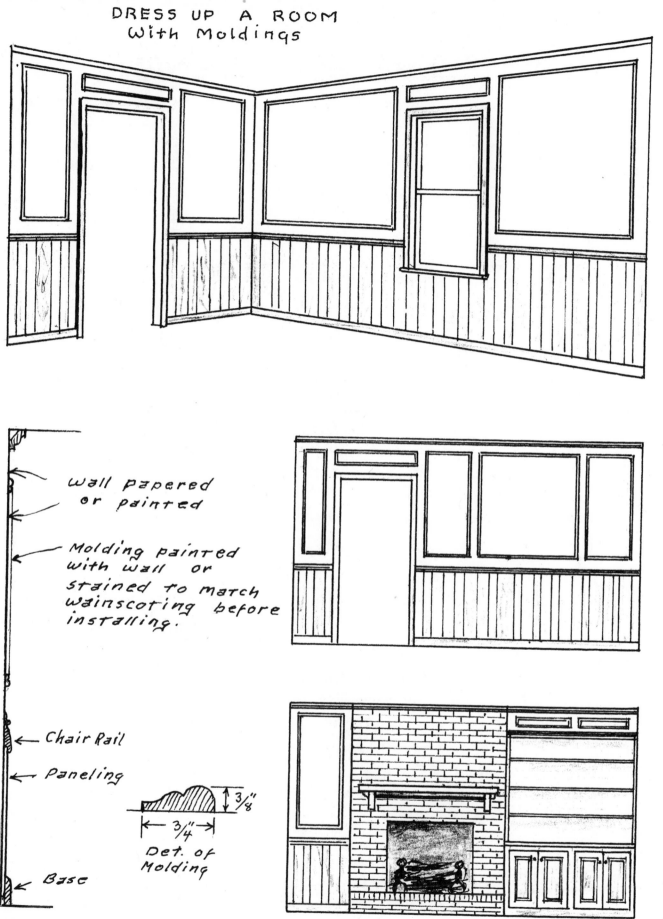

DRESS UP A ROOM
With Moldings

Wall papered
or painted

Molding painted
with wall or
stained to match
wainscoting before
installing.

Chair Rail

Paneling

Base

3/8"

3/4"

Det. of
Molding

Figure 7-1

DRESS UP A ROOM
With Moldings

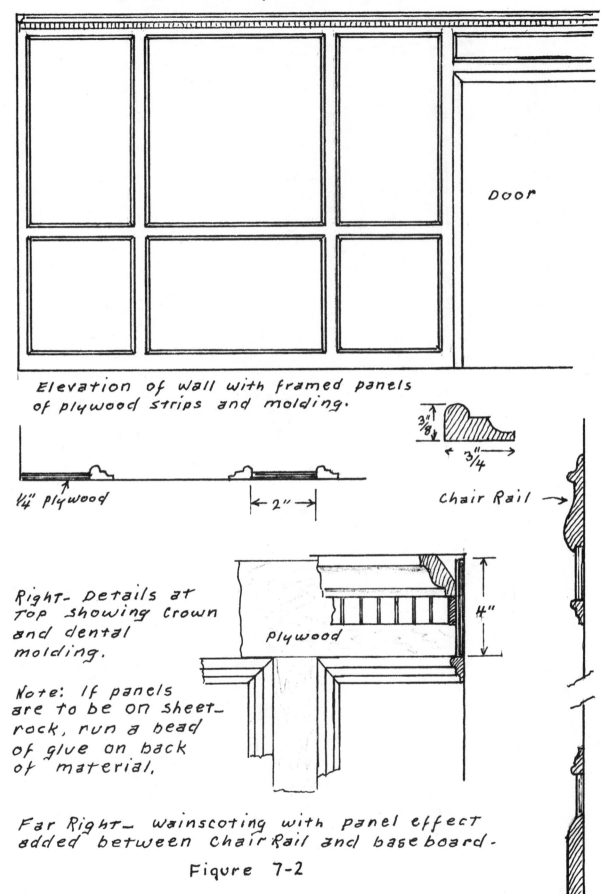

Elevation of wall with framed panels of plywood strips and molding.

Door

1/4" plywood

|← 2" →|

3/8"
3/4"

Chair Rail →

Right- Details at top showing crown and dental molding.

Plywood

4"

Note: If panels are to be on sheetrock, run a bead of glue on back of material.

Far Right- wainscoting with panel effect added between Chair Rail and baseboard.

Figure 7-2

MANTELS

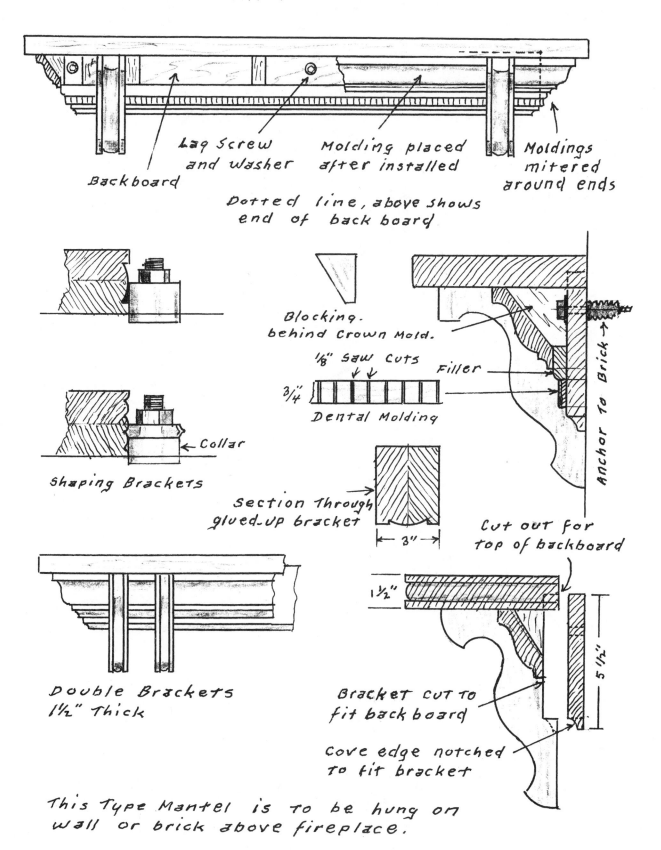

Lag Screw and Washer

Backboard

Molding placed after installed

Moldings mitered around ends

Dotted line, above shows end of back board

Collar

Shaping Brackets

Blocking behind Crown Mold.

⅛" Saw Cuts

¾" Dental Molding

Filler

Anchor To Brick

Section Through glued-up bracket

3"

Cut out for top of backboard

1½"

5½"

Double Brackets 1½" Thick

Bracket cut to fit backboard

Cove edge notched to fit bracket

This Type Mantel is to be hung on wall or brick above fireplace.

Figure 7-3

CAP-TYPE MANTEL

This type is fastened on top of brick by nailing through leaf into wood pegs driven in the holes of the brick or through the front into wood blocking.

The width of the leaf, backboard and moldings are variable. But the leaf should be 7" to 7½" longer than the brick top.

wooden pegs or Blocks

cove molding

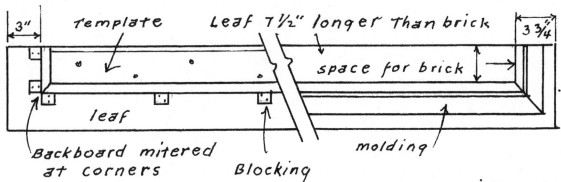

3"

template   Leaf 7½" longer than brick   3 3/4"

space for brick

leaf

Backboard mitered at corners

Blocking

molding

Cut a 1"x 4" slightly longer than the top of the brick and tack or clamp it to the leaf as a template for fastening the backboard.

width of brick

Nail here

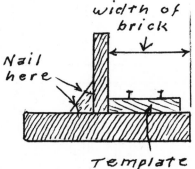

Template

Cut the miters on the backboard and tie it to the leaf with the triangular blocks that have been cut to fit the back of the crown molding. Coat the edge of the board and the blocks with glue.
The crown and dental molding can now be added but leave the cove at the bottom edge off until installed.

Figure 7-4

COLONIAL ENTRANCE

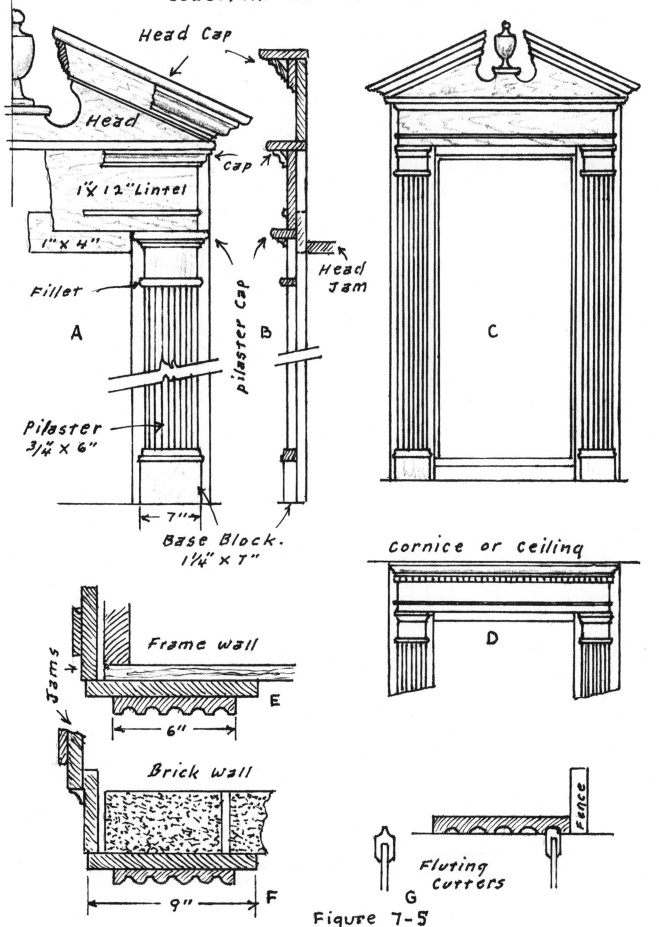

Head Cap

Head

Cap

1"X 12" Lintel

1" X 4"

Fillet

A

Pilaster Cap

B

Head Jam

Pilaster
3/4" X 6"

7"

Base Block.
1 1/4" X 7"

C

Cornice or ceiling

D

Jams

Frame wall

6"

E

Brick wall

9"

F

Fluting Cutters

G

Fence

Figure 7-5

MOLDINGS MADE WITH DADO

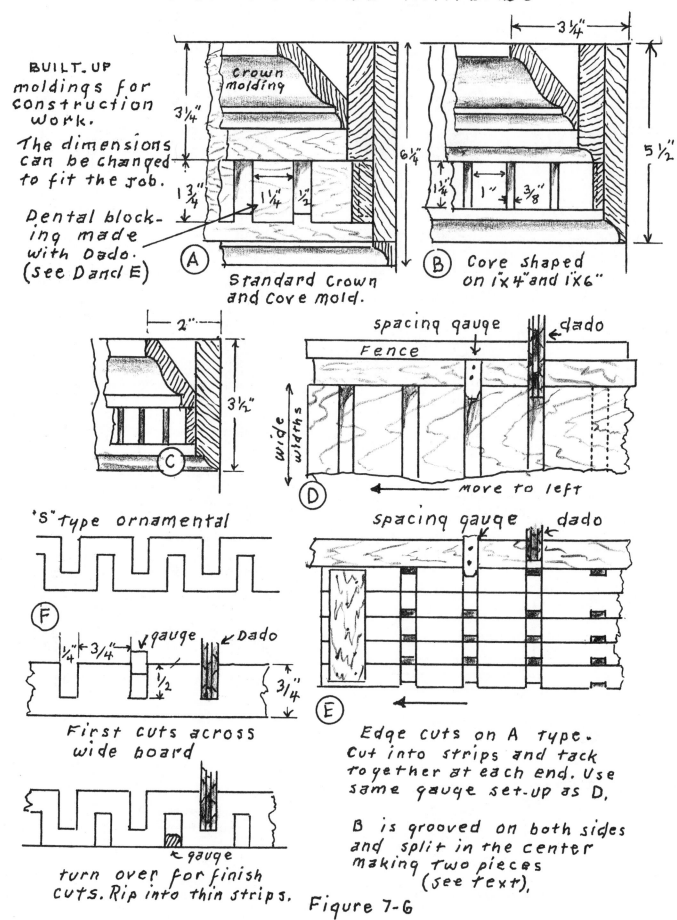

BUILT-UP moldings for construction work.

The dimensions can be changed to fit the job.

Dental blocking made with Dado. (see D and E)

3¾"

1¾"

1¼"   ½"

(A) Standard crown and cove mold.

3¼"

5½"

1¼"   1"   ⅜"

6¼"

(B) Cove shaped on 1"x 4" and 1"x 6"

2"

3½"

(C)

spacing gauge   dado

Fence

wide widths

move to left

(D)

"S" type ornamental

(F)

¼"   ¾"   gauge   Dado

½"   3¼"

First cuts across wide board

turn over for finish cuts. Rip into thin strips.

gauge

spacing gauge   dado

(E)

Edge cuts on A type. Cut into strips and tack together at each end. Use same gauge set-up as D.

B is grooved on both sides and split in the center making two pieces (see text).

Figure 7-6

mold also has a cut on the bottom edge to give the effect of separate blocks with smaller ones in between. Cut the board that has been notched into strips of the desired width and fasten them together with scraps of ¼" plywood as shown (E). Be sure that the ends are flush and square so the edge cuts will join the flat ones. Turn the back strip toward the saw so the gauge can engage the cut that was made on the flat side (not the one on the edge). This should insure the two cuts being in line if the gauge has not been moved from its first position and fits closely in the grooves.

The other one (B) is dadoed on both sides, cut into strips, and then split, making two pieces ¼" to ⁵⁄₁₆" thick. The edge cuts are omitted on these thin strips.

Smaller variations of this type molding can be used in cabinet or furniture work for finishing the tops of bookcases, china cabinets, gun cabinets, and mantels.

Figure 7-6F is an ornamental mold made by cutting both sides as shown and ripping into thin strips. The problem with making this type is that it is very easy to break as the length along the grain is only ¼". A tough, fine-grained wood and a sharp saw are required. Another problem is installing, as nails may split the molding in the short turns. Glue may work out from underneath, causing the stain to spot so use the glue carefully. Apply with the fingertip or small piece of sponge rubber on the back side and press in place.

STAIRWAYS

There are many types of stairs and many ways to build them. Over the years I have had experience with most of them. Since this is not a book on stairways, I will try to explain and illustrate (Figures 7-7 and 7-8) only one method that is simple, attractive, inexpensive, and can be adaptable to most stairway construction. As most stairs are carpeted today, No. 2 pine can be used for the treads instead of expensive hardwood. Two 2" x 6" boards can be used as stringers or carriages. Blocking sawn from a 1" x 6" board is set on top as supports for the treads (Figure 7-7). The treads are 2" x 12" or two 2" x 6" boards, so there is no need for the center stringer.

A wall is constructed at the outer side, stopping at the top of the eighth tread (Figure 7-7, Step 1). This gives a place for the handrail (which is about 7' long) to stop just below the ceiling. Only 14 balusters will be needed. A round wall rail with metal brackets may be used on up to the top of the stairway, or a full length one can be fastened to the wall on the other side.

As any good carpenter knows, one of the most important things in stairway building is the layout. For the benefit of those who have no previous experience, I will explain the procedure.

The one shown here is for an 8' ceiling. Add 10" or 11" for the distance from the bottom of the ceiling to the upper floor. Divide the total (8' 10") by 14 (the number of risers). We see that 7⁵⁄₈" will be fairly close for the riser height. If you wish to be more accurate, take a board about 10' long and stand it on the first floor and mark it even with the upper floor. Then with dividers, mark off 14 equal spaces. This will give the exact rise to the top of each tread. To keep the bottom and top tread the correct distance from the lower and upper floors, cut 1⁵⁄₈" off the bottom of the strip (or the thickness of the treads). This gives the height of the blocking that the treads will be nailed to.

The 2" x 6" carriages are to be cut to the proper angles and length so they fit at the top about 9" below the upper floor level and on the lower floor at the proper place. To determine the length, we multiply the number of treads by the "run," which is 10". There are 13 treads (not counting the upper floor) so we have 130" from the wall to the outer edge of the bottom pitch block (Figure 7-8, Steps 6 and 9). The bottom block is cut to 6" height to allow for the thickness of the tread; therefore, the point of the 2" x 6" will be about 2" short of 130". The length on the floor from the wall to the end of the carriage is 10' 8". Mark the distance on the floor.

With a tape, measure from this mark to the one at the top (9" below the upper floor). This is the length of the carriage at the long points. Cut only one of them and try it in place to check for fit. With a framing square, using 15¼" x 20" (double the rise and run), mark the top end on the 14¼" side of the square and the bottom end on the 20" side. Cut and set in place by temporarily tacking to the floor at the bottom.

Make a pitch board (Figure 7-8, Step 9G), which will be used as a pattern to cut the pitch blocks. The rise, 7⁵⁄₈" is one side and the run or top is 10". The bottom or the side that lays on the 2" x 6", should be close to 12⁹⁄₁₆". Lay it on the carriage and check with a level as shown. If it checks out, cut 26 of them from ¾" x 6" board lumber (Figure 7-8, Step 7G).

Use the 2" x 6" carriage for a pattern to cut the other one. Start at the top end and mark the positions of all the pitch blocks by using the long (or bottom) edge of the pattern. Each length should be 12⁹⁄₁₆". At the bottom, if the pattern extends about 2" beyond the point of the 2" x 6", you are close enough. If it is as much as ½" over or under the 2", the difference can be divided and taken up by slightly altering the 12 marks above.

Nail the carriages in place. The walls should already be finished, so nail them directly over the wall board into the studs.

The skirting boards, which are ¾" x 11¼", are fitted to rest on top of the carriages. (A 10" board may be used instead, by blocking it up an inch or two.) After they have been fitted at the top, make horizontal cuts at the bottom where they rest on the floor. Make a vertical cut on the closed or wall side about 2" out past where the edge of the first tread will be. The vertical cut on the other one will be made later to fit against the newel post. The location of the first tread determines the position of the post that should extend past it enough to cover the edge of the carpet as it turns down to the floor. Nail the skirting boards in place. The furring strips that are used on the outside of the open 2" x 6" carriage can be used to tie the skirting board

STAIRWAY

With Housed Stringer

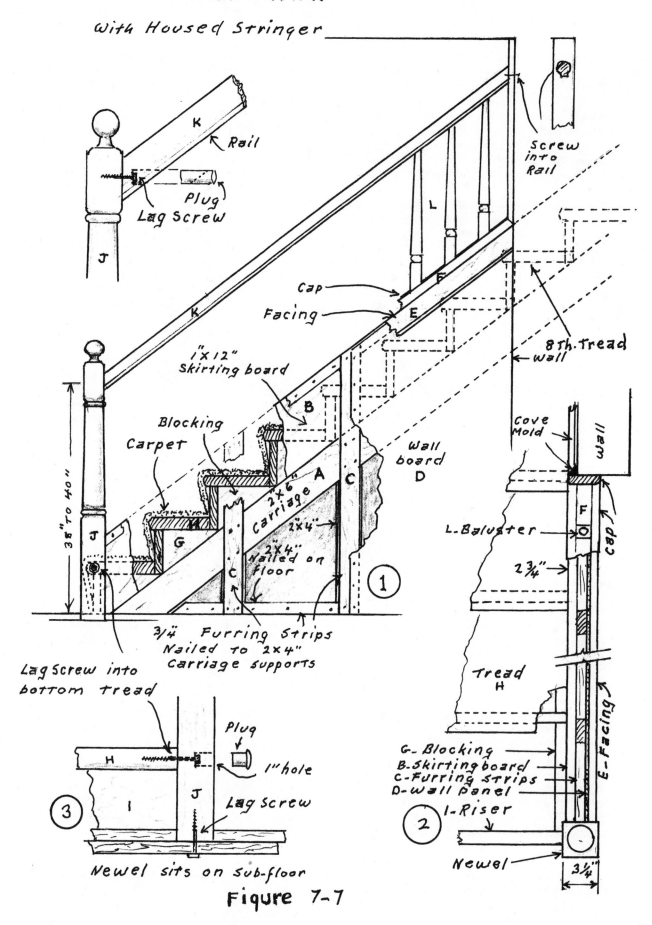

Rail

K

Plug

Lag Screw

J

Screw into Rail

L

K

Cap

Facing

E

8th. Tread

wall

1"X 12" Skirting board

B

Blocking

Carpet

Wall board D

2"X6" Carriage

A

C

2"x4"

2"x4" Nailed on floor

G

C

①

38" to 40"

J

Lag Screw into bottom tread

3/4" Furring Strips Nailed to 2x4" Carriage supports

Cove Mold

wall

L. Baluster

F

2 3/4"

cap

Tread H

G_ Blocking
B. Skirting board
C- Furring strips
D-Wall panel
I-Riser

②

E-Facing

Newel

3 1/4"

Plug

1" hole

H

I

J

Lag Screw

③

Newel sits on Sub-floor

Figure 7-7

STAIRWAY

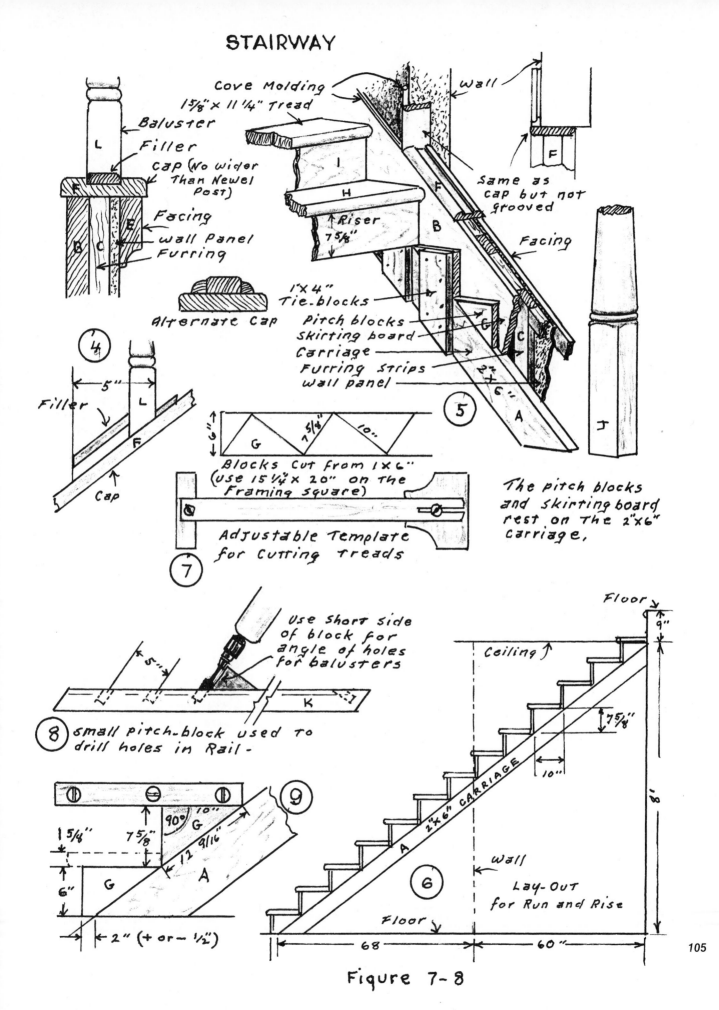

Cove Molding
1 5/8" x 11 1/4" Tread

Baluster

Filler

Cap (No wider Than Newel Post)

Facing

Wall Panel
Furring

L

F
E
B
C

Alternate Cap

Riser
7 5/8"

I

H

F

B

Wall

F

Same as cap but not grooved

Facing

1"x 4" Tie-blocks
Pitch blocks
Skirting board
Carriage
Furring strips
wall panel

C
C
C

2"x 6"

5

A

2"x 6"

J

4

5"

Filler

L

F

Cap

6"

G

7 5/8"

10"

Blocks Cut from 1x6"
(use 15 1/4" x 20" on the Framing square)

Adjustable Template for Cutting treads

7

The pitch blocks and skirting board rest on the 2"x6" carriage.

Use Short side of block for angle of holes for balusters

5"
2"
3"

K

8 small pitch-block used to drill holes in Rail-

90° 10"
G

1 5/8"   7 5/8"
12 9/16

6"   G   A

2" (+ or - 1/2")

9

Floor

Ceiling

7 5/8"

10"

A 2"x6" CARRIAGE

Wall

6 Lay-Out for Run and Rise

Floor

68   60"

9"

8'

105

Figure 7-8

to the carriage at the open part. Nail the pitch blocks to the skirt, taking care that they join at the marks previously made on the carriage. Short 1″ x 4″ blocks tie the pitch blocks to the carriage. Saw the bottom pitch block to fit the floor with the top about 6″ above the floor.

Cut the first riser, which will be 6″ wide. The rest can be 7½″. Keep them flush with the top of the pitch blocks. Cut the first tread and second riser, lay them in place, and position the newel post. Let it extend out in front of the edge of the tread about ¾″. Saw the vertical cut on the skirting board to fit against the square base of the newel post. Chisel out a socket in the floor for the post to sit in (Figure 7-7, Step 3) and cut the bottom off so the distance from the floor to the center of the handrail is 38″ to 40″ high (1). Drill a 1″ hole about halfway through at the bottom for the lag screw that fastens it to the tread. Another one is used to fasten it to the subfloor from underneath.

Continue with the treads and risers, working upward. Nail the bottom edge of each riser to the back edge of the tread. Figure 7-8, Step 7 shows a template that will help in cutting the treads. It can be adjusted for each one and used as a pattern to mark them by.

The "housed stringer" shown in the drawings is built so its thickness will be about ½″ less than that of the newel post (Figure 7-7, Step 2). The post shown here is a standard one that is 3¼″ x 3¼″ at the base. If a larger one is used, the thickness of the stringer can be adjusted by using thicker furring strips between the carriage and wall panels. The facing strip (E) which is 3″ or 4″ wide with a molded edge, is fitted between the newel and the offset in the wall.

Keep the top of all parts even so the cap will fit properly. It can be the same width as the newel or a little less. The cap is either plowed to receive the bottom of the balusters or a small molding is nailed on each side with filler blocks cut in between each baluster (Figure 7-8, Step 4). A piece of the same material is mitered to the cap and turns up the wall for the handrail to be fastened to. One edge will extend past the inside of the wall about ¾″. A cove molding will be placed behind it and will join to the one on the top edge of the skirting board. Tack the wall board (or cap) in place temporarily as it will be removed later so the handrail can be fastened to it from the back side.

I have found that it is better to make a wooden miter box for stairway work since the two angles that are used most are determined by the rise and run of the treads. By sawing these cuts in the box, you will save time by not having to shift from one angle to another as with a metal miter box.

Mark the cuts on the sides of the box, using 15¼″ on one end of a framing square and 20″ on the other (double the rise and run). The box can be used to cut the rails, balusters, fillers, and molding.

Cut the rail on the short angle (7⅝″) to fit between the newel and the vertical wall cap as it lays on the grooved cap. If the wall and newel are plumb, it should fit when raised to the proper height. If in doubt, cut a pattern on a strip 2″ or 3″ wide and try it first. Keep the rail position parallel with the grooved cap so all the balusters will be the same length.

Drill the holes in the rail to receive the round ends of the balusters (Figure 7-8, Step 8).

Saw one of the balusters at the bottom end on the same angle that the rail was cut, leaving 3″ to 5″ of the square part. Set it in the groove of the cap and against the newel. Mark at the top allowing for the depth of the holes in the rail.

Since the balusters are tapered, check the diameter at the point where they enter the rail. This will determine the size of the holes to be drilled. The balusters should be about 5″ apart, or half the run of the tread. With this type stringer, however, they can be spaced as you like as long as they are vertical and uniform.

Mark the height of the top of the rail on both the newel and the cap molding that turns up the wall. Take the wall cap down and fasten the rail to it with screws from the back side. Be sure that it is centered and square. Set it in place and fasten to the wall. Fasten the rail to the post with a lag screw (Figure 7-7).

Set the top baluster first. Work it into the hole in the rail and into the groove at the bottom. Plumb with a short level and fit a piece of filler between it and the wall cap. Except for the bottom one, the pieces of filler will be the same length. The bottom of the balusters can be toenailed into the cap keeping the nail heads below the top of the fillers. A little glue should be used on the fillers as they are nailed in place.

Plug the holes in the newel as shown in Figure 7-7.

TOOLS AND 8 ACCESSORIES

Here are a few ideas on how some useful tools and accessories can be made from scrap and junk materials.

Old files, drill bits, scrap aluminum, and other metal can be recycled and put to further use. Worn files make good wood chisels and turning tools. Grind to shape and add handles, which can be turned in the lathe. Short pieces of 5/8" or 3/4" conduit can be used as ferrules or bands around the handles to prevent splitting.

MOLDING HEADS AND CUTTERS

Shaper cutters can be made from short pieces of files and used in heads that take one or two cutters. The single cutter molding head shown in Figure 8-10 can be made of scrap aluminum. Scraps of metal molding, old window, screen door frames, and other scrap aluminum are cut up, melted, cast into blanks, and machined to shape.

Figure 8-12 shows how this can be done with only a hair dryer, a bucket of sand, some tin cans, and charcoal. The machining can be done on a wood-turning lathe if a metal lathe is not available.

I am also including some ideas on maintenance of wood-cutting tools. I have always done my own tool sharpening and general maintenance of jointer knives, shaper cutters, and band and circle saws. I found out years ago that some of these jobs required special tools and jigs to do a better job and save time.

For example, a narrow band-saw blade could not be filed in a clamp made for handsaws. Nor could its teeth be set with a regular saw set.

These problems were finally solved with a clamp and saw set, which I made especially for this purpose, resulting in many extra hours of service with the blades.

Even if a professional tool sharpening service is available, a set of jointer knives must be accurately reset in the head by the owner. This is usually a tedious, time-consuming job.

I found that many time-saving methods and gadgets can be worked out if a little thinking and tinkering is done when confronted with such problems. Some of the methods and gadgets that I have developed may be helpful to the reader. These and other do-it-yourself projects are explained and illustrated below.

Figure 8-1A shows shaper cutters being made from pieces of old files. Break into pieces by clamping the desired length in a vise and breaking off the excess by tapping lightly with a hammer. Grind the desired contour on one end then hold at an angle to grind the cutting edge. Finish by honing with an oilstone. If the cutter has a curved pattern as an ogee (left), a slip stone will be needed to hone the inside curves of the cutting edge.

Some molding heads consist of two slotted collars and two matching knives (Figure 2-8). Shown in Figure 8-1B are two methods that can be used to grind the matched pair.

To make the cabinet door cutter (Figure 8-1C), it is necessary to dress a thin grinding wheel as shown in Figure 8-1A (right). If a dresser is not available, an old carbide masonry drill will do a fair job of shaping a grinding wheel.

Notice that the rounded edge of the door being shaped (Figure 8-1C) has less curve than that made by standard cutters. This is advantageous as there is less of the inner core exposed and the rounded edge is easier to sand.

JOINTER KNIVES

A good jointer is one of the most important tools in any woodworking shop if it is properly maintained. For it to do precision work, the front and rear tables must be aligned with each other and the knives sharp and accurately set in the head.

Figures 8-2 and 8-3 show some simple jigs that will make the job of sharpening and resetting easier. If the jigs are made and used as shown, they will aid in keeping the three knives in uniform size with straight and sharp cutting edges, and accurately reset in the head (Figure 8-3).

Make the parts shown before the knives are removed from the head for grinding because the jointer will be needed in making and fitting the jigs. The set-up is shown in Figure 8-2A and B. First build a shelf in front of the grinder, 4" to 5" wide and about 12" long for 6" knives. Place it with the top surface about 3/4" below the center of the wheel. Make the jig or guide as shown by straightening and rabbeting the two edges.

One edge will be used for "jointing" (or straightening) the knives and should be rabbeted a little less than the width of the knife. The other edge is rabbeted about 1/4".

The grinding wheel should be true with a medium or fine grit. Clamp the guide to the shelf so the knife edge just touches the wheel (A). Slide each knife along the guide until all are the same width. Take off just as little as necessary to straighten, and remove any gaps that may be along the edge.

MAKING AND
GRINDING SHAPER CUTTERS

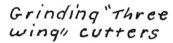

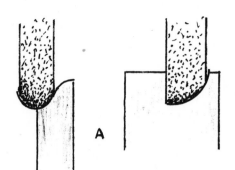

Grinding OGEE and cabinet door cutters with shaped grinding wheels.

A

Grinding "Three wing" cutters

To make two cutters alike, drive three brads in board. mark around edge. grind other one To match the mark,

or

draw design on tape and grind to shape.

B

Masking Tape

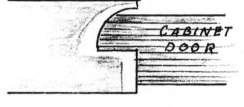

CABINET DOOR

C

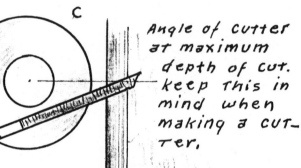

Angle of cutter at maximum depth of cut. keep this in mind when making a cutter.

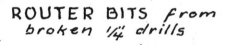

ROUTER BITS from broken 1/4 drills

D

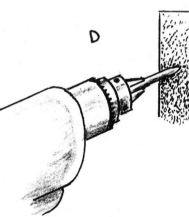

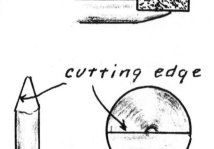

cutting edge

Router Bits made from old drill bits. use drill to turn while grinding to shape. then grind half of the tip away. to give it clearance, leave the cutting edge as is, but grind away a little around the rest of the point. to sharpen, hone the flat side

Figure 8-1

SHARPENING JOINTER KNIVES

Clamp Jig to Table

Jig. Hardwood block 3" or 4" wide, 12" long for 6" jointer knives

Shelf built up in front of grinder 3/4" below center.

"A" Jointing — Slide along jig until all are same width with straight edges.
B Hollow grinding — Grind until a narrow visible edge remains on the cutting edge — Do not grind to a sharp edge.

pins
Screw
clamp plate
Filler

Honing jig holds knife for correct angle of honing. This leaves a slight heel behind the cutting edge that helps prevent gapping and dulling. Hone with even strokes until sharp.

HONING IN HEAD

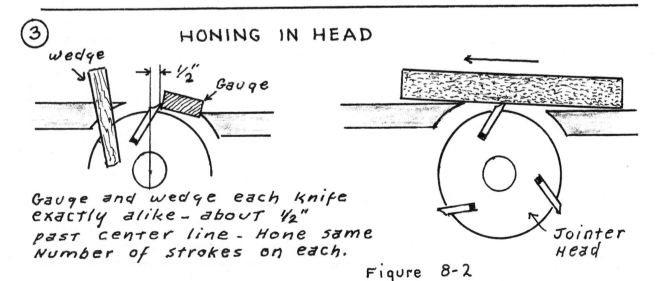

wedge

1/2"

Gauge

Gauge and wedge each knife exactly alike — about 1/2" past center line — Hone same number of strokes on each.

Jointer Head

Figure 8-2

SETTING JOINTER KNIVES

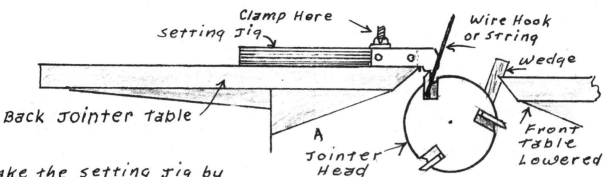

Clamp Here

Setting Jig

Wire Hook or String

Wedge

Back Jointer table

A

Jointer Head

Front Table Lowered

Make the setting jig by using a correctly set knife as a guide (see text).

Wedge (or lock) the head with the knife about ¼" from the edge of the table

Cut the jig as shown (C) and place the two pins as guides.

Clamp in place with the pins against the table, make the two plates, and fit to the edge of the knife on each side.

To set the sharpened knife, pull up with the hook into the notches and tighten.

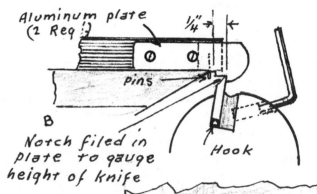

Aluminum plate (2 Req'.)

¼"

pins

B

Notch filed in plate to gauge height of knife

Hook

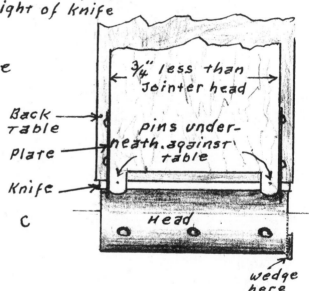

¾" less than Jointer head

Back Table

pins underneath against table

Plate

Knife

C

Head

wedge here

SETTING PLANER KNIVES

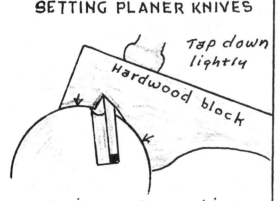

Tap down lightly

Hardwood block

Set knife a little high. Tighten lightly at ends. Tap down and tighten

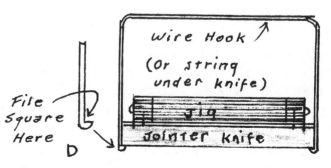

Wire Hook

(Or string under knife)

Jig

Jointer knife

File Square Here

D

110

Figure 8-3

Turn the guide around and set it so the grinding wheel will start cutting on the old bevel (B) a little closer to the heel than the cutting edge. Touch the knife lightly to the wheel and check this before proceeding.

When the guide is properly set, start at one end and slide the knife all the way across with even pressure against the wheel. By holding the knives in your hands, you will be reminded to dip in water more often and prevent overheating.

The curvature of the wheel will hollow grind the knife. Check the work after each pass to keep the grinding uniform across the length of the knife. Keep the grinding away from the cutting edge. If it starts to grind into the edge before the knife has been hollow ground, shift the guide a little closer to the wheel by tapping it lightly.

Continue until there is only a very narrow uniform line along the edge. By leaving this thin edge (which will be finished with an oil stone), you will be assured that the three knives are the same width and have straight cutting edges.

Clamp the knife in the jig shown (Figure 8-2, Step 2) and hone until sharp. Notice that the angle of honing leaves a small heel behind the cutting edge (D). The block of wood holds the stone at the correct angle for the heel.

The jig for setting the knives in the jointer head is shown in Figure 8-3. It will work on most jointers if carefully made. The best method is to fit it to a knife that is already accurately set in the head.

Check for this by laying a straight-edged block 10" or 12" long on the back table with about 1/3 of it hanging over the front table. Turn the head slowly by hand.

The block should move about 1/8" as the cutting edge of the knife tips it. Make two marks about 1/8" apart at the point where the knife moves the block. Use them to check both ends of the knife to be sure it is set parallel with the top of the table. If none of the knives are found accurate enough to fit the jig to, adjust the back table, or one of the knives until it is as described above and use it in the following procedure.

Lock the head by lightly tapping a small wedge at one end between it and the frame. The edge of the knife should be about 1/4" from the edge of the back table (Figure 8-3A and B).

Cut a piece of 3/4" plywood 10" or 12" long and 5 1/4" wide for a 6" jointer (or 3 1/4" for one that has 4" knives). Two small pins are placed underneath at one end to serve as stops or guides. They are to assure the jig is accurately set each time it is used. Cut the pins down to 1/8" long and saw out the excess wood between them as shown (Figure 8-3C).

Cut two plates from aluminum or other thin metal as shown (Figure 8-3B). They are fastened to each side of the jig to gauge the height of the knife as it is tightened in the head. Notice that a notch is filed in the bottom edge and when the jig is in place it will extend about 1/8" below the table level. The notches should be smooth and have sharp inside corners so the knife edge will have a definite point of contact with the plate when it is pulled up into it.

Clamp the jig on the back table with the pins against the front edge. Hook the plates over the knife and fasten with two screws. Be sure the cutting edge of the knife is tight in the notch. This will assure that it is reset to the same height after it has been sharpened. By making short slots in the plates and using screws with larger heads, the plates can be adjusted slightly if needed. Check both sides carefully before removing the knives for grinding.

A hook made from a wire clothes hanger is used to lift the knife up into the notch. It has short hooks at the ends that fit under the knife (Figure 8-3D). If there is not enough space for the wire between the head and frame, a piece of string can be used by laying it in the slot under the knife and pulling up on both ends.

Do not remove the jig until all three knives are set. Drop the knife in the slot with the hook or string under it and turn the head back until the knife is under the jig.

SAW SET FOR BAND SAWS

It's easy to file a band saw if you have a good vise or clamp to hold it (Figure 8-6), but have you ever tried setting the teeth in a narrow blade? In Figures 8-4 and 8-5, I have tried to detail the construction and operation of a saw set that I designed and have been using for years. Of course, if you do not have many saws to keep in shape, this may not be a worthwhile project. For the professional or saw filer, it should be a great help in maintaining band saw blades.

It is designed for saws up to 1/2" wide, but can be made to take wider ones by using wider plates in the "hammer and anvil" assembly, or by cutting a groove in the wood base to lower the saw enough for the "set" to engage the teeth. Shims are used under narrow blades to raise them to the correct height.

It sets two teeth with each stroke of the lever: one forward and the other to the back making it unnecessary to go around the saw twice as is done in filing. It also has a self-feeding ratchet attachment that moves the blade into the correct position for setting the two teeth. However, this can be omitted and it can be fed manually.

The essential part of the saw set is the "hammer and anvil." They are made up of four plates of 1/8" steel (Figure 8-5, Step 4). The ends are filed in a way that, when the saw is clamped between them (by pushing down the lever), the teeth are bent to the side (see Steps 4 and 5).

Fillers are used between the plates to space them for different size teeth. Saws with 3/16" to 1/4" teeth will require a 1/8" filler between the plates. For larger ones, extra fillers will be needed. They can be in 1/16" thicknesses if desired. When fine-tooth saws of 1/8" are to be set, the fillers are removed from between and placed on the outside of the plates (Step 5). Rough cut three of the plates about 2 3/4" long and the other one 3 3/4". Grind and file them as shown in Step 4 until they match at the ends with a 15° angle beveled back on one, and an "overhang" on the other.

SAW SET FOR BAND SAWS
Sets two teeth with each stroke of lever

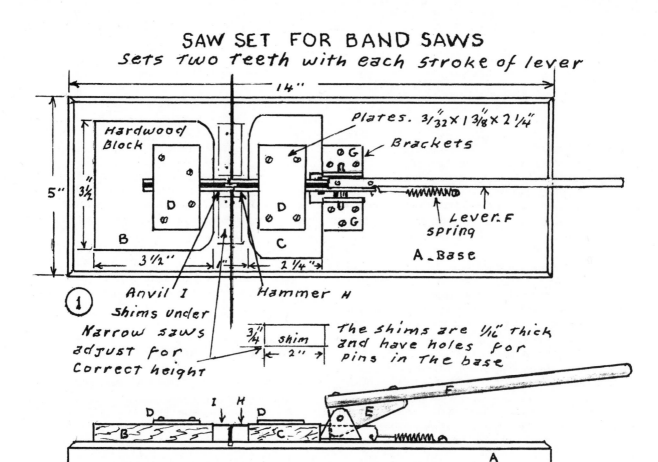

Hardwood Block

Plates. $3\frac{1}{32}'' \times 1\frac{3}{8}'' \times 2\frac{1}{4}''$

Brackets

5''

$3\frac{1}{2}''$

D

B

D

C

G

G

Lever. F

spring

A_Base

$3\frac{1}{2}''$

1''

$2\frac{1}{4}''$

14''

① Anvil I
Shims under
Narrow saws
adjust for
Correct height

Hammer H

$\frac{3}{4}''$ shim
2''

The shims are $\frac{1}{16}''$ thick
and have holes for
pins in the base

D   I   H   D

B   C   E   F

A

② Base_$\frac{3}{4}''$ plywood(A)   The blocks around the anvil
and hammer, are hardwood, $\frac{1}{2}''$ thick or the
same thickness as the height of the two units.

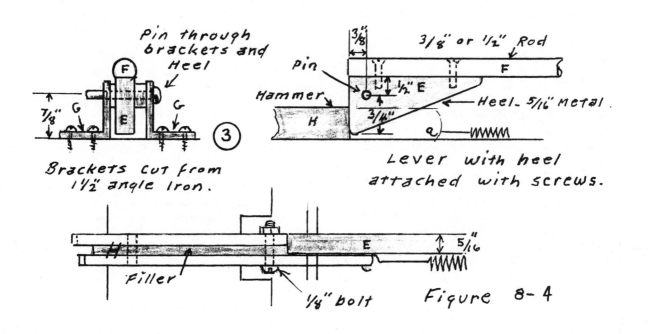

Pin through
brackets and
Heel

F

G   E   G

$\frac{7}{8}''$

Brackets cut from
$1\frac{1}{2}''$ angle iron.

③

$\frac{3}{8}''$

$\frac{3}{8}''$ or $\frac{1}{2}''$ Rod

Pin

F

Hammer

$\frac{1}{2}''$ E

H

$\frac{3}{4}''$

Heel_$\frac{5}{16}''$ metal.

Lever with heel
attached with screws.

H

Filler

E

$\frac{5}{16}''$

$\frac{1}{8}''$ bolt

Figure 8-4

SELF-FEEDING ASSEMBLY

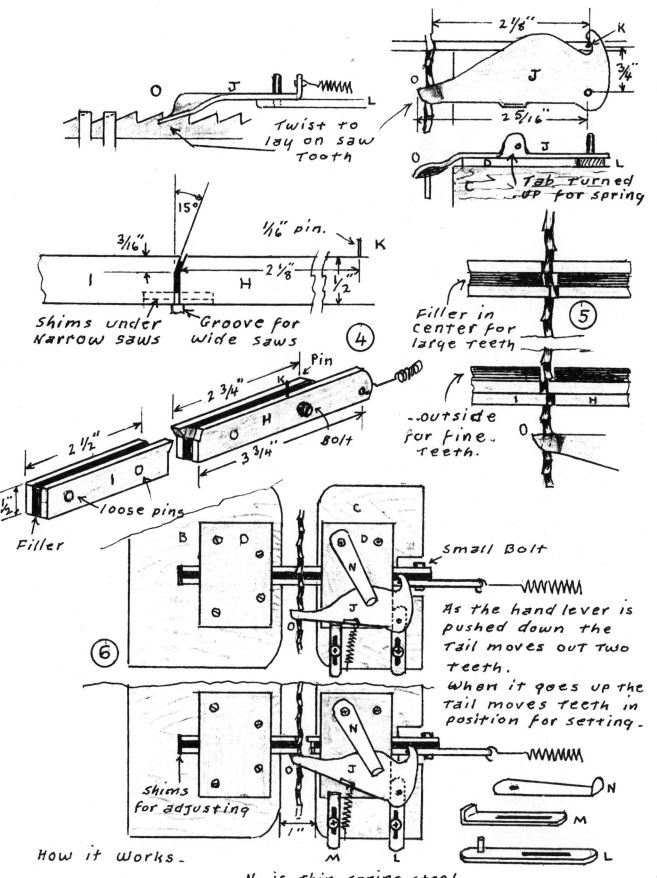

Twist to lay on saw Tooth

2 1/8"

K

3/4"

O   J   L

2 5/16"

O   D   J   L

C

Tab Turned up for spring

15°

3/16"

1/16" pin.   K

I   H   2 1/8"   1/2"

Shims under Narrow saws

Groove for Wide saws

(4)

Filler in center for large teeth

(5)

..outside for fine teeth.

Pin

2 3/4"   K

2 1/2"   O   H

I   O   Bolt

3 3/4"

1/2"   O

Filler   loose pins

B   D   C   D

N

J

O

(6)   small Bolt

As the hand lever is pushed down the Tail moves out two teeth.
When it goes up the Tail moves teeth in position for setting.

N

J

O

Shims for adjusting

1"

M   L

N

M

L

How it Works.

N is thin spring steel. holds J in place.

Figure 8-5

113

BAND SAW FILING CLAMP

The one shown here is for saws 10' to 14' long. Reduce size to 24" if your blades are shorter.

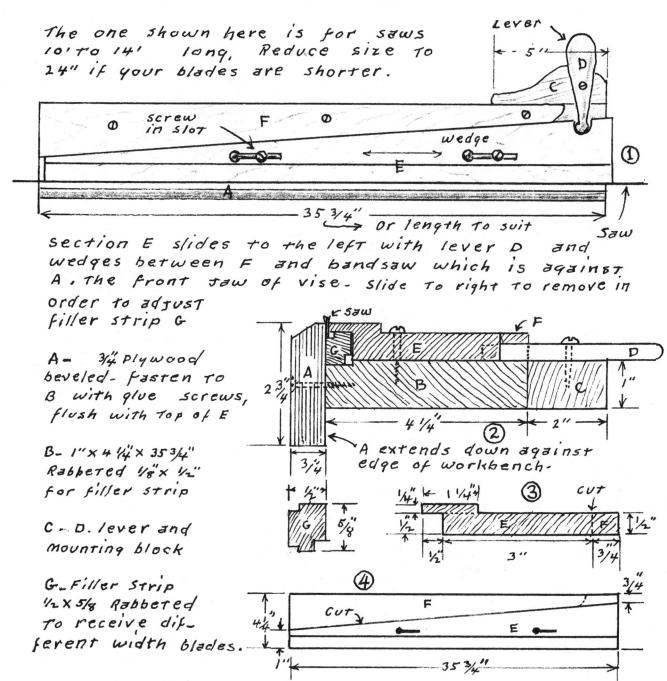

Section E slides to the left with lever D and wedges between F and bandsaw which is against A, the front jaw of vise. Slide to right to remove in order to adjust filler strip G

A— 3/4" Plywood beveled- fasten to B with glue screws, flush with top of E

B— 1" x 4 1/4" x 35 3/4" Rabbeted 1/8" x 1/2" for filler strip

C - D. lever and mounting block

G— Filler strip 1/2 x 5/8 Rabbeted to receive dif-ferent width blades.

E and F. Wedge Assembly— Rabbet as shown in ③ or glue 1/4" x 1 1/4" strip to top front edge. Cut on angle as shown ④. Sawed edges should be straight and smoothed Drill two 1/2" holes with slots added as shown ①,
to Assemble; Pull assembly against A. fasten F with 3 or 4 screws. Place the two roundhead screws in the slots of the wedge E, so they will slip through the 1/2" holes

Figure 8-6

FILING BAND SAWS

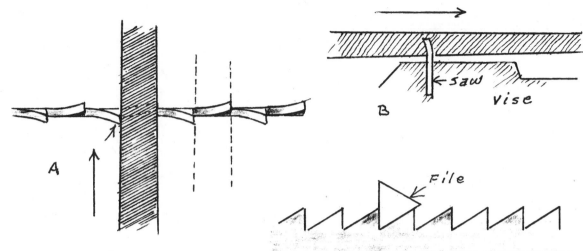

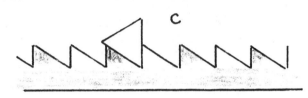

A Band saw is easy to file
unless it is hardened or
a "skiptooth" All that is
needed is a good vise and
a file. Let the file lay
against both teeth and
push square across, against the cutting edge of the
tooth that is leaning toward you (small arrow) then
skip over to the next cutting edge (dotted lines)
Continue filing every other tooth. use uniform pressure. Twist blade wrong side out and file other
teeth. Usually one stroke between the two teeth
is enough. Hold file level B. Use file larger than
depth of teeth C. After blade has been filed several
times it may need jointing. Hold stone lightly against
teeth while saw is running, Then file until sharp.

HAND SAWS

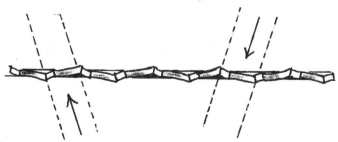

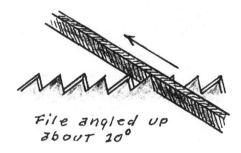

File angled up
about 10°

Joint. by sliding flat file over points
of teeth, (hold file level) Drawings
show angle of file being pushed
against cutting edge. File just
enough to leave sharp point.

Figure 8-7

SAW VISES for FILING

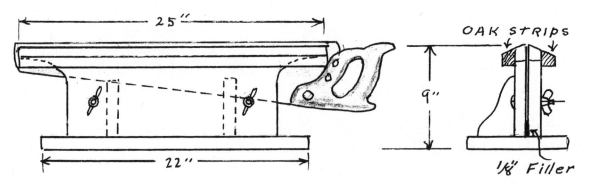

OAK STRIPS

25"

9"

22"

1/8" Filler

If you file your own handsaws, here's a good
vise that is easily made. Saw two pieces of
3/4" plywood as shown above - Add oak strips
on top edges to help stiffen the jaws.
Bevel about 25°.   Add base and braces.
Use large wing nuts or hand wheels to tighten.
Clamp to work bench with C clamps.

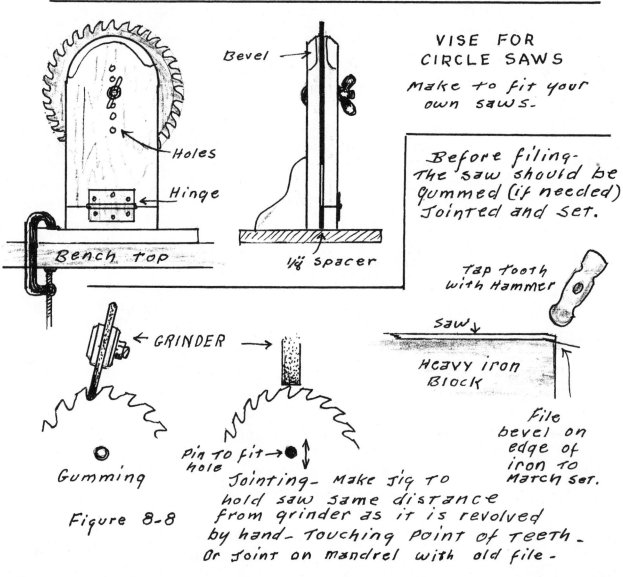

Bevel

Holes

Hinge

Bench Top

1/8" Spacer

VISE FOR
CIRCLE SAWS
Make to fit your
own saws.

Before filing
The saw should be
gummed (if needed)
jointed and set.

Tap tooth
with Hammer

Saw

Heavy iron
Block

File
bevel on
edge of
iron to
match set.

← GRINDER →

Pin to fit →
hole

Gumming   Jointing- Make jig to
hold saw same distance
from grinder as it is revolved
by hand- Touching Point of teeth.
Or joint on mandrel with old file.

Figure 8-8

116

SOLDERING BAND SAW BLADES

If you choose to
solder your broken
bandsaw blades. A
Jig like this is
needed to hold
the ends in alignment.
If you use a torch to
melt the solder The
Hammer and anvil are
needed to press the
Joint while the solder
Cools. they should be
in perfect alignment.
If tongs are used, omit
the hammer and anvil.

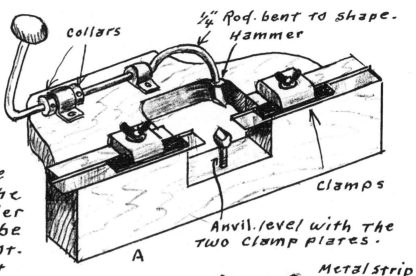

Collars   ¼" Rod. bent to shape.
           Hammer

Clamps

Anvil. level with the
two clamp plates.

A

Metal strip

B   Clamp   piece
              of
              Metal
              Molding
              for
              Clamp
              Plate

METAL PLATE

FILE

WOOD BLOCK

Filing Taper on
ends of band saw.
Taper length equal
to one tooth.   D

C   Hammer- made from
     piece of ½" Rod.

     File To
     shape

Anvil.
from Leg
screw

small piece of sheet
silver solder coated
with paste of borax
powder and water-
between saw ends.

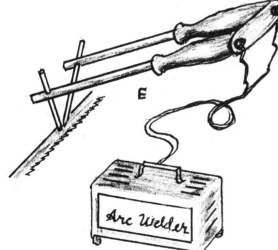

E

F

Arc Welder

Electric Torch-
Does good Job but
Take care or it will
burn the blade.

A pair of heavy Tongs
heated red hot, and
clamped over Joint.
Hold until cooled—
Or use a gas or electric
Torch (shown at left) First
heat hammer, then blade
until solder melts. Drop
hammer and hold until
it cools. Practice on scraps
of old blades before using.

Figure 8-9

MOLDING HEADS

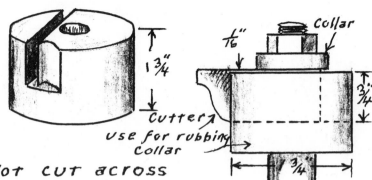

Here's a couple of the handiest shaper molding heads you will probly ever own. They are made of 1 3/4" or 2" aluminum

A

The head "A" has a slot cut across the face to fit cutters made from pieces of old files, which make excellent cutters. Cut the slot just deep enough so that about 1/16" of the edge of the cutter extends up above the top, A collar is used to clamp it in the head, and the teeth along the edge of the file keep it from slipping. A setscrew on the side holds the cutter in place while not in use, or for setting up when not on the shaper spindle. The lower part of the head is used as a rubbing collar on curved work.

For Chip Clearance

To reduce vibration- drill hole fill with lead

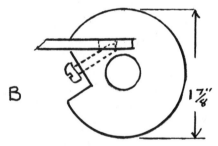

B

The head (B) as shown here is a coping head and has a threaded hole to fit spindle. By bushing up underneath with collars, it can be tightened on the top of the spindle. see coping on the shaper. Figure 2-6 It uses Sears cutters at right. If you choose, drill 1/2" center hole and use for regular shaping.

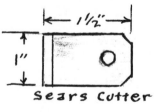

Sears Cutter

The advantage of these heads is that only one cutter has to be made. In a few minutes you can grind one to match other moldings, or of your own design at no expense. Take some old files, break in a vise, and grind to shape. Both ends can be used if you wish.

Figure 8-10

why not
MAKE THEM YOURSELF?

If you do not have a metal cutting lathe, you can turn aluminum on your wood turning one by using tools made from old files. Turn at about 2500 R.P.M.

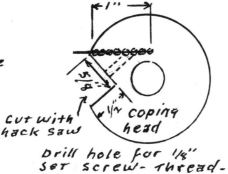

Drill a series of 1/8" holes 3/4" deep- and a 3/8" hole as shown

Cut blanks from 2" dia. stock- Drill 1/2" center hole. (29/64" hole if it's to be threaded for a coping head)

Cut with hack saw

coping head

Drill hole for 1/8" set screw- thread.

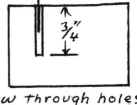

saw through holes with hack saw

Place a piece of sheet metal in saw cut- saw down beside it- add another piece and saw the other side Finish with file.

1 3/4" to 2" Dia.

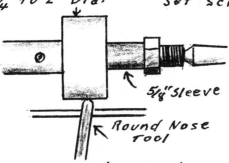

5/8" sleeve

Round Nose Tool

Fasten on arbor and turn- true face and sides. Remove from arbor finish around edge of hole with file or sander.

Hole must be angled so the set screw engages the hole in cutter-

RUBBING COLLARS
from Aluminum

Drill 1/2" hole in stock

Hack saw

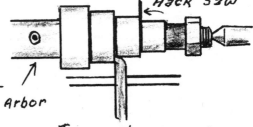

Sleeve to fit bearing and spindle-

Arbor

The best Rubbing Collars of all are ball bearings. If they do not have 1/2" hole they can be bushed. Arrange so outer rim turns with material being shaped.

Turn three or four different sizes. Cut part way through with hack saw while turning- Remove and finish sawing.

Figure 8-11

119

MELTING AND CASTING ALUMINUM

In this simple forge

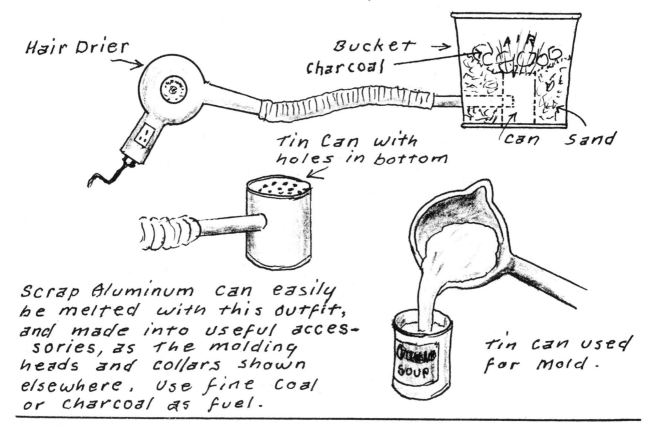

Hair Drier

Bucket
Charcoal

AIR

can   Sand

Tin Can with
holes in bottom

Scrap Aluminum can easily
be melted with this outfit,
and made into useful accessories, as the molding
heads and collars shown
elsewhere. Use fine Coal
or charcoal as fuel.

SOUP

tin Can used
for Mold.

CUTTING ON THE GRINDER

Silicon Carbide Masonry Blades
make good Cut-off wheels
for your grinder, Ask a
brick mason for some
discarded blades.
They can also be used to gum saws and
sharpen other Carbide tools, as masonry
drills and router bits.
An old masonry drill can be used as a "dresser"
To true up your regular grinding wheels.

Figure 8-12

SHEET METAL BREAK

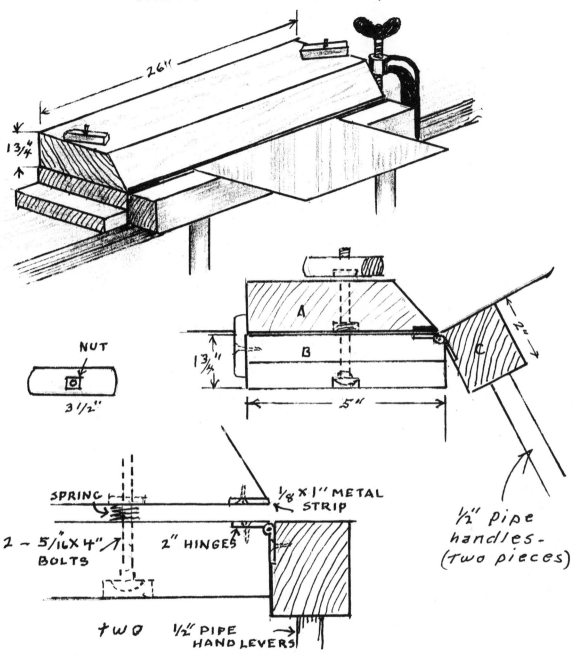

26"

13/4"

NUT

3 1/2"

A

B

13/4"

5"

2"

C

1/2" pipe
handles-
(two pieces)

SPRING

1/8 X 1" METAL
STRIP

2 ~ 5/16 X 4"
BOLTS

2" HINGES

two 1/2" PIPE
HAND LEVERS

Make size to suit. use hardwood and heavy-
duty hinges. Mortice them into parts B
and c. The spring is not necessary but it
helps by pushing the top up so the metal
can easily be pushed under it.

Figure 8-13

ADJUSTABLE MITER BOX
For light work

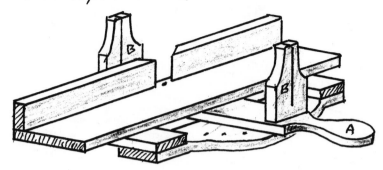

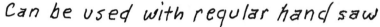
Can be used with regular hand saw

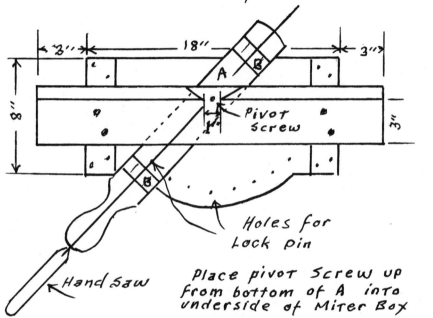

3" ◄── 18" ──► 3"

8"

3"

Pivot Screw

Holes for Lock Pin

Hand Saw

Place pivot screw up from bottom of A into underside of Miter Box

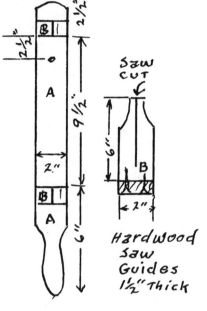

2½"

2½"

9½"

2"

6"

A

B

A

B

A

Saw Cut

6"

B

2"

Hardwood Saw Guides 1½" Thick

Handy Helpers

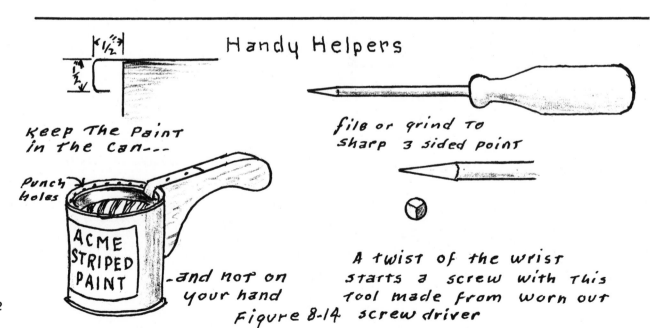

1½"

Keep The Paint in the Can---

Punch Holes

ACME STRIPED PAINT

--and not on your hand

file or grind to sharp 3 sided point

A twist of the wrist starts a screw with this tool made from worn out screw driver

Figure 8-14

TWO OLD-TIMERS

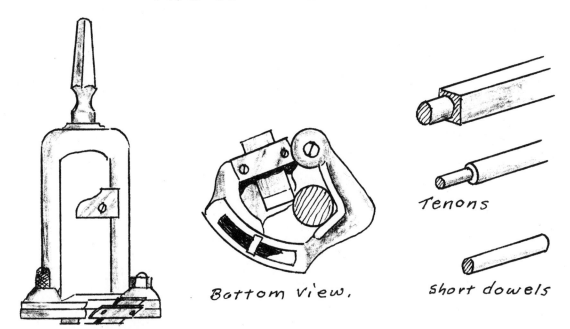

Tenons

Bottom View.

Short dowels

Here are a couple of old hand tools I would not
do without. They take a little elbowgrease to use
but do a good job when properly sharpened and
adjusted. The Hollow Auger, above, will do its particular job quicker than any other method when
there are only a few pieces to be tenoned.
  The Scraper below cannot be beat for smoothing
     joints in glued-up panels or cabinet fronts
and cleaning boards of scratches, dirt, and
pencil marks.

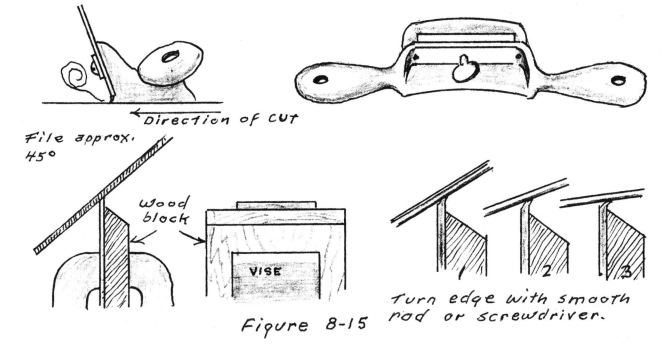

Direction of cut

File approx.
45°

Wood
block

VISE

Turn edge with smooth
rod or screwdriver.

Figure 8-15

The other two are the same except they are reversed in order to set the other tooth in the opposite direction.

Notice that the long plate has a hole in the outer end for a spring that pulls the hammer back after each stroke of the lever. Be sure it is beveled as shown in Figure 8-5, Step 4 and not with the overhang.

The fillers can be made of aluminum or other soft metal and should be the same length and width as the "setting plates," except all beveled back, away from the saw teeth. Make one 1/8" filler and one or two 1/16" for each unit if it is to be used on saws with teeth larger than 1/4".

When the plates and fillers are all shaped as shown (Figure 8-5, Step 4), clamp each unit together to drill for the pins. Be sure they are flush at the "setting" end and edges. Drill through all the pieces of each unit at the same time so they will be uniform when pinned together. A small bolt is used at the end of the (H) unit as shown in Steps 4 and 6 to hold the plates tightly together. The pins should be at least 1/8" and just long enough to go through the unit.

With the pins in place, grind the other end of the anvil until all the layers are flush. Remove the long plate from the hammer and grind the remaining plate and fillers flush.

The anvil lays in a slot cut in the hardwood block (B) and the hammer is between two blocks. The metal plates (D) hold them in place. They should fit in the slots close enough to keep them aligned with each other but with just enough clearance for the hammer to slide back and forth freely, and to allow easy removal for different settings. After it has been tried out and is working properly, the ends of the plates can be hardened for longer life.

Figure 8-4, Step 3 shows the lever and bracket assembly as I made it but it can be made a number of ways as long as the heel pushes the hammer tightly against the saw teeth and the lever is strongly anchored to the base with sturdy brackets.

Temporarily fasten all parts in place and try out on an old saw. The stroke of the lever can be adjusted by placing metal shims in the slot at the end of the anvil (Figure 8-5, Step 6).

SELF-FEEDING ASSEMBLY

The self-feeding assembly (Figure 8-5) has only one moving part, which is the "birdlike" plate (J) cut from sheet metal. Its "beak" hooks over the small pin set into the edge of the long plate of the hammer in Step 4 (K) and the tail engages the saw teeth and moves them into position to be set (O).

The "bird" pivots on a pin through its eye. The pin is fastened in a slotted plate (L) the same thickness as the plates (D). The other slotted plate with the end bent up (M) is for adjusting the "sweep" of the tail for different size teeth, so it will catch every other tooth. A small spring pulls the tail back after each stroke and a thin piece of spring steel (N) holds the bird in place. It pivots around to one side so the bird can be lifted off the pin for ease in adjusting. It is a good idea to first make a working pattern of the bird out of thin metal (a piece of a tin can). A heavier one can be made from it later when it is working. Don't forget to leave the tab on the back edge that the small spring is fastened to.

Figure 8-5, Step 6 shows the operation of the feeder. The tail of the birdlike plate moves in and out as the lever goes up and down.

The tail has to slide out over the points of two teeth and pull the second tooth in flush between the first two plates where it will be set, or bent toward the hand lever. The other tooth should be between the two back plates and set in the opposite direction if the proper fillers are in place. Notice the welded joint in the saw blade as there may be two adjoining teeth set in the same direction. If so, skip over a tooth and continue.

Don't expect it to work perfectly the first time. Changes and adjustments will probably have to be made. Assemble all parts with screws so they can be removed for altering or replacing.

The other illustrations in this chapter (Figures 8-6 to 8-15) are included as helpful hints or ideas and are self-explanatory.

MAKE YOUR OWN POWER TOOLS 9

I have always been a pack rat, saving everything that might be of use later—not only pieces of wood of all kinds, but junk parts, such as bearings, sleeves, rods, bolts, and angle irons salvaged from discarded appliances, old motors, and automobiles.

When I decided to make a machine or tool, I would go through the assortment of odds and ends, picking out what I thought could be used and adapted the design of the particular project to fit the parts. Although the finished product could not always be described as a thing of beauty, it usually served its purpose. If not, it went back to the junk pile and I to the drawing board.

In the following drawings, I have tried to illustrate how some useful machines and accessories can be made with a combination of wood and metal parts at little expense.

Light metal work can be done on a wood lathe with a few accessories, such as a three- or four-jawed chuck and a 60° tail center; I have a small metal-working lathe, which made the job easier. For small work, a tapered work arbor with a chuck can be used to mount the stock for turning. Old files ground at an angle of about 45° make fairly good turning tools. The procedure is shown in Figure 8-11 for turning aluminum. Soft steel can also be turned, such as fitting the ends of a shaft into bearings or turning a shoulder or taper but turn at a slower speed, take light cuts, and keep the tools sharp.

Where precision is required, as fitting a shaft into a bearing, turn a little oversize and finish by slowly moving a flat file over the work while it is turning. Check often by trying the bearing on the shaft for a drive-on fit.

If you wish, you can take the parts to a machine shop but I have tried to show how these items can be made without expensive tools or machine shop work. It may be advantageous to buy the mandrels ready made, especially for the shaper and jointer that will run at higher speeds. The slower machines such as lathes and sanders can be made as shown or to fit the parts available.

SHAPER

I built the spindle shaper (Figures 9-1 and 9-2) over 25 years ago and it is still in use in my shop. It is simply two wooden boxes or columns, one inside the other. The inner one has just enough clearance to permit it to freely slide up and down inside the outer column.

The top or table is a piece of ³/₄″ plywood covered with Formica. It is fastened to the top of the inner column by means of a framework of 1¹/₂″ x 2¹/₂″ strips notched together (Figure 9-2). The base is made of 2″ material and the details are shown. The outer column is fastened to it with bolts as shown or you may use lag screws.

I made the shaper for heavy-duty work and the outside column is about 10″ square but a smaller version can be made and a solid piece, as a 4″ x 4″ used for the inner column if desired.

An old vise screw (or similar) is used to adjust the height of the table. It has a hand wheel fastened to the bottom end that can be turned through an opening in the base. The screw goes through a nut or threaded plate on top of the base and fits in a socket inside the inner column (Figure 9-1A), which can be a metal cup or plate. I used an old thrust bearing and turned the end of the screw to fit inside.

The locking device is a lever going through one corner of the outer column. When tightened, it is forced against a metal plate on the corner of the inside one that is beveled to 45°. This pushes the inner column to the opposite corner and holds it in position.

The lever can be made with a long bolt bent at a right angle. A nut is inset inside the box to engage the threaded end (see Figure 9-2E).

The mandrel should have a long ¹/₂″ spindle so standard cutters can be used. It is mounted as shown in Figure 9-1D.

The motor should be at least ³/₄ hp 3450 rpm and is mounted on a 2″ board which has slots for lag screws that permit adjusting for belt tension (Figure 9-2G). The motor mount rests on top of a support block as shown, with the motor and spindle pulleys aligned with each other.

The fence (Figure 9-1C) is bolted to the table at one end and a C-clamp is used at the other. The two plates are slotted in order to adjust for different size cutters. A flat groove is plowed along the slots to countersink the screw heads (see Figures 9-1A and C).

LATHE

The lathe (Figures 9-3 and 9-4) is constructed of odds and ends that should be easy to find around the shop or from a junk dealer: a few pieces of pine and hardwood, two pieces of angle iron about 3′ long (these can be cut from an old bed rail), a couple of ball bearings (of which one should be a thrust bearing), and a piece of galvanized ³/₈″ or ¹/₂″ water pipe about 9″ long for the hollow spindle.

SPINDLE SHAPER

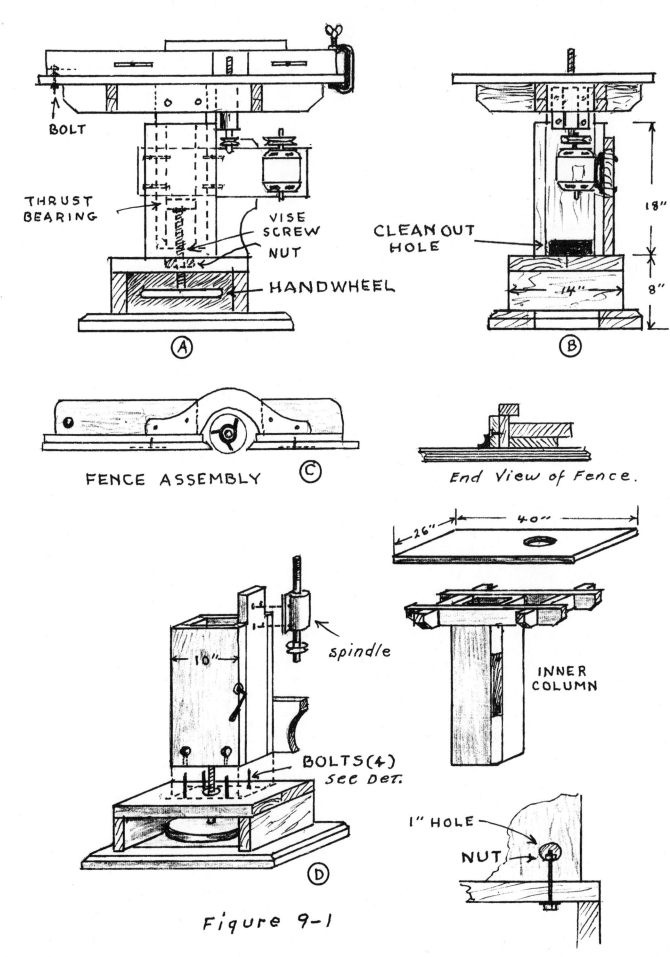

BOLT

THRUST BEARING

VISE SCREW NUT

HANDWHEEL

(A)

18"

8"

CLEAN OUT HOLE

14"

(B)

FENCE ASSEMBLY (C)

End View of Fence.

40"

26"

INNER COLUMN

10"

spindle

BOLTS(4) see det.

(D)

1" HOLE

NUT

126

Figure 9-1

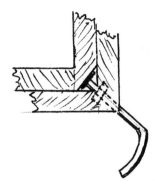

Install locking device before the other side of column is installed

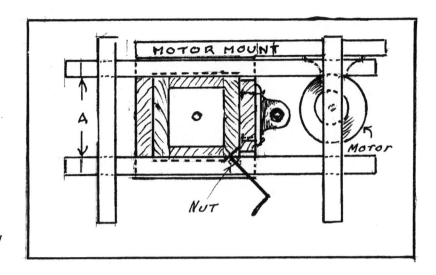

Ⓔ looking Through Top, At two columns, Mandrel, Motor, Motor mount, Top braces, and locking device.

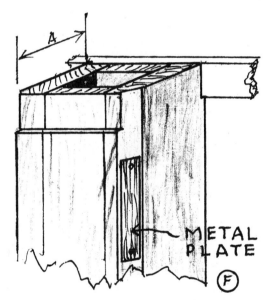

Ⓕ

Top of inner column has shoulders cut on two sides to help support the Table braces. The dimensions A in both drawings are to be the same.

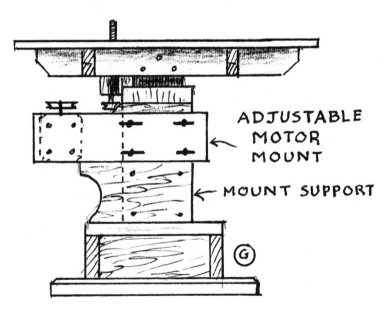

BACK SIDE

Figure 9-2

127

TURNING LATHE

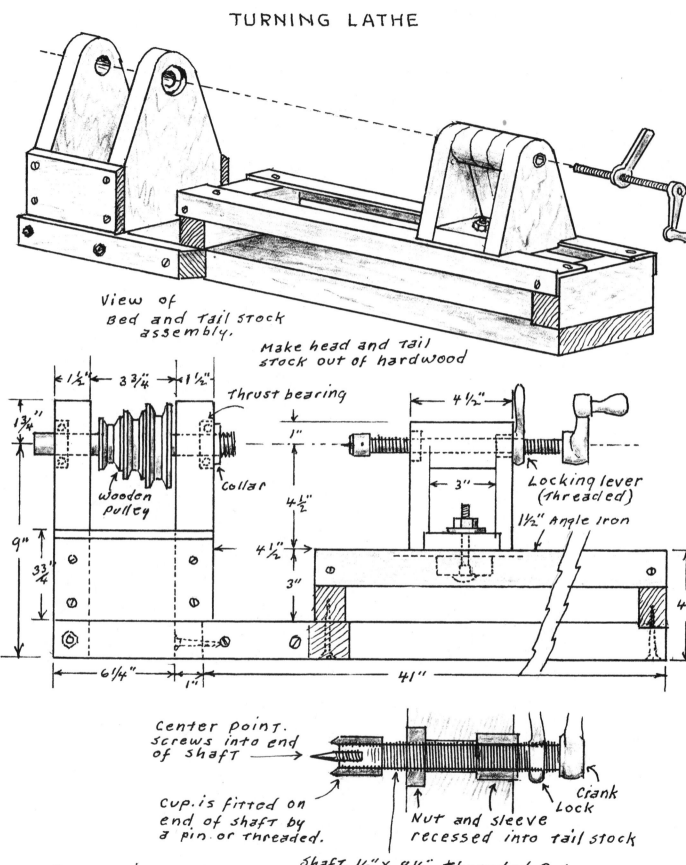

View of
Bed and Tail Stock
assembly.

Make head and tail
stock out of hardwood

1½"   3¾"   1½"

thrust bearing

13¾"

Collar

Wooden
pulley

4½"

4½"

Locking lever
(threaded)

3"

1½" Angle iron

9"

3¾"

4½"

3"

6¼"

1"

41"

4½"

Center point.
screws into end
of shaft →

Cup is fitted on
end of shaft by
a pin or threaded.

Nut and sleeve
recessed into tail stock

Crank
Lock

Shaft. ½" x 8½" threaded Rod

For Details of Tool Rest,
see "Things for the Lathe"   Figure 9-3

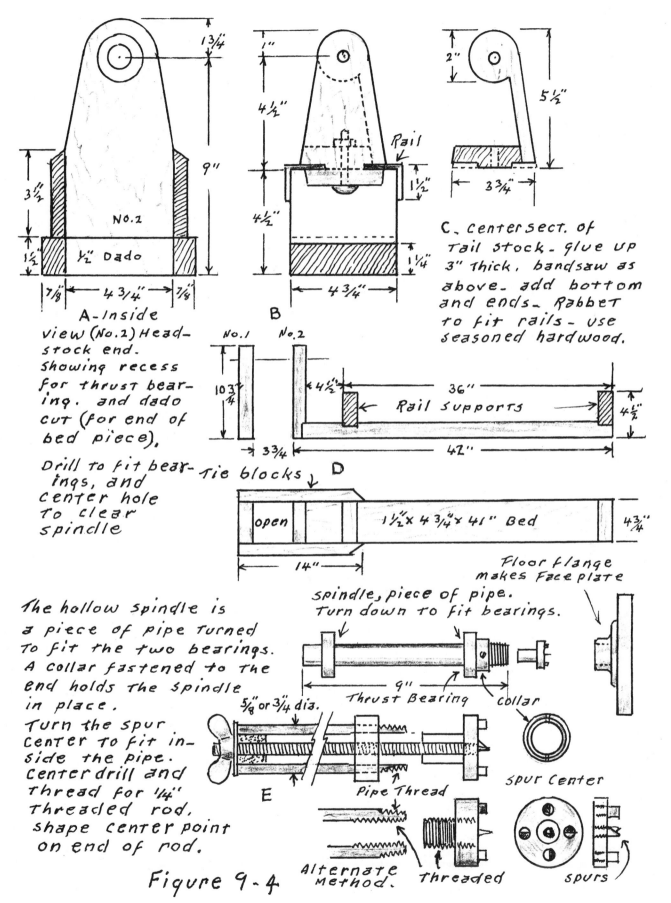

13¾"

1"

2"

4½"

Rail

5½"

9"

3½"

NO.2

½" Dado

1½"

4½"

1½"

1¼"

3¾"

⅞"

4 3/4"

⅞"

4 3/4

A-Inside
view (No.2) Head-
stock end.
Showing recess
for thrust bear-
ing. and dado
cut (for end of
bed piece).

B

C. center sect. of
Tail stock. glue up
3" Thick, bandsaw as
above. add bottom
and ends. Rabbet
to fit rails. use
seasoned hardwood.

No.1   No.2

10¾"

4½"

36"

Rail supports

4½"

Drill to fit bear-
ings, and
center hole
To clear
spindle

3¾"

42"

Tie blocks

D

open

1½"× 4 3/4"× 41" Bed

4¾"

14"

Floor flange
makes Face plate

the hollow spindle is
a piece of pipe Turned
To fit the two bearings.
A collar fastened to the
end holds the spindle
in place.

spindle, piece of pipe.
Turn down to fit bearings.

9"

Thrust Bearing

Collar

Turn the spur
Center To fit in-
side the pipe.
Center drill and
thread for ¼"
Threaded rod,
shape Center point
on end of rod.

5/8" or 3/4" dia.

E

Pipe Thread

Spur Center

spurs

Alternate
Method.

Threaded

Figure 9-4

For the tail stock, use a piece of ½" threaded rod about 9" long, a nut to fit, a short sleeve or bushing with a ½" hole and a handwheel or crank for the outer end. A few other small parts will be needed for the cup and spur centers but they can be fitted as you choose as long as they hold the work while it is being turned. It is essential that they are accurately centered, especially in the headstock spindle. The bed can be made of pine, but the headstock should be hardwood, as the bearings need to have a "drive" fit into their seats.

The sharp-edged sleeve around the end of the tail shaft serves as the cup center. The center point can either be seated in a ¼" hole or screwed into a threaded one by making it on the end of a short piece of threaded rod. This will prevent it from being pulled out of the shaft when turned work is being removed from the lathe.

The headstock spindle is made by turning the outside diameter of the pipe for a close fit in the bearings and pulley. Try to find bearings and a pulley with ⅝" or ¾" holes. If a ⅜" pipe is used the o.d. should be a little over ⅝". A ½" pipe is usually about ¹³⁄₁₆".

Whichever size pipe you use for the hollow spindle, the diameter should remain as large as possible because one end will need to be threaded with a standard pipe thread to receive the face plate.

A collar is fastened on the end between the threads and the thrust bearing. Another one may be needed on the other end to prevent endplay (see Figure 9-4E).

The headstock spur center is essentially a small disc about 1" in diameter with a shank that fits into the spindle. It has a sharp pointed insert in the center and four spurs around the edge to engage the work stock.

I made the one shown in Figure 9-4 by drilling four equally spaced holes, threading them, and screwing in short pieces of threaded rod. The protruding ends were filed to shape to form the spurs as shown (E).

A ¼" threaded rod can be used to hold the center in place. By filing or grinding a sharp point on the end, it can also serve as the center point. Another use for the rod is to fasten work to the face plate. The face plate is a disc of ¾" plywood with a pipe flange fastened in the center. When first tried on the turning spindle, it may have a wobble. If so, either turn the face of disc true, or remove the disc from the flange and true the flange as it turns on the spindle.

Drill a hole in exact center for the threaded rod. The center can be located by starting the hole with a sharp pointed turning tool.

The tool rest can be made as shown in Figure 9-5. It is made up of two or three wooden brackets that support the beveled strips. The brackets are bolted to the lathe bed and the strips lie in the notch as shown (C). By making several different lengths of the "rest strips," one can be chosen for the full length of the turning.

Illustrated in Figures 9-5 and 9-6 are a few other ideas for the lathe that may be of use to the home craftsman. The threaded rod through the spindle is the best way I have found to fasten work to the face plate. Of course, the work will have to be center drilled for the rod to go

through it. In most cases it can be plugged with a piece of dowel after it is finished. Figure 9-5D is an example of how the rod is used to turn a wooden bowl.

Figure 9-5E shows some turning tools that can be made. The "gouge" is from an old wrist pin from an automobile engine, which can be found at any garage.

These pins can also be used to make sleeves to fasten accessories to motor shafts as shown in Figure 9-7F, if they have the correct size hole through them. Heat to draw the temper, drill, and thread for setscrews.

The other turning tools shown in Figure 9-5 are made from old files. Others not shown such as "round nose," "parting tool," and "spear point" are easily made on the grinder. Leave the temper as is and they will stay sharp longer.

USING JUNK MOTORS

Figure 9-7 shows how a small motor from a junked appliance can be made into a useful shop tool. Mount it on a bed as shown (A) and add the tail stock, and it will serve as a small lathe. The headstock spur can be bought from Sears or made from a ½" sleeve by cutting the four teeth or spurs around the edge of one end and adding a center point. A thrust bearing should be used between the sleeve and motor to relieve pressure against the motor bearings (A). Details of the bed, tail stock, and tool rest are shown (B and C). Make size to suit.

The work arbor (Figure 9-7D) permits using a chuck and many small accessories such as wire brushes, sanding drums, rotary files, and drills. Larger accessories can be used by mounting them directly on the arbor. The arbor may need to be supported on the outer end by the tail stock center. This can be done by making an extra shaft for the tail stock with a 60° center or just a center that will screw on the shaft. A polishing pad, sanding disc, and buffing wheel can be fastened on ½" shafts or bolts (F). They are attached to the motor shaft with a sleeve and setscrews.

The sanding drum (Figure 9-7E) is made by drilling a ½" hole in the center of a block of soft wood. Mount on the arbor and turn to diameter desired. Drill a ⁵⁄₁₆" hole near the edge and saw a slot through the edge of the drum into the hole for the ends of the sandpaper to slip through. A ¼" dowel pushed into the hole holds the sandpaper.

A larger sanding drum is shown (Figure 9-7G), which is excellent for finish sanding. I use one like this to sand the curved sides of guitars and other curved pieces where hand sanding is usually required. It has a piece of thin rubber-backed carpet material about ½" thick, glued around the outside of the wooden drum, which serves as a cushion. This greatly prolongs the life of the sandpaper and permits more uniform sanding over irregular surfaces. A narrow strip is left between the ends of the cushion so the paper can be fastened directly to the wood cylinder with staples. I found that No. 100 grit floor sandpaper is best for general use.

THINGS FOR THE LATHE
that you can make

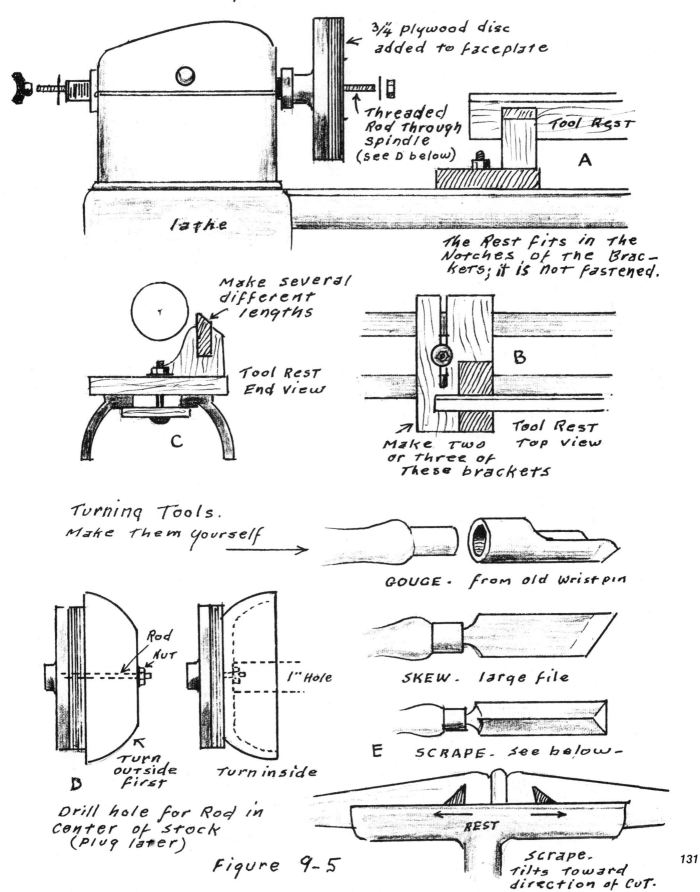

3/4 plywood disc added to faceplate

Threaded Rod Through spindle (see D below)

Tool Rest

lathe

A

The Rest fits in the Notches of the Brackets; it is not fastened.

Make several different lengths

Tool Rest End view

C

B

Tool Rest Top view

Make two or three of These brackets

Turning Tools. Make them yourself

GOUGE. from old Wristpin

SKEW. large file

SCRAPE. see below

E

Rod

Nut

1" Hole

Turn outside first

Turn inside

D

Drill hole for Rod in Center of stock (Plug later)

Figure 9-5

scrape. tilts toward direction of cut.

REST

131

THINGS FOR THE LATHE

Two used ball bearings make a good steady-rest for slender turnings. ...and does not burn the wood. Drill the holes equal distance from center, and so the bearings can be adjusted to about ½" of each other.

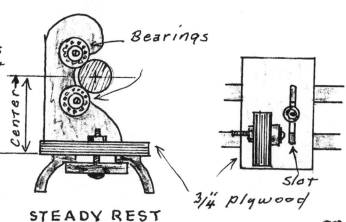

Bearings

Center

STEADY REST

Slot

¾" plywood

When there are several spindles to turn with tenons on the ends- A "stop" clamped to the tool saves time.

Ball bearing

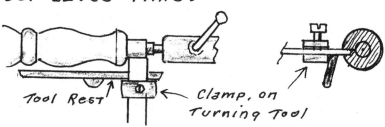

Tool Rest

Clamp, on Turning Tool

The small bolt with the two washers. permit adjusting the bearing to correct position Turn a small section about the middle of the stock- ease the "rest" up to it, until both bearings turn.

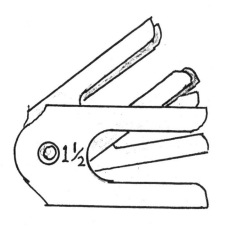

◎1½

Gauges for small Turning made from scraps of Formica

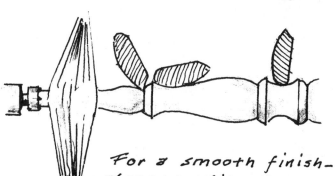

For a smooth finish- after sanding, use a shaped block of soft pine. Then polish with a piece of cloth.

Figure 9-6

JUNK MOTORS
"Put Them To Work"

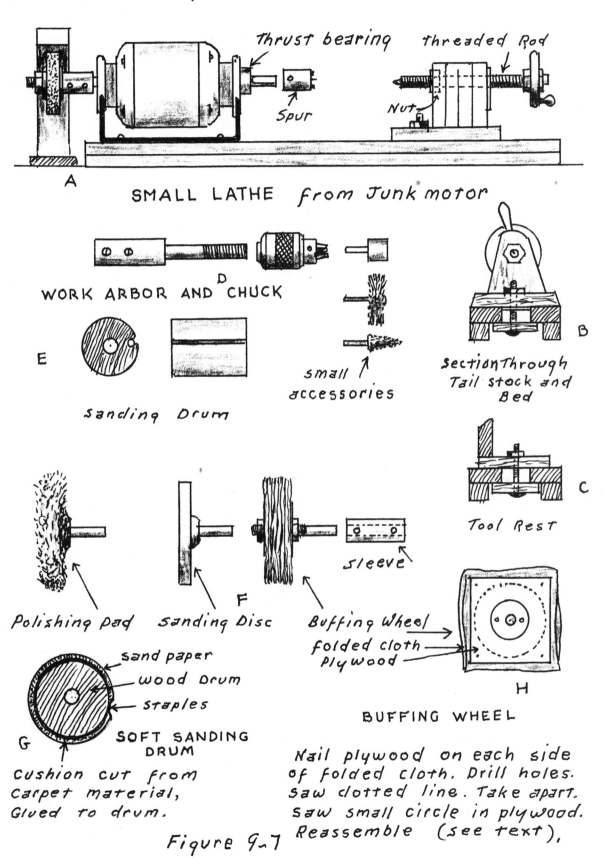

Thrust bearing

threaded Rod

Spur

Nut

A

SMALL LATHE from Junk motor

WORK ARBOR AND CHUCK

D

E Sanding Drum

small accessories

B Section Through Tail Stock and Bed

C Tool Rest

Polishing Pad   Sanding Disc   **F**   Buffing Wheel   Sleeve

folded cloth
Plywood

H

sand paper
wood Drum
staples

G SOFT SANDING DRUM

Cushion cut from
Carpet material,
Glued to drum.

BUFFING WHEEL

Nail plywood on each side
of folded cloth. Drill holes.
Saw dotted line. Take apart.
Saw small circle in plywood.
Reassemble (see text).

Figure 9-7

BUFFING AND POLISHING WHEELS

Various sizes of buffing wheels can be made from scrap cotton cloth. Even old worn-out workpants can be recycled by cutting them up and folding to the desired thickness. I found that from 1″ to ½″ thickness is best. Fasten the fold between two pieces of ¼″ plywood by nailing through each corner and clenching the nails. Be sure the cloth is tightly compressed to prevent it from twisting around the drills when the holes are drilled through it. Drill the center hole to fit the shaft on which it is to be used and two ¼″ holes, one on each side of the center for stove bolts (Figure 9-7H). Slip a short piece of dowel or rod in the center hole and cut the outside diameter (dotted line). Remove the pieces of plywood, resaw (small circle), and reassemble.

These are fine for polishing pieces of wood as well as metal. For metal, use buffing compound, which can be bought from Sears. The polishing pad (Figure 9-7F) can also be purchased. It is sheepskin with a cloth backing that fits over a rubber sanding disc.

JOINTER

The jointer shown in Figures 9-8 and 9-9 can be made of wood and a few metal parts including a mandrel. The motor should be at least ½ hp and 3450 rpm.

I made one similar to the one shown to take out on jobs where a considerable amount of cutting and fitting had to be done. I found it of great help in installing cabinets, stairways, and other millwork that couldn't be completed in the shop. With the proper cutters, it does a good job of jointing and rabbeting and it makes a good shaper for straight work by using available molding cutters.

As you can see, it is simply a molding head and mandrel mounted on a stand with adjustable tables or ledges on each side. It works like a shop jointer but cuts only 1″ wide. However, this is usually enough for most edge-jointing work.

SANDER

Figure 9-10 shows a handy sander that can be made with a "junk motor" and the end bells taken from another one that has good bearings. The motor is fitted with a drum by means of an arbor (D). Another drum is mounted on a mandrel made by bolting the two bells together as shown (C and D) with a board between serving as a mount. They are mounted on a table (A) so standard belts (for portable belt sanders) can be used.

A shoe or block of wood is fitted between the pulleys and is about ¼″ above the top of them. It is slightly beveled at each end to reduce wear on the sanding belts and has a base block that is slotted so it can be adjusted or easily removed. The board that the bells are fastened to goes through a slot in the table and is bolted at the bottom. A spring is fastened underneath to keep the belt tight on the drums.

This sander can be used in several ways. A disc can be added to the outer end of the motor shaft. Curved pieces can be sanded where the belt goes around the drums and by adding the attachments shown (Figure 9-10E). It does a good job sanding the rounded edges of lipped cabinet doors.

The belts can be split for this job, making two narrow ones. A special shoe is made by rounding out a groove or trench through the center (E), to fit the curve of the door edge.

A frame is made to fasten on top of the table, to hold the doors at the correct angle (see Figure 9-10E and dotted lines on B). It is cut out on the bottom edge to clear the belt but two short blocks are added at the bottom ends in line with the bottom of the trench in the shoe to keep the edge of the door level with the sander.

The shoe is adjusted by means of the slot in the base so it is in line with the frame. Guides may be needed underneath the shoe to keep the narrow belt in the groove (C and E).

The drums can be made as shown (D) by drilling holes in blocks of wood about 2½″ square and 4″ long (or width of the belt). Drill one to fit the arbor for the motor, as shown (D) and the other for the shaft through the bells. Set up a temporary tool rest and turn on the motor shaft. It can also be turned by placing a pulley on the other shaft. Make about ⅛″ crown on the face of the drums. Gluing a piece of rubber around the motor drum will help prevent the belts from slipping.

Another sander is shown in Figure 9-11. It is made from an old floor sanding machine. It does an excellent job sanding both flat and curved work.

BAND SAW

Like the other machines in this chapter, the 12″ band saw is made of a few pieces of wood, a mandrel, two bearings, and a few other odds and ends. I have built two of these in the past, the one shown here, and one with 16″ wheels. I used the large one ten or twelve years and sold it to a person who used it another ten years.

If a larger than 12″ wheel size is needed, the dimensions given here can be changed proportionally. A heavier frame will be needed, as well as larger bearings, mandrel, and longer blades, which should be about 10′ for a 16″ size.

Figure 9-12 shows the general dimensions of the frame, the location of the wheel shafts, and an outline of the wheel guards, which can be made as you choose, as long as they cover the cutting edge of the saw.

The frame is made of three of four layers of board lumber glued together to a thickness of about 3″. The upper part should be hardwood, as extra strength is needed in the arm to prevent it from twisting when tension is placed on the saw blade.

JOINTER

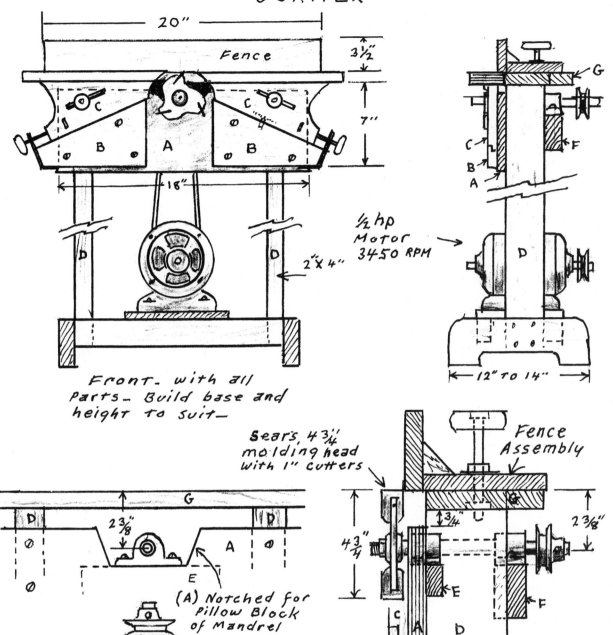

20"

Fence

3½"

7"

C   C

B   A   B

18"

D   D

½ hp
Motor
3450 RPM

2"×4"

Front. with all
Parts. Build base and
height to suit.

G

C
B
A

D

12" to 14"

Sears, 4¾"
molding head
with 1" cutters

Fence
Assembly

G   D   G

D   D

2⅜"

2"×4"   F

A

E

2⅜"

F

¾"

4¾"

E

F

C

B   A   D

(A) Notched for
Pillow Block
of Mandrel

Shaft   Pillow
Blocks

D   D

A   E   A

B   B

Top of Cutter flush with
Top of The board (G)
Front board (A) is
fastened to the 2"×4"
legs and ¾" below
The top of them.

Mandrel, 8" or 9" long
Mounted at top of stand.
Buy one ready made if
you can. if Not make as
shown.

This Jointer does
accurate work. as
Jointing up to 1" Thick,
Rabbeting and Molding

Figure 4-8

135

JOINTER

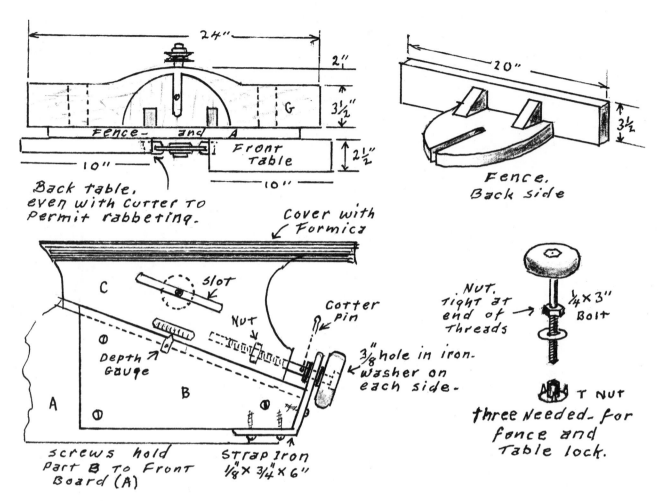

24"

2"

3½"

2½"

Fence and Front Table

G

A

10"

10"

Back table, even with Cutter to permit rabbeting.

20"

3½"

Fence, Back side

Cover with Formica

C

Slot

Nut

Cotter Pin

Depth Gauge

A

B

3/8" hole in iron. washer on each side.

screws hold Part B To Front Board (A)

Strap Iron ⅛" × ¾" × 6"

Nut. Tight at end of Threads

¼ × 3" Bolt

T Nut

three Needed. for fence and Table lock.

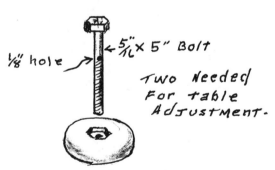

⅛" hole

5/16" × 5" Bolt

Two Needed For table Adjustment.

Saw and Turn handwheels. Drill and Chisel for tight fit over bolt head

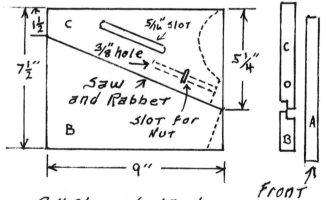

1½"

C

5/16" slot

3/8" hole

5¼"

7½"

Saw and Rabbet

B

Slot for Nut

9"

C

A

B

Front Board A
7¼" × 20-22"

3¼" Plywood Stock. Make Two - Right and left - Sand rabbet Joint for smooth and accurate Adjusting.

The slot for locking hand wheel Must be parallel To angle Cut. The hole drilled for the Adjusting handwheel must be too. drill and chisel a small slot for a nut inside.

Note- The front and back table MUST be in perfect Alignment. Check with straight edge as you fasten The B blocks.

Figure 9-9

TWO JUNK MOTORS
—and One of them wouldn't Run.
But they were used to build this
Handy Sander

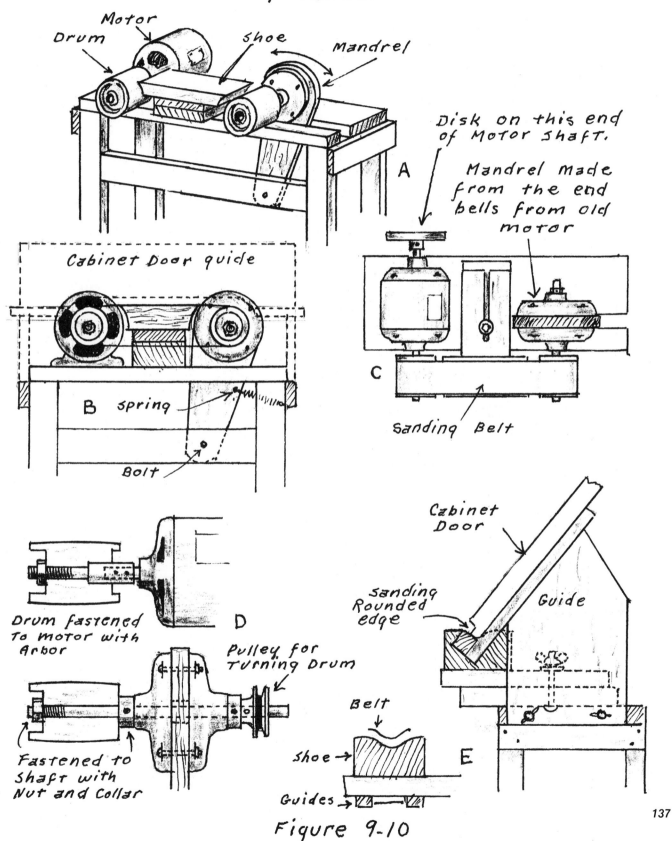

Motor

Drum

Shoe

Mandrel

A

Disk on this end
of Motor Shaft.

Mandrel made
from the end
bells from old
motor

Cabinet Door guide

B   spring

Bolt

C

Sanding Belt

Drum fastened
To Motor with
Arbor

D

Fastened to
Shaft with
Nut and Collar

Pulley for
Turning Drum

Belt

Shoe→

Guides→

E

Cabinet
Door

Sanding
Rounded
edge

Guide

Figure 9-10

TABLE SANDER
Made From old Floor Sander

This Could be The Handiest Machine in Your Shop. (I've used one for 30 years)

Slot Cut in Top for Drum

3/4" Plywood

switch

2"x 4" legs

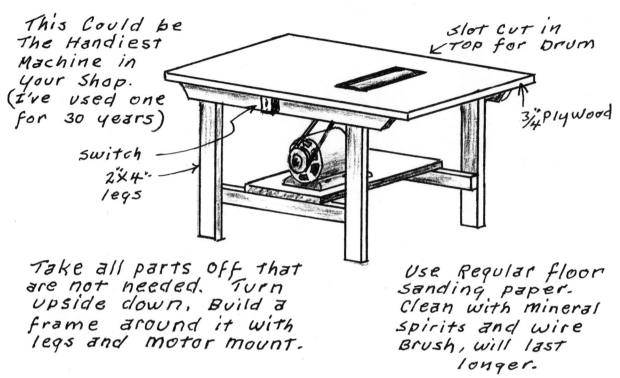

Take all parts off that are not needed. Turn upside down. Build a frame around it with legs and motor mount.

Use Regular floor sanding paper. Clean with mineral spirits and wire Brush, will last longer.

Formica Top

Old Floor Sander

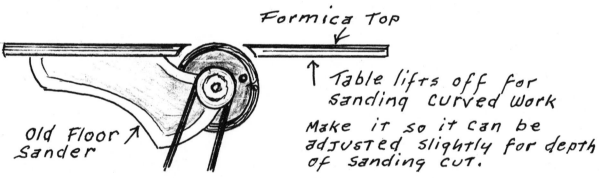

↑ Table lifts off for sanding curved work

Make it so it can be adjusted slightly for depth of sanding cut.

PULLEYS MADE OF WOOD

Glue up layers of hardwood. Drill Center, Saw To Rough diameter. Mount on Motor Shaft. Turn.

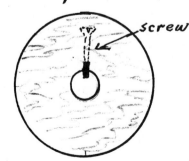
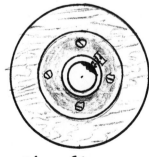
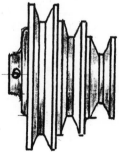

screw

saw slot for key seat or...

...pipe flange Drilled and Mounted on end.

Figure 9-11

BAND SAW

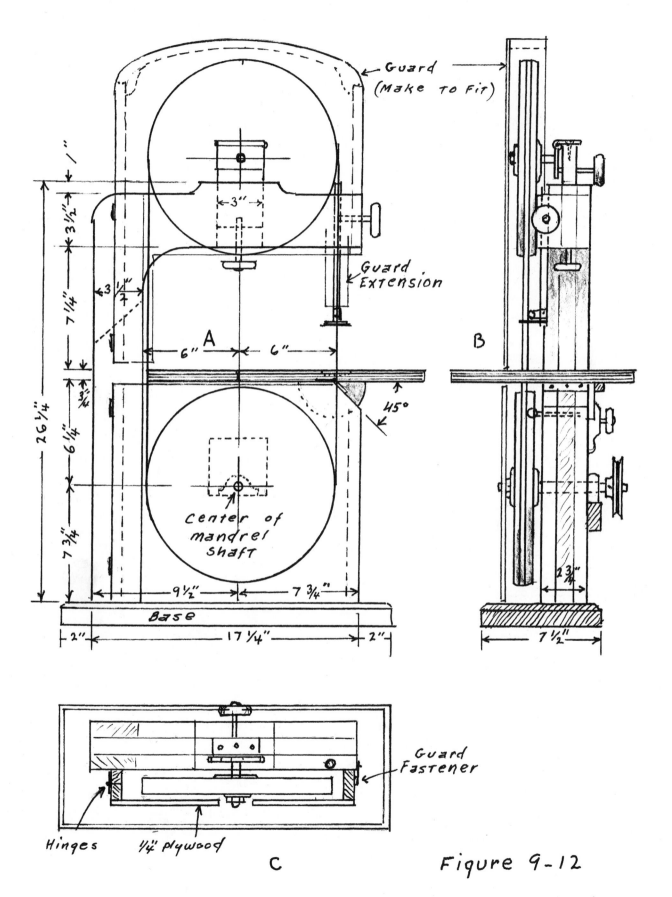

Guard
(Make to Fit)

3"

Guard
Extension

A

6"   6"

45°

Center of
mandrel
shaft

B

2 3/4"

1"

3 1/2"

7 1/4"

3 1/4"

26 1/4"

3/4"

6 1/4"

7 3/4"

9 1/2"   7 3/4"

Base

2"   17 1/4"   2"

7 1/2"

Guard
Fastener

Hinges   1/4" plywood

C   Figure 9-12   139

Use smooth unwarped boards of the same thickness, coat heavily with glue, and clamp until dry.

Figure 9-13 shows how the boards are lapped at the turn of the arm as they are laminated for extra strength.

The lower wheel base can be pine but should be built up as shown for strength and to prevent warping. Provisions should be made for whatever type mandrel that is to be used. The drawings show a cutout space in the base to permit the use of a "housed" type that is fastened with screws through holes in its base. Any type or method that has good bearings should be satisfactory if it is properly installed. Be sure the center of the shaft is located as shown in Figure 9-12.

Although the given dimensions are for an 80" saw blade, a longer blade may be used by raising the arm. The two pieces that fasten to the base can be made longer or slotted as shown in Figure 9-13. This will allow some vertical adjustment if needed.

The wheels are made of $3/4$" plywood with circular strips of $1/4$" plywood glued around the edges on both sides, to give a thickness of $1 1/4$" at the rim (see Figure 9-14) rough cut to $12 1/4$" diameter. The procedure for turning the face to exact size will be covered later.

The upper wheel has a laminated hardwood hub, which is glued into a 3" hole cut in the center of the wheel (Figure 9-14). It is made by gluing two or three pieces of white oak or maple together for a thickness of about $1 5/8$". Rough saw to a $4 1/4$" diameter.

The bearings are seated into each side of the hub, and must be accurately aligned with each other. The method I use is shown in Figure 9-14. A $1/8$" pilot hole is first drilled through the center and the bearing seats are bored from it. Note, however, in Step 3 how one of the bearings can be used as a guide by partially recessing it in a block that is clamped to the drill press.

An expansion bit can be used to bore the seats if the bearings are of an odd size. Adjust the bit so the bearings will have to be driven in place by placing a block of wood over it and lightly tapping with a hammer. Try the set-up on scrap material before drilling the hub.

Because it will be turned to shape in the lathe as shown (Figure 9-14A and B), the $1/8$" pilot hole will need to be redrilled to fit the rod that holds it to the face plate or an arbor on which it can be mounted for turning. If the arbor is used, a $1/2$" hole will be needed.

Cut a 3" hole in the center of the upper wheel with a circle cutter and turn the hub for a tight fit as shown (A). Glue the hub in the wheel. The lower wheel has a hole to fit the mandrel shaft and $1/2$" thick wooden plates on each side (C).

Both wheels are trued up by using the lower wheel mandrel shaft as a lathe. A temporary tool rest is added to one side of the frame. Turn to size with a slight crown as shown in Figure 9-14. The crown is needed to keep the saw blade tracking in the center of the wheel.

The upper wheel hub may have to be redrilled to fit on the mandrel shaft. This will cause no problem since it will turn on the bearings that will be centered in the previously drilled seats. Figure 9-13 shows the details of the upper wheel mount. It is a hardwood block that slides up and down in an opening in the arm. Take care when making the arm to leave the opening as shown. It should be centered with the wheels, plumb, and square.

The mount is adjusted vertically by a handwheel underneath. A short stiff spring is placed on the end of the handwheel shaft as shown (Figure 9-13D). It helps keep an even tension on the saw blade as well as absorb jolts if chips should fall between the saw and wheel. A metal plate is fastened underneath the arm, which is drilled and threaded for the handwheel shaft (B and G).

A heavy loose-pin hinge is used to mount the wheel shaft to the block. The shaft can either be turned down on the end and peened in a hole drilled in the hinge (Figure 9-13A–C) or threaded with a nut used on each side. The other end is drilled and threaded for a retaining screw and washer. Another handwheel is used to tilt the wheel for proper tracking of the saw blade. The guide and thrust wheel assembly is shown in Figure 9-15. It is a flat plate about $1/8$" thick and 2" x $2 1/2$", with a $1/4$" slot sawed out of the center (A). It is fastened to the bottom of a $1/2$" rod, which is about 10" long. The two slotted guides are fastened to the plate with screws so they can be adjusted to fit against the sides of the blade.

The thrust wheel (Figure 9-15) can be a small ball bearing or a roller cut from a piece of rod and center drilled. It is fastened to another slotted plate, which is attached to the side of the rod. The slots permit adjusting the thrust wheel to the back of the blade. The roller must turn freely on its shaft, which can be a small machine bolt, screwed into the plate.

The rod will need to be ground flat on one side in order for it to remain straight with the saw. A suggested method is shown (Figure 9-13F). The rod fits into a sleeve which is inset in the arm. It must be parallel to the center line of the two wheels, and about 1" behind the back edge of the saw or just inside the outer layer of the arm. The rounded block is added to the arm to hold it in place.

The lower thrust wheel can be made as shown in Figure 9-15C or as you wish as long as it turns freely and is adjustable. Some of the better band saws have both thrust wheel and guides underneath the table. They should be located so they will not interfere with the tilting of the table.

The table is fastened to the frame with a loose-pin hinge. It has a half circle of $1/2$" plywood fastened to the underside with a locking clamp (see Figure 9-15D), which is used to lock the table in position.

A recess is cut in the top, around the blade for an insert made of $1/4$" plywood. It is removed when the table is to be tilted for angle or bevel cuts.

The wheel guards are $1/4$" plywood fastened to strips of $3/4$" wood. The left side is two strips hinged together. One of them is fastened to the frame with screws. The right side is in one piece with a hook or latch, which is used to fasten it to the frame (Figure 9-12C). An adjusta-

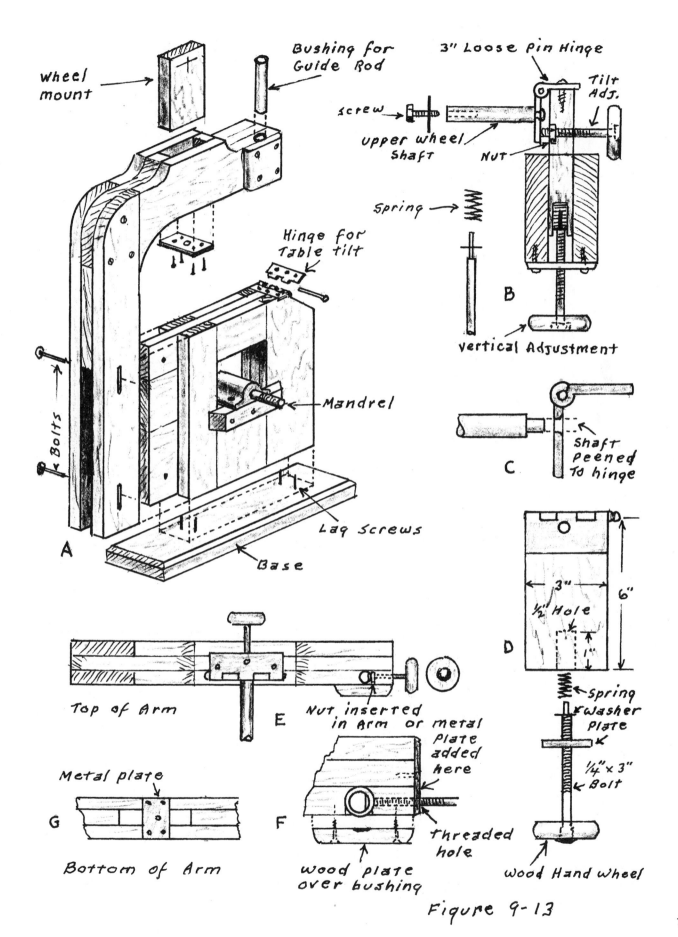

wheel mount

Bushing for Guide Rod

3" Loose Pin Hinge

Tilt Adj.

screw

upper wheel shaft

Nut

Spring

vertical Adjustment

B

Hinge for Table tilt

Mandrel

C

Shaft Peened To hinge

Bolts

Lag Screws

Base

A

3"

½" Hole

6"

1"

D

Top of Arm

E

Nut inserted in Arm or metal plate added here

Spring
Washer
Plate

¼" x 3" Bolt

Metal plate

G

Bottom of Arm

F

threaded hole

wood plate over bushing

Wood Hand wheel

Figure 9-13

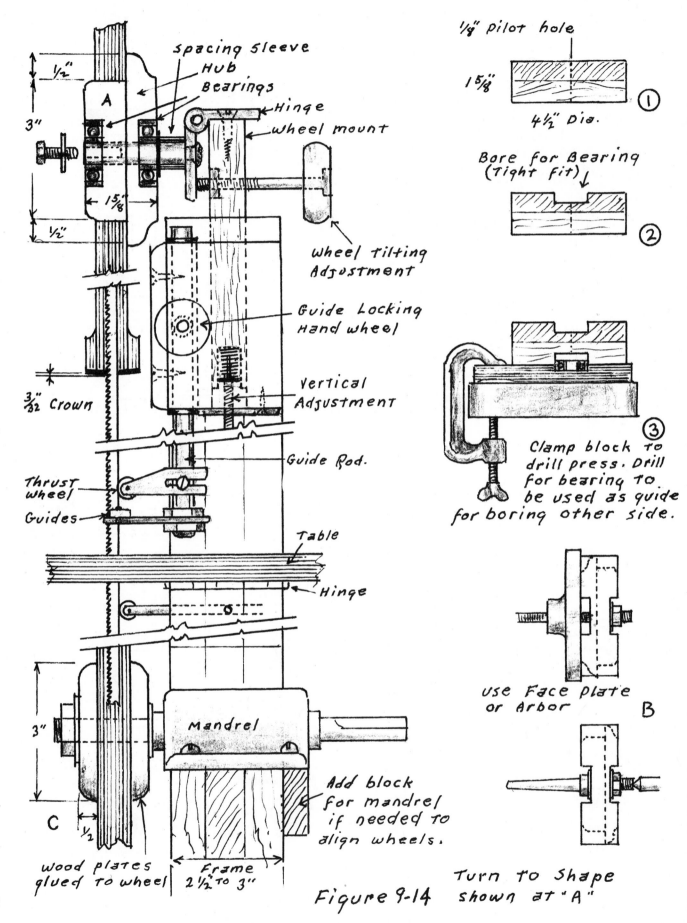

spacing sleeve
Hub
Bearings
Hinge
Wheel mount

A

½"
3"
1⅝"
½"

Wheel Tilting Adjustment

Guide Locking Hand wheel

Vertical Adjustment

3/32" Crown

Guide Rod.

Thrust Wheel
Guides

Table

Hinge

Mandrel

3"

C

½"

Wood plates glued to wheel

Frame 2½" to 3"

Add block for mandrel if needed to align wheels.

⅛" pilot hole

1⅝"

4½" Dia.

①

Bore for Bearing (Tight fit)

②

③

Clamp block to drill press. Drill for bearing to be used as guide for boring other side.

use Face Plate or Arbor

B

Turn to Shape shown at "A"

Figure 9-14

142

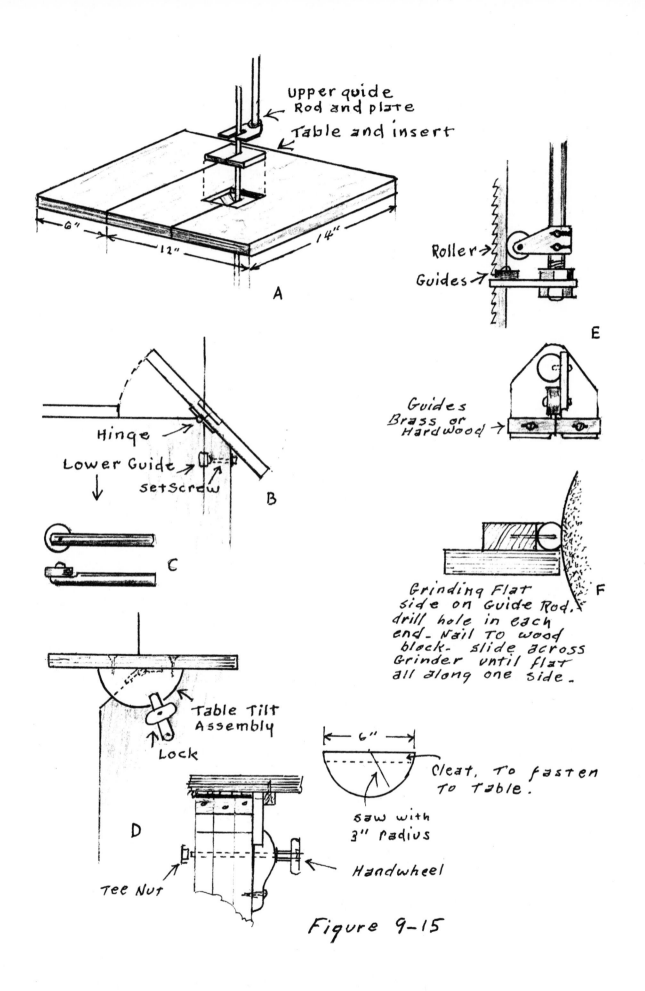

upper guide
Rod and plate

Table and insert

6"

12"

14"

A

Roller

Guides

E

Hinge

Lower Guide

set screw

B

C

Guides
Brass or
Hardwood

Grinding Flat
side on Guide Rod,
drill hole in each
end. Nail TO wood
block. slide across
Grinder until flat
all along one side.

F

Table Tilt
Assembly

Lock

D

6"

Cleat, To fasten
To Table.

saw with
3" radius

Tee Nut

Handwheel

Figure 9-15

ble extension should be added to cover the blade between the guide and the arm. It can be made of sheet metal and fastened to the rod just above the thrust wheel plate.

After the wheels have been trued up, they should be fitted with rubber tires to provide better traction, and help retain the set in the saw teeth.

Cut bands from an old truck innertube about 2″ wide. Stretch over the wheels using rubber cement or contact glue. Trim off the excess with a sharp knife.

Be sure the wheels are in line with each other. The lower one can be aligned with the upper by shifting the mandrel. Blocking can be added to either side of the cutout in the frame for added thickness if needed to support the mandrel.

With a blade on the wheels and enough tension to hold it fairly tight, turn several rounds by hand. Adjust the upper wheel "tilt" until the blade runs in the center. It should center both wheels. If not, they are not aligned properly. Check all parts for accuracy and sturdiness.

When the blade is tracking properly, adjust the guides. They should lightly touch each side of the blade. The thrust wheel is set about 1/16″ from the back edge. It is supposed to turn only when the saw is being used. Do not use the machine until the wheel guards and extensions are installed as shown in Figure 9-12.

APPENDIX: METRIC CONVERSIONS

TO CONVERT	TO	MULTIPLY BY
Length in inches	millimeters (mm)	25
Length in feet	centimeters (cm)	30
Square inches (in^2)	cm^2	6.5
Square feet (ft^2)	m^2	0.09

EQUIVALENTS

inch	millimeter
$1/16$	1.59
$1/8$	3.18
$3/16$	4.76
$1/4$	6.35
$5/16$	7.94
$3/8$	9.53
$1/2$	12.70
$9/16$	14.29
$5/8$	15.88
$11/16$	17.46
$3/4$	19.05
$13/16$	20.64
$7/8$	22.23
$15/16$	23.81
1	25.40

INDEX